THE NORTHERN SILENCE

THE NORTHERN SILENCE

JOURNEYS IN NORDIC MUSIC
AND CULTURE

ANDREW MELLOR

YALE UNIVERSITY PRESS
NEW HAVEN AND LONDON

Copyright © 2022 Andrew Mellor

All rights reserved. This book may not be reproduced in whole or in part, in any form (beyond that copying permitted by Sections 107 and 108 of the U.S. Copyright Law and except by reviewers for the public press) without written permission from the publishers.

All reasonable efforts have been made to provide accurate sources for all images that appear in this book. Any discrepancies or omissions will be rectified in future editions.

For information about this and other Yale University Press publications, please contact:
U.S. Office: sales.press@yale.edu   yalebooks.com
Europe Office: sales@yaleup.co.uk   yalebooks.co.uk

Set in Adobe Caslon Pro by IDSUK (DataConnection) Ltd
Printed in Great Britain by TJ Books Ltd, Padstow, Cornwall

Library of Congress Control Number: 2022934793

ISBN 978-0-300-25440-2

A catalogue record for this book is available from the British Library.

10 9 8 7 6 5 4 3 2 1

For Jack, Jennifer and Jude

Contents

	List of Plates	*viii*
	Map	*x*
	Prelude. *Tapiola*	1
1	Landfall	12
2	Performance	58
3	Off Piste	114
4	Nordic Noir and Snow White	164
5	Scandinavian by Design	212
	Postlude. Silence	261
	Notes	*281*
	Acknowledgements	*285*
	Index	*291*

Plates

1. Björk performs at Lowlands Festival, August 1996. Photo by Frans Schellekens. Getty RMA:508572397, Frans Schellekens / Contributor.
2. Emilia Amper plays her nyckelharpa. Photo by Henrik Peel. From artist with permission.
3. Geirangerfjord. Photo by Chunyip Wong. Getty EPL:1171977818.
4. Faroe Islands. Photo by Jose Gieskes. Getty FPX:1149537935, Jose Gieskes / 500px.
5. Anna Thorvaldsdottir. Photo by Saga Sigurdardottir. Wise Music / Saga Sigurdardottir.
6. Silence Festival, 2016. Photo by Andrew Mellor.
7. Essen Opera. Photo by Eva and Pertti Ingervo. Eva and Pertti Ingervo / Alvar Aalto Museum.
8. Musiikkitalo, 2011. Photo by Arno de la Chapelle. Musiikkitalo / Arno de la Chapelle.
9. Oslo Opera. Photo by Dag Sundberg. Getty IBK:83986860.
10. Musikkens Hus.

PLATES

11. Lordi celebrates victory at the 2006 Eurovision Song Contest, Athens. Photo by Sean Gallup. Getty ENT:57667046.
12. Sakari Oramo at the BBC Proms, 2017. Photo by Chris Christodoulou.
13. South Jutland Symphony Orchestra. Photo by Patricio Soto.
14. *Mahagonny* at the Royal Danish Opera. Photo by Thomas Petri.
15. Marimekko, Paris Fashion Week 2017. Alamy 2DHCE7K, Abaca Press / Alamy Stock Photo.
16. Sámi in Pajala, Sweden. Alamy R4NW9K, Cavan Images / Alamy Stock Photo.

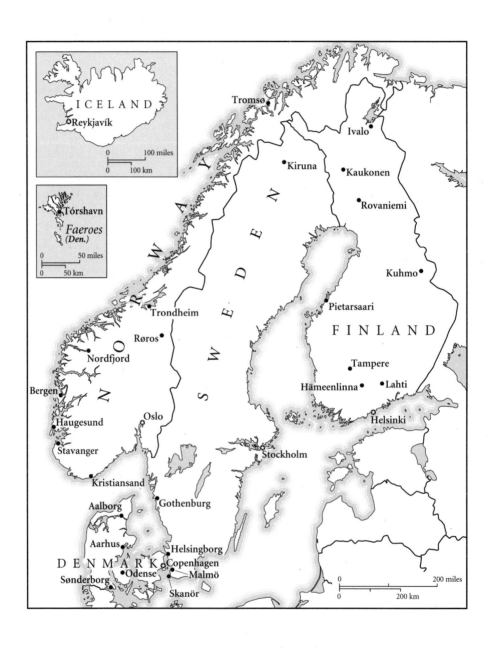

Prelude. *Tapiola*

From the glass walls of Helsinki Airport, Finland's forests resemble a dado rail separating the horizon from the sky. But the country's ancient woods are different. They are altogether more inhospitable, inaccessible and unkempt. They don't start or finish; they come into being and drift elusively away again. The deeper you venture in, the more their base rhythm shifts. Those neat forests harvested for timber and pulp in suburban Helsinki are clipped and consistent. Finland's old-growth forests are sprawling and unruly, littered with glacial boulders and standing pools.

I am clambering through one such forest with two Finns, Pekka and Esa. We are on the outskirts of the town of Pietarsaari, high on the country's west coast in the district of Ostrobothnia. It is late November, around midday. The sun has emerged, but will remain visible for a few hours at best and will cleave resolutely to the horizon while it does. Its position there actually makes the forest lighter: rays filter sideways through the trees, particularly near the forest clearings where no canopy can interrupt them. I have not experienced this particular kind of light in a wood before. It illuminates millions of tiny particles in the air. It is bracing and *em*bracing, a visual equivalent to submersing yourself in lake water.

Pekka Hako is a musicologist, folklorist and educationalist from Helsinki and wants to talk about this distinctive late autumnal light. He is a bear of a man, unmistakably Finnish from the drooping legato of his spoken English to his high cheekbones and Nokia gumboots. He mentions the Finnish architect Alvar Aalto, born not far from here. 'Aalto tried to recreate this effect in many of his buildings,' Pekka half-shouts as he walks some metres ahead, negotiating rocks and dodging squelching mud, gesticulating with his left arm to signal he's speaking. 'He considered the sun's position at latitudes like this and tried to find ways of getting its light to infiltrate buildings in the same way, using latticing and panels. He wanted just the quality of light we have here.'

Aalto wasn't the only one. This lustrous, piercing sideways light leads me to music – to the last major piece for orchestra by the Finnish composer Jean Sibelius. In *Tapiola*,[1] Sibelius created what seems on the surface to be an orchestral depiction of Finland's spirit of the forest, as set out in the country's folkloric poetry. At its simplest, *Tapiola* can be interpreted as a journey deep into one of these woods. It carries with it the heaving undertow of forest winds and creaking trees. It makes oblique references to mystery critters lurking in the half-darkness. It saturates your ears with a sense of the unseen and the unknown. It disorientates at macro and micro level: underneath the orchestra's elusive twists and turns, the entire musical structure sits uneasily in its own key.

Despite the fear and foreboding, *Tapiola* eventually comes good. In the score's final bars, the orchestra reaches outwards in an almost physical embrace. Its string sections divide and spread-eagle, alighting on notes just far enough apart to affect the musical equivalent of a damp, luminous glisten. The music shifts key for the first and only time – into the major. As an evocation of autumnal Nordic light momentarily filtering through forest trees, the final bars of *Tapiola* get closer than Alvar Aalto ever would. We are left with the reassuring impression of the forest as a foe turned friend.

After those crepuscular chords, *Tapiola* disappears into the silence from which it emerged. Sibelius would do the same. For more than thirty years following *Tapiola*'s first performance in 1926, the composer wrote little he deemed fit for public exposure. Were the warning signs there? *Tapiola* has only one half-melody, itself built mostly from repetitions of a single note. Despite that valedictory shift from minor to major, the piece effectively remains within the confines of a single key, a design feature almost unheard of in music at the time. The whole score is alarmingly short on actual musical material. Little wonder silence followed *Tapiola*. As one musicologist has written, 'Sibelius reduced his music more and more until, in the end, there was none.'[2]

Silence, it's tempting to speculate, had proved itself too intrinsic a part of Sibelius's musical language for him to resist embracing it fully. Or perhaps, from his home in the woods, he let *it* embrace *him*. The composer had explored the eloquence and energy of silence in plenty of works before. In some, he uses it more obviously. But in *Tapiola*, silence is the natural state over which each and every sound treads discourteously, right from the rumbling kettledrum with which it sneaks into being. Here, Sibelius uses silence not as a rhythmic lubricant or a dramatic device pitched in counterpoint to extreme noise. Rather, it lies under each and every note, like the inaudible breathing of the forest. Playing the silence, the best conductors know, is how to play *Tapiola*.

Silence is more prominent in the northernmost reaches of Europe, in urban as well as rural environments. Sometimes it is real and pure. Sometimes it lingers despite the noise – the deafening silence of poetic fantasy; stasis charged with ferocious thought. Like the forest of Tapiola, it can exist internally as well as externally. Sibelius's life after *Tapiola* was filled not with silence, as legend dictates, but with attempts to fill it – with a world of stillborn noise ultimately suffocated by a silence more powerful.

After our walk in the forest, Esa, Pekka and I amble back towards the centre of Pietarsaari, a bilingual town known by its Swedish-speaking majority as Jakobstad. We pass an elegant white building that once produced the cigars complicit in the cancer that nearly killed Sibelius. We head downtown to Campus Allegro, a series of civic buildings joined together in 2013 by a spectacular architectural canopy that forms an indoor street. We line up at the open canteen, load plates with herring and berries, and settle down at a table to eat. There is very little cold or standoffish about Pekka or Esa. When I speak, they listen, and vice versa. When there's nothing to be said, we eat without words, listening to the half-silence all around.

'How do you know when you've met a Finnish extrovert?' the old joke goes. 'He's looking at *your* shoes, not his.' Writing about human behaviour and creativity in nationalistic terms is cumbersome, clichéd and can border on the offensive. But anyone who has spent a significant amount of time in Finland is likely to acknowledge that the joke works because, to some degree, it is rooted in truth. I have met some Finns who are gregarious chatterboxes and have encountered a number of quiet Americans too. If the Finnish joke enshrines a stereotype, it is a stereotype born of a canon of behaviour that has been observed for decades and is increasingly owned by self-knowing Finns. 'You can practically be arrested for speaking to strangers in Helsinki,' the Finnish conductor Esa-Pekka Salonen once said, drawing a stark comparison with his new home, Los Angeles.

Salonen is one of a swathe of Nordic classical musicians to have fulfilled contracts outside their home countries in the last three decades, a gargantuan talent export that has transformed the experience of classical music for many in mainland Europe, Britain, the United States and beyond. In 2021, individuals from Finland, Denmark or Sweden were employed as lead conductors at six of the United Kingdom's sixteen professional symphony orchestras and its only full-time, salaried choir. British and American orchestras commission more music from Nordic composers than from German and Italian ones combined. Once a month, a pub in London presents the most interesting new bands from the Nordic region in a club night that has garnered a cult following. It's never long before the Eurovision Song Contest gravitates back towards the Nordic region – for many, its spiritual home.

Perhaps the best-known Nordic musician of all is Björk Guðmundsdóttir, a singer and composer from Iceland identifiable by her first name alone and recognizable in an instant from the darkness that lingers behind her eyes. Björk encapsulates the wider popularity of Nordic culture across genres and also the cult of Nordic fandom: she looks different, sounds different and appears entirely rooted in the nature and folklore of a mysterious, faraway land. For the more rational, Björk is outstandingly talented, creatively brave, personally honest, uncommonly broad-minded, largely unfettered by notions of reputation and evidently takes her work extremely seriously.

Publicists have seized on those ideals in an age when the commercial music industry wants to squeeze yet more money out of its remaining assets and classical music badly needs a change in image. As a pop musician who once sang Schoenberg at the Salzburg Festival, Björk straddles both domains. But it's in classical music that we've seen the bigger explosion of interest in Nordic artists and repertoire. Dozens of classical concert promoters and orchestras in the United Kingdom (UK), and many in the United States, Australasia and the Far East, have presented Nordic music strands with accompanying imagery of swirling aurora borealis or flat lakes lined with forests.

Plenty of those who have taken to fetishizing Nordic lifestyles to sell music, furniture, fiction or holidays have homed in on parallel aspects of life in the North. Up here, we are told, you find a slower alternative to the fast lane of European and American capitalism, one that manages to remain innovative and progressive nonetheless. We are pointed towards the significance of nature and the continued dialogue with indigenous traditions including music, storytelling and non-sacred ritual. For all that intangible and questionable folklore, there is also hard political reality. This is the landmass on which the social democratic project of high tax, high wages and a full provision of public services from cradle to grave has held out. It seems an inescapable truth that the politics of universal entitlement born in postwar Scandinavia have played a pivotal role in the success of Nordic musicians – first at home, then abroad. Have those politics influenced the sound of their music, too?

Back at Campus Allegro, Esa and Pekka walk me through the indoor street, where an orchestra of preschool string players is giving an informal performance for an audience of office workers and retirees. At an atrium at the far end, they show me a remnant of the forest we visited that morning: a huge glacial boulder that was plonked here by the biggest crane Pietarsaari has ever seen, not long before the complex was topped-out. The artist Benjamin Orlow was asked to put his mark on the rock and opted to embroider it with a strip of red neon twisted into the shape of handwriting. It spells out a simple sentence: 'I can do anything I want.'

Standing in the boulder's basin-like clearing, you are surrounded by a constellation of commercial, educational and cultural institutions. In one direction is the University of Applied Sciences, its art school Novia specializing in the creation of works from animal fur. Less than twenty yards in the other direction is the Pietarsaari Music Institute, fully equipped with pipe organs, Steinway pianos and iMac computer suites. Without stepping into the cruel Ostrobothnian outdoors, you can access a cinema, a library, the headquarters of a local bank and a fully equipped modern concert hall. There, the following night, Esa will play his trombone in a performance of Beethoven's Pastoral Symphony given by the town's orchestra of professionally trained musicians, the Pietarsaari Sinfonietta. All this in a metropolis of under 20,000 souls.

It was never the plan that the Nordic countries would export classical music and musicians to the world – that orchestras in Los Angeles, San Francisco, Seattle, Minneapolis, Ottawa, Toronto, Bogotá, Tokyo, Seoul, Paris, Montpellier, Lyon, Rome, Prague,

Saarbrücken, Cologne, Detmold, Leipzig, London, Manchester, Birmingham, Bournemouth, Glasgow, Cardiff, Wellington and Auckland would have chief conductors drawn from a region with a collective population smaller than that of Texas. Evidence on the ground in Scandinavia, Finland, Iceland and the Faroe Islands tells you how it has come to pass. These countries are strewn with music schools, professional orchestras, fit-for-purpose concert halls and modern opera houses. Much of that infrastructure was born of a political movement that sees culture as part of the welfare state, as a source of sustenance for the largest possible number of people in strangely shaped, difficult-to-traverse countries where isolation and weather could easily conspire against mental health. The question, then, is whether the eggs of civic infrastructure came before the chickens of human creativity and original artistic thinking.

It was the proliferation of new and beautiful performance venues, experienced as a tourist rather than a critic, that piqued my interest in the musical life of the Nordic countries, leading me to explore how classical music up here is supported and presented. Later, attending performances as a journalist, it became clear these buildings were physical manifestations of something deeper. The more I reported from the Nordic region, the more I recognized that the arts, and classical music in particular, occupy a different position in national conversations here.

More than a decade on, now a Scandinavian taxpayer, I have found myself immersed not just in the musical life of the North, but in everyday life here. I have become familiar with the region's strange combination of progressiveness and closed-mindedness, asceticism and aspiration, complacency and hunger for self-improvement. I have experienced the dark side of Nordic societies and grappled with the sometimes chilling truths that Brand Scandinavia likes to conceal. Gradually subsumed into Nordic ways, I have seen the joys and frustrations of these systematic societies mirrored in the way their music is made, shared and even written.

Never has that music lost its allure, even as I've considered its reluctance to shake off some central ingredients apparently instilled by the likes of Sibelius. The strange state of *Tapiola* – in which each bar evolves out of the natural impulses of its predecessor, in which instrumental texture and colour are as important as harmony and rhythm, in which the music itself appears to suggest that the ideal sound is no sound at all – has influenced composers throughout the world. But its effect in the Nordic region, I have become convinced, has been transformative.

There was something in Sibelius's music, in particular, that told people from Reykjavík to Rovaniemi that this was *their* language, *their* sound, even as that sound proved so alluring to folk with no connection to the North whatsoever. *Tapiola* was written for Sibelius-obsessed Americans, and there were plenty across the Atlantic who sensed something separatist in it – who heard music that spoke, to paraphrase one contemporary critic, of another way of existing.[3] Certain composers in Scandinavia, Finland and Iceland have become fixated with the organic design features perfected in Sibelius's late works. Many claim no connection with his music whatsoever while still writing scores that appear to breathe the same air, even if they employ entirely different methods. Others have convinced themselves that *Tapiola*'s sense of distillation represents the music of the North in its purest, most honest form – a vision of Nordic functionalism equivalent to an Arne Jacobsen chair. Is it possible that we hear in the music what we see in the design, even if we're not conscious of it?

Long after the sun has disappeared in Pietarsaari, Esa and Pekka walk me to that quintessentially Finnish of watering holes: an American-style sports bar. Inside are musicians from the festival I'm here to report on. Despite the proliferation of flat screens and framed memorabilia, plenty of customers are determined to avoid any distraction from the business of getting drunk. Others have turned out to witness a rare occurrence in European sport, the sight of two Nordic soccer teams playing one another in the Europa League. Nobody told the music festival, which has arranged for the violinist Pekka Kuusisto to take to the small stage beneath the biggest of the big screens and play an hour-long set.

At a certain point, the game between Finland's HJK (Helsingin Jalkapalloklubi) and Denmark's FCK (FC Copenhagen) is switched off. The lights are lowered, the hubbub subsides and Kuusisto starts to loop and overlay folk songs on his fiddle, occasionally singing in a plain voice with his eyes clasped shut. Nobody complains, a few leave and a group of teenagers in one corner try to contain hysterical laughter. The overwhelming majority, however, sit attentively – apparently as transfixed by the performance as they were by the game.

Nordic classical music, even more so its 'contemporary' sub-genre, might never attain the mainstream appeal of the popular music that shares its DNA. But there's something about the work produced by progressive Nordic musicians of all genres that evidently cuts through the communicative troubles endured by equivalent music elsewhere. That is partly connected to the conditioning of audiences, like those in the Pietarsaari sports bar, by the cultural aspirations of the Nordic region's education system, its civic institutions and its principled media. Then again, the rest of us seem to enjoy and admire contemporary Nordic music too. In the 2010s, little Denmark produced two winners of the so-called Nobel Prize for Composers, the University of Louiseville's Grawemeyer Award. Both write music that, in its own way, treats silence as a commodity.[4]

In 2017, I made a radio programme about *Tapiola* for the BBC. Via my inbox, I was quickly reminded that many listeners prefer Sibelius's orchestral alchemy to be left to speak for itself, unfettered by thoughts of cultural, geographical and personal context. Music is music. *Tapiola* is no less chilling, fortifying or tantalizing if you have no idea of the provenance of its composer or the starting point of his inspiration. The piece is as much an exercise in pure musical architecture – or even an abstract state of mind – as it is an image of the 'Northland's dusky forests' referred to at the top of the score. That is what makes it so fascinating and so universal.

But *Tapiola* is called *Tapiola*, and Sibelius chose to build his home in the woods. Those facts present us with plenteous clues as to why this strange and compelling piece does what it does to our brains and bodies. That is the approach I have taken to the musical scores, albums and traditions discussed in this book, united by little more than their illustrative potential, their clear national significance or my pleasure in listening to them. There is no reason the ideas proposed here should foreclose any other, contradictory responses to the music, the infinity of which is what makes the works themselves so universal and so resilient.

As a travelling journalist rather than a laboratory musicologist, I have become increasingly absorbed in the topography, traditions, mindsets and wider cultures of the Nordic countries and how they have shaped the music made here. I have had the opportunity to spend many hours with Nordic musicians, and to walk alone in various corners of the region with the fruits of their labours playing in my ears. The longer I have been here, the more familiar I have become with the societal nuances of these half-dozen countries, bound together by history, geography, language and culture. All the while, those external factors have not drifted away from the music. On the contrary: each has consistently lubricated my understanding of the other.

After numerous dispatches from the Nordic countries, it seemed about time I gathered some snapshots of that process together – to tell some stories and trace some parallel lines, including my own linear journey to understanding this music better. After 15 years reporting from the region, 7 of them living here, I have had plenty of stereotyped ideas about Nordic art and society overturned, but just as many reinforced or subtly realigned. Naturally, some simplification is necessary when introducing six countries with distinctive cultures under one banner, and I'm confident each of those countries feels secure enough in itself to accept the odd flippant remark by way of broad characterization. Otherwise, what I report on here is what I have seen with my eyes, heard with my ears and interpreted through the lens of my lived experience. Nordic music, especially its classical sub-genre, is a rich, varied and sprawling subject and this book makes no attempt to provide a comprehensive view of it. By necessity, plenty of talented and important musicians are left out. The silence can speak for them.

Nordic / Scandinavian

References in the text to 'Scandinavia' refer to Denmark, Norway and Sweden – the three Scandinavian kingdoms bound by common linguistic and political roots. Finland and Iceland, regarded locally as separate from Scandinavia, will be referred to in the text as such. The term 'Nordic countries' incorporates all five nations together with the Faroe Islands – like Greenland, an autonomous country within the Kingdom of Denmark.

1

Landfall

"Scandinavia is a collection of countries we can't tell apart."
A. A. Gill

Landing a plane at Haugesund Airport takes mettle as well as skill. The runway is squeezed between jagged rocks on the straight edge of Norway's south-west coast, the bit that stares blankly at the Shetland Islands. As you approach by air from the southeast, a chaotic miniature mountain range consistently veers up and falls away again, as if from the pages of a child's pop-up book. From a window seat, it's impossible to know if you're seconds or minutes from touching down.

That's assuming you can see anything. Rain is as near to constant as anywhere on the continent here. Mist and precipitation can reduce visibility to a few metres. Winds are often fiercely strong. This time, in November 2006, you could see land from around fifteen metres above it. But still the aircraft wobbled, dipped and shimmied awkwardly when the tarmac appeared. At the last possible moment, a surge of throttle yanked it back into the sky like a marionette.

The go-around provided a useful aerial tour of a small but representative patch of Karmøy, where western Norway dissolves into the North Sea and straggles of thin, rocky land meet thousands of islands scattered like biscuit crumbs. This is the forbidding landscape of Scandinavian stereotype, mythically if not factually representative of a corner of the continent traditionally left off the beaten track, in every sense.

Much of Norway's west coast looks like this. Patterns of islands and peninsulas are strewn around an ocean either confrontationally frothy or overwhelmingly bleak. Significant, directional stretches of road are rare. Only recently has the Norwegian state started to construct slender bridges between inhabited spits and islands, negating the constant need to board ferries to cover even modest distances. Even in our age of connectivity, communities in this part of Norway are isolated by logistics more than by kilometres.

Bergen, the country's second city and former capital, nestles between fingers of steep rock protruding into the water. There is no way to enter the town that isn't spectacular, but my coach drive north from Haugesund resembled traditional methods: around mountain and over fjord, via wheel and hull. Through the ferry windows, it was impossible to decipher where water stopped and mist started. Sometimes, the outline of a vast mountain could be picked out in the enveloping greyness. Only on subsequent visits could I fill in the blanks: the colossal peaks, sheer hillsides and serene snaking fjords.

For now, there were real-life Norwegians to observe. Scandinavians, we are informed by history and legend, are Europe's great survivors – a people whose fearless view of the world stood them in good stead through the first great land-grab of historical record and has continued to, even through the ruptures of the twentieth century and the moral quandaries of the twenty-first. On the ferry's rudimentary main deck, Norwegians poked hot-dogs into their mouths, lathered with ketchup and mustard from industrial-sized dispensers. Fizzy lager or acrid black coffee washed them down. Conversation was minimal from the businesspeople, truckers and teenagers, mutually unwound by the journey's slow tempo – or so it seemed. They looked calmly into the wind and rain with a sort of well-worn respect. To them, it wasn't weather, it was nature – the great enemy and the great inspiration.

Norway's most famous composer, Edvard Grieg, was native to these parts. In his day, the late 1800s, painters and musicians were holding this area of the country aloft as the 'real' Norway – the cradle of its identity and an inspiration to those who would stand up and be counted in the face of colonial rule from Denmark and Sweden. But, as the singers sang and the exhibitions were organized, locals were leaving Norway in their thousands. They'd had enough of isolation, poverty, bitter cold and months without seeing the sun. No song or painting was going to persuade them it was worth staying.

One of those who left, and persuaded many to follow, was a musician himself. On the square in Bergen that bears his name stands an image in bronze of Ole Bull, violin under chin. Bull was the André Rieu of the nineteenth century, the first musician to dress up indigenous Norwegian music (folk tunes, in other words) and present it to the general populace in concert. In 1852, the publisher Christian Tønsberg issued a picture book titled *Norwegian National Costumes* in support of the burgeoning nationalist movement.[1] Its appendix included six folk tunes transcribed into musical notation by Bull. Among them was the first attempt at notating a melody born on a Hardanger fiddle, the distinctive folk instrument indigenous to this corner of Norway.

Flushed with success as his countrymen struggled, Bull staked everything on a grand idea: a scheme to cross the Atlantic himself and colonize a huge patch of Pennsylvania he referred to as New Norway. In the United States his delusions of grandeur saw him name one district Oleana and construct a hilltop dwelling he christened Valhalla in another. But those same delusions soon got the better of Bull and after a series of misjudgments the whole enterprise collapsed. He was forced back to Bergen where he used what remained of his fortune to build an elaborate villa overlooking a slither of the North Sea.

Bull's cajoling of the folk music of western Norway's valleys and mountains into the concert hall may have broken new ground. But its most significant effect was to inspire Grieg, who would inject the spirit of that music into notated scores that soon took their place among those of the European masters. Grieg gave Norway its first outward-facing musical voice. But his career demonstrates what a musical backwater his homeland was for much of the nineteenth century.

In the absence of a suitable institution at home, Grieg was sent to Felix Mendelssohn's conservatory in Leipzig to learn the craft of the composer, German-style. After graduation in 1862, he moved to Copenhagen, the Danish capital and the nearest the Nordic region had to a cosmopolitan musical hub. It was here, encouraged by an enclave of Norwegians and generously aided by Bull, that Grieg began to consider how he might use his homeland's vernacular tunes and dances in the forging of original concert music – music that would also lend weight to Norway's burgeoning calls for emancipation from foreign rule.

Grieg made a go of it. He returned to Norway a success, widely recognized and installed in his own fjord-side villa outside Bergen. By now his music had become highly sympathetic to the nationalist cause almost by instinct, mostly by borrowing methods from the folk music propagated by Bull. Grieg's music was rural rather than urban, Norwegian rather than Danish, full of the clarity and freshness that would come to characterize the Nordic in art. It had freed itself from the calorific excess of German music while utilizing that music's most advanced techniques. Grieg's Piano Concerto borrowed the design of the concerto by the German Robert Schumann. But while the two works are overtly similar in style, Grieg's manages to sound entirely different, deploying characteristic musical tricks to conjure up an unmistakable sense of wide, open spaces. Norwegian painters sought the same ends on canvas, obsessing over dramatic views of mountain, sea and sky and the peasant authenticity of the country's west coast.

Grieg's musical image of Norway bore an umbilical connection to its landscape. He was soon drawn into the emerging national obsession for outdoor pursuits that has become a key plank of the nation's image today. In 1887, having enjoyed a walking tour to the hotbed of Norwegian folklore that was the Jotunheim Mountains, the composer wrote to his Danish colleague Niels Ravnkilde: 'I would not swap this for a dozen Gewandhaus concerts.' The reference was to the prestigious orchestra in Leipzig with its links to Bach and Mendelssohn. Grieg had become more sensitive to sound, more individual, more fearless. Norway's landscape was making him a more recognizably Norwegian composer, in his own mind and on the pages of his scores.

▲

A few hours after leaving Haugesund, my bus pulled into Bergen's squat concrete bus station where a group of teenagers were on hand, deep in optometric conversation and sucking fervently on cigarettes. The walk into the city took me past the back of a shopping precinct and the crosshatch of streets where Bergen, for a moment, resembled a modern European metropolis. From every other angle, the place felt somehow unreal, a model village up-scaled to almost life-size. The fairytale clapboard terrace that lines the main harbour stopped just before you'd expect it to. The city-centre mountain, Fløyen, roared into the sky and yet was conquerable, in sneakers, in an afternoon.

The next morning, the last hotel guest at breakfast, I got talking to the Australian chef, also in his twenties. He had arrived in Norway while travelling and been captivated by its unlikeliness, too intrigued to leave. 'I've seen plenty of visitors sitting right there, where you're sitting, looking out and wondering how a place like this can even exist,' he said, unable to conceal that touch of smugness that comes by default to foreigners who have made their homes in beautiful places.

He was a stout man with a hairy, rotund face whose proportions were as generous as his spirit. He had stayed in Bergen, ten months and counting, for 'fresh air, outdoor sports, the girls and a job that lets me off at two' – not inconsiderable bargaining chips even for an Australian. Later that day, I sat in the window of the city centre McDonalds and watched as a steady procession of smiling Norwegians trotted past in the direction of Fløyen, which sprouts up from the concrete sidewalk less than 50 yards away (Bergen literally means 'the hill'). Three teenagers at the table next to me finished their Big Macs, slung on their backpacks and joined the climbers.

I turned right out of McDonalds towards the city's cathedral – an atypical Norwegian church, built of stone rather than wood and sporting a spray of stained glass around its altar. In the porch, I bought a CD of choral music by Grieg. It cost as much as the flight from London to Haugesund but seemed worth the outlay – a proper musical souvenir, recorded by Bergen's cathedral choir under its conductor Magnar Mangersnes three years earlier. This being 2006, I took the plastic disc back to the hotel and listened to it on a portable CD player.

The headline piece was Grieg's *Four Psalms*. The English title is misleading, as the word 'salmer' in Norwegian more accurately translates as 'hymns'. Grieg's texts come not from the Old Testament but from poetry by the Danish theologians Hans Adolf Brorson and Hans Thomissøn and their Swedish counterpart Laurentius Laurentii Laurinus. Their metrical verses speak of faith, sin, the resurrection and paradise. I knew a handful of Grieg's orchestral works but the *Four Psalms* came as a surprise. There was a vulnerability about the music that I took as a quality – the same quality I saw and heard all around me in Norway and would continue to over the years, even if I would come to define it in less patronizing terms.

The singing on the recording sounded different from that of polite English choirs. The Bergen ensemble's lighter and more breathy sound brought a soft edge to the music – a vibrating resonance, something suggesting the shroud of mist that had enveloped the ferry the day before. It was sensitive but earnest singing, in tune with the sentiments of the texts. Grieg wrote the collection in 1906, a century before my trip, months before he died and a year after Norway finally declared itself an independent country. Its score calls for a choir of four voice parts with an integrated male-voiced soloist. On this recording, the soloist sang with a stern, oaky voice.

If nature and folksong are everywhere you turn in Nordic music, the Lutheran church is often not that far behind – from Dietrich Buxtehude's baroque cantatas to Abba's disco hits. It was Denmark that imposed Lutheranism on Norway and Iceland. Sweden, in turn, installed it in Finland. The fit was good: a version of Christianity that shunned hierarchies, disliked overt display, fostered resolve and in more recent times presented no theological obstacles to anointing women. The plain interiors of the Nordic region's Lutheran churches are an obvious precursor to its celebrated interior design aesthetic. Their clear-glass windows suggested to the faithful that they look not for transubstantiationalist miracles to see God's work, but to the divine beauty of the natural world outside.

Of all the territories it had lost to Luther's teaching, Rome was least bothered about Scandinavia – an outpost so far north it barely existed on the cultural map; it was presumed so full of violent, pillaging heathens it was probably unsalvageable anyway. The reasoning might have been wrong but the judgement was probably right, and it extends to historiography. Only recently have the Nordic lands and their artists, writers, philosophers and composers been deemed worthy of serious critical and academic attention. Besides, the Nordic people were far too busy searching their own souls to offload the contents thereof onto others. That much is clear from Grieg's *Four Psalms*.

Grieg's own opinions on religion remain uncannily representative today. He was sceptical of dogma and suspicious of the church's authority, as disdainful of its higher echelons as Martin Luther had been before him. But he felt culturally tethered, however loosely, to the institution of the church even if his spirituality was founded on the sanctity of man's private relationship with God – another Lutheran conceit reflected directly in the design of the *Four Psalms*, its introspective, individual soloist surrounded by a choral community.

That soloist is a baritone, the vocal range of the average adult male, even a pint-sized one like Grieg. When he steps out from the ensemble to sing of hopes and fears, the soloist personifies the individual's relationship with an all-seeing God. But he also gives the music a sudden depth and perspective. Grieg consciously placed a certain musical distance between these two elements in his piece, the individual and the masses. The call-and-response and echo techniques Grieg used in so many of his works had their origins in the herding calls that allowed for communication across Norway's valleys. For Grieg, they spoke of metaphorical distance: then and now, the echo of history, the sense of something lost. 'It is the feeling of looking backwards and forwards at the same time,' the Norwegian baritone Johannes Weisser explained to me in 2010, 'melancholy combined with hope.'

That sentiment pervades much of Grieg's music. No sooner had Norway achieved complete independence in 1905 than the world started to industrialize and old certainties were questioned. Those Norwegians who had stayed put had been forced to grapple with radical ideas proposed by the Danish philosopher Søren Kierkegaard, who challenged one of the very foundations of society – the authority of the church – while arguing that a truly virtuous life came with a side order of unavoidable mental torture. Norway, meanwhile, was modernizing before it had been afforded the chance to mature.

The most overtly Norwegian ingredients of Grieg's *Four Psalms* are the tunes themselves. They had existed long before Grieg did, and came to him via Ludvig Mathias Lindeman, an organist who set out to collect indigenous melodies from various parts of Norway in 1848, compensated for his troubles by a government stipend. One of the locations he visited was Valdres, a centre of Norwegian folk music not far from the Jotunheimen Mountains where Grieg liked to hike. The composer found the tunes in Lindeman's publication titled *Older and Newer Norwegian Field Melodies Collected and Arranged for Piano*.[2] In his *Four Psalms*, Grieg applied his tried and tested method of unlocking the harmonies he believed implicit in all Norwegian folk tunes. Most of the composer's works reflect, at their heart, his quest to 'express my impression of the hidden harmonies in our folk melodies'.

But Grieg did more. There are plenteous techniques borrowed from folk music in the *Four Psalms*, beside those echo effects. They include drones created by continuous notes in fixed positions (sometimes a drone of two notes at a set interval), harmonies that smooth the way from whole tones to half tones and hints of the individual frolicking ornaments that would have sprouted when the tunes were sung communally in church. Grieg invested the melodies themselves with focus, structure and expressionistic directness. But he dressed them with just a little more harmonic sophistication than he had let on — the sort that allowed for subtext and friction, especially when grinding major and minor keys up against one other. Grieg even extended the implied distance between the soloist and the choir by having one sing in the minor mode of a particular key at the same time as the other sings in its major mode, and vice versa.[3]

We might speculate, too, that there was a serving of politics in Grieg's last published work. *Guds søn har gjort mig fri* ('God's Son Hath Set Me Free') ends its litany of resolve with seven spirited repetitions of the word 'free': a celebration of Norway's recent liberation? *Jesus Christus er opfaren* ('Christ is Risen') is riddled with clashing harmonies that don't resolve: hints of Norway's collective existential and religious crisis? The last of the four, *I Himmelen* ('In Heaven Above') is a picture of heavenly bliss wrought from earthly diligence. The choir's voices are bound extraordinarily tightly: a warning to the nation's communities to buckle-up as the wrecking ball of industrialization started to swing?

What sounds most Norwegian of all in the *Four Psalms* is also that which retains such startling currency in Norway today: the residual melancholy that comes from knowing a place and seeing it change, and the relative reassurance that can be experienced when sharing that feeling with others. Grieg couldn't have predicted that his native land would transform itself more rapidly than any other nation in Europe, in every year subsequent to his death and counting. It's difficult to be in Bergen, an old city made rich by a new industry, and not feel the tenacious melancholy of the *Four Psalms* – however beautiful the view.

◢

By 2008, I was working as a journalist on a music magazine. I had returned to Norway in the intervening years and in February 2010 was sent on assignment to Tromsø, its northernmost major city. Tromsø lies 350 kilometres inside the Arctic Circle, at the point where the country's land mass starts to curve eastwards to meet the extreme ends of Sweden, Finland and Russia.

Three hours into the flight from London, the captain's voice sounded over the intercom. In a jaunty Norwegian accent, he invited passengers to look out of the plane's left side windows. 'You will see our most spectacular weather feature: the aurora borealis.' Even through the glass and plastic of an aircraft window, the Northern Lights were indeed spectacular. They resembled a gargantuan curtain of green light, rippling and shimmering with energy. They hung there like an apparition, before the plane banked and descended in preparation for its approach.

We landed late at Tromsø, way past midnight. I took a taxi into the city, driven by a Syrian member of Norway's imported working class of Middle Eastern and Baltic nationals. Despite the late hour, he insisted on making a short detour, stopping at a research facility on the side of a hill, in front of which stood a huge polar bear frozen forever by taxidermists. In its reinforced glass case, the beast reared up resplendent on hind legs, its paws gesturing like the hands of a conductor. Below us, whitened by snow and ice and glowing with yellow electric light, Tromsø resembled an Arctic Budapest in miniature, its city and mountain sides separated by a spindly, altitudinous bridge that rose like the peak on a seismograph.

The driver, Karam, told me of Tromsø's fishing industry, its techno music scene, its indigenous Sámi population and its proud litany of 'world's northernmosts' (brewery, university, league football team, Burger King – all higher up than the highest point in Alaska). 'Remember, you can't outrun one of those,' he said, pointing at the polar bear. I took the comment to be flippant but realized later it was simply advice. As we talked, the Northern Lights materialized again, this time in the full force of their magnificence, coursing through the sky apparently right above us. It was less enchanting this time, more overwhelming – a visual representation of the most imposing music imaginable, and yet entirely silent.

Tromsø is relatively mild for its latitude, a benevolence of the Gulf Stream. Still, February's standard -7°C, limited daylight and omnipresent whiteness were enough to teach you that the northern Nordic winter is less a season than a grand, immersive installation that alters every sense. You get wise to the practicalities quickly, learning to base your wardrobe on cotton and down and having a method for taking it all off fast in well-heated cafés and bars.

Mental adjustment takes a little longer. I got my first sense of it as I listened to the Spanish harpist-singer Arianna Savall and the Norwegian fiddler-singer Petter Udland Johansen in the panelled boardroom of the Tromsø Savings Bank. Their concert titled 'Peiwah' formed part of the festival I was here to cover, Nordlysfestivalen (The Northern Lights Festival). Peiwah drew the fishing communities of northern Norway and Catalonia together by delicately weaving their respective folk tunes in one continuous thread. A small, warm, wood-lined building in a cold climate does something to human concentration and interaction, even before you throw intimate live music into the mix.

Around the corner from the bank was the Rorbua Pub, a raucous, smelly old bar which also formed the setting for a talk show beamed live to the nation once a week while punters went about their business in the background (from the corner, another stuffed polar bear supervised proceedings). In this place, representative of a utilitarian resolve that casts Tromsø a long way from prettified Bergen, I met Ole, a retired lorry driver, and his friend Vibeke, a former nurse. Ole had the direct, fearless gaze of someone who had grown up in the wilderness while Vibeke's face steadily shook off its veneer of sorrow as more alcohol was poured into it. They spoke to me in good English about the forecasted blizzard: what sort of snow it would bring, how the airport would keep its runway open, where not to go once it arrived. On my last night in town the heavy snow duly blew in and the festival's closing party became a lock-in, the Tromsø Big Band playing into the small hours as the snowline crept up the windowpanes. Low volume jazz and focused improvisation were what seemed to get cold Tromsø listening hardest – antidotes to the cold that so easily drains cohesive thought.

A few nights previously at Tromsø's Culture House, the violinist Ragnhild Hemsing had given a concert that merged Grieg's Violin Sonata No. 2 with the folk tunes that inspired it, playing on both a classical violin and a Hardanger fiddle. There was a dance element too. In a newly commissioned work by Lasse Thoresen, a composer as reliant on Norway's folk tradition as Grieg was, the dancer Hallgrim Hansegård contorted his body in cahoots with an inanimate milk urn, his moves conceived as a result of considerable research into the precise physical language of the folk dances known as 'halling'. Less than a year earlier, Hansegård had danced with another fiddler, Alexander Rybak, as part of Norway's winning act at the 2009 Eurovision Song Contest in Moscow.

Thoresen's piece was titled *Yr*, a pun referencing both anticipation and drizzle (more Bergen than Tromsø). It was played on a normal violin strung according to a folk fiddle's tuning system, in this case 'gorrlaus' (bottom to top, the strings tuned F-C-A-E). The distinctive tuning took the violin out of the domain of the concert hall but the piece itself had plenty of mountain mud on its shoes, looking out over long distances as it spun a yarn of joy and sorrow, patience and fortitude. The music served as a good reminder that the Norway idealized by the national romantics was a tough place to be.

One moment, *Yr* indulged the liberties beloved of twenty-first-century composers (notes between notes, scratches, grinding discords). The next, it dug into the preferred devices of the folk musicians: open intervals, drones on one string accompanying weaving melodies on another, rhythmic drive stemming from the heel-end of the bow – many of the same devices used in Grieg's sonata. After *Yr*, Hemsing switched to her Hardanger fiddle to play 'Hulder Tune' from Vang, a melody from a district to the east of Bergen where Lindeman had done his tune-collecting and from where Hansegård had got his dance moves (a 'hulder' is a seductive enchantress common to Norwegian mythology).

The openness, resonance and freshness of the Hardanger fiddle is a tonic, especially for those accustomed to veneered concert violins. These are instruments that semaphore, as if from hill to hill, yet remain capable of deep sensitivity. Their clarity is built on the resonance of overtones – the often-inaudible notes produced by certain frequencies – rather than brute force, while the old tuning systems immediately shift the music they play onto a different paradigm. Before Grieg and the many other Nordic composers who felt a responsibility to dignify folk music by making it 'classical', instruments like the Hardanger fiddle were what gave the Nordic region its own distinctive sounds.

◢

Norway's most extensive collection of musical instruments can be found in a stately villa, perched on a hill on the Lade Peninsula, just north-east of the city of Trondheim. The house once belonged to Trondheim grandee Christian Bachke, who fell in love with a Russian named Victoria Rostin in 1919 while she was up from Oslo visiting her older sister (who had initiated the family tradition for falling in love with Trondheimers three years earlier). The Rostin sisters were born into money but had found themselves marooned in Europe at the outbreak of the First World War and sought refuge in Oslo. The older sister, a singer named Valentina, had made the journey to Trondheim in 1916 and never returned. Victoria went to visit her in 1919 and stayed too, marrying Christian and getting the run of his villa, Ringve.

Norway was officially neutral during the First World War but allied to Britain, which took charge of its merchant shipping operations. The next global conflict would afford the country no such luxuries. In April 1940 a Nazi armada sailed calmly up the Oslo Fjord and took control of the nation. Certain pockets, including Trondheim, resisted hard. Norway's National Day is now celebrated on 17 May, ostensibly marking the end of Swedish rule on 8 May 1905. It is actually the day on which the Nazi occupation ended forty years later.

Meanwhile, German troops had demanded the Bachkes give up their estate to make way for a makeshift airstrip on the peninsula. They had not bargained on the formidable Victoria, who negotiated hard to save the building and was promptly suspected of collusion in a Norway bristling under occupation. Denmark had fallen to Hitler's forces more quickly, physically joined to Germany and less well positioned to resist. Sweden remained neutral while Finland, not long free from Russia, was drawn into fighting intermittently for both sides.

When her husband Christian died in 1946, Victoria set about converting their villa into a museum of musical instruments collected on her various trips around the world or sourced via fertile relationships with certain Copenhagen dealers. Her project became the talk of the town. The museum, known as Ringve, still stands and survived a fire in 2015. It is now Norway's national museum for music and instruments.

Trondheim is a good place for it. Another former Norwegian capital, the city sits on a fjord at the mouth of a river, squat in comparison to Bergen and more ready to divide its quaint old districts from its aspiring steel and glass ones. In Trondheim, violinists aren't immortalized in bronze. They walk the streets, instruments slung over shoulders, on the way to compete in the city's string quartet competition, to play in one of its two professional orchestras, to appear in its zippy chamber music festival – or perhaps to work a shift as a Ringve guide.

All manner of keyboard, string, woodwind, brass and percussion instruments reside in this creaking villa and its outbuildings, charting the development of an art form and the Nordic countries' sluggish participation in that development throughout the twentieth century. There are plenty of instruments imported from abroad, but the region's own folk heritage gets pride of place. The museum's most interesting specimens suggest how instrumental music in this part of the world was first heard, which naturally leads visitors to wonder what that music actually sounded like.

On a visit in 2009, one of the collection's Hardanger fiddles was played for me by a student guide, its resonance all the more palpable in a small, wood-panelled room. The instrument emerged from its namesake region, just south-east of Bergen, at the turn of the eighteenth century. It started out as a vessel for the lullabies, laments, dances and herding calls that underpinned the cycle of life in rural Norway – tunes seasoned with the drones, recurring open intervals and delicate ornamental elements adopted by Grieg. Soon the Hardanger fiddle made its way into church, leading the bridal procession at weddings. Florid decorations grace the instruments' necks and scrolls, but the more eagle-eyed will notice extra strings placed underneath the standard four. These remain untouched by the player, but resonate with overtones in acoustic sympathy with the bowed strings above, lending drones extra depth and giving melodies a touch more zing – the present, evocative sound I had heard from Hemsing in Tromsø.

The contraption that really caught my eye in Ringve is associated with Sweden. The nyckelharpa resembles the love-child of a Hardanger fiddle and a hurdy-gurdy. It incorporates the resonating strings of the former, but the sound it produces when bowed ups the ante again: richer, fizzier, punctuated by the clickety-clacks of mechanical frets activated by keys resembling dinosaur teeth. The British Swedophile Andrew Brown has likened its sound to 'an accordion on the verge of tears'.

The precise geographical origins of the nyckelharpa are unknown, but wherever it came from, it survived only in Sweden. Specifically, in the Uppland district north of Stockholm where it served much the same function the Hardanger fiddle had in central Norway. Courtesy of a handful of pioneering revivalists, by the 1900s the nyckelharpa had developed from an instrument with a single melody string to a fully chromatic device with a considerable range – and that striking sound.

This 'new' nyckelharpa was capable of more than the simple polkas that formed the mainstay of Swedish folk music. In 2011, the nyckelharpist Emilia Amper was nominated for a Grammy for her recording of a miniature concerto for the instrument by composer Johannes Rusten, performed with the Trondheim Soloists. The piece, *Abrégé*, weaves tunes in the traditional folk style around a string orchestra with a charming combination of the lyrical and the mechanical – the very anatomy of her instrument. 'It's hard to put words to the sound of the nyckelharpa,' Amper told me that year, 'but I would say it has a lovely fullness and roundness, with a crispy and silver-glittering treble at the same time.'

The nyckelharpa survived its fling with endangered-species status. There have been no such brushes with oblivion for the last of the national folk instruments I saw at Ringve. The kantele is a plucked, zither-like device from the eastern Baltic that Finland has long declared its own. Given the rapid development of the instrument from around five strings to up to thirty, no two handmade kanteles are the same. Of the few I saw at the museum, the most handsome had 24 strings – a stern lump of spruce and hardwood in the form of a bird's wing.

Finland's folkloric Old Testament, the epic poem known as the *Kalevala*, dictates that the first kantele was fashioned by the wizard Väinämöinen from the jawbone of a giant pike. It was then strung with hair plucked from the mane of Big Brown, the demon Hiisi's wayward steed (standard *Kalevala* fare). The sound of the kantele is just as exotic. Quite unlike that of any classical instrument, it is probably closest to that of the Hungarian cimbalom, whose strings are not plucked but struck with metal rods. Like the cimbalom, the kantele carries with it the slightest whiff of Christmas bells.

The instrument and the legend of its provenance demonstrate Finland's relationship to Scandinavia, physically attached but standing culturally apart. Despite its sometime colonial rule by Sweden, republican Finland had few political links with the monarchies that neighbour it to the west before the post-war emergence of a Nordic political alliance, and no linguistic links beyond its bilingual use of Swedish. The Finnish language is closer to Hungarian and Japanese than to Germanic Scandinavian. Likewise, the process of nation building that Finland experienced in parallel with Norway delivered very different musical results. For that, we have Finland's sorcerous folk traditions to thank.

Early kantele players would dispense music that appeared never to begin or end; its hypnotic, mutating streams of variations accompanying shamanistic vocal recitations of the various tales that came to form the *Kalevala*. Grieg used the lullabies, herding calls and hymns of the mountain regions he knew to cultivate concert music as if from Norwegian soil. Jean Sibelius, Finland's first internationally significant composer, would imitate the cyclic, mutating patterns of the Finnish rune singers and kantele players as he reimagined the structural possibilities of the symphony. But only after he'd consciously imitated the sound of the instrument itself.[4]

Finland achieved full independence as a country even later than Norway but in much the same manner, slipping unobtrusively from the grasp of an otherwise-engaged Russia in 1917. Folk tunes, jangling kanteles and magical stories populated by unfortunate souls and all-powerful animals have retained startling currency in Finland's cultural life, as much as any equivalent in Norway, a country that protects its cultural traditions far more fiercely. In Finnish music, traditional mythical elements pop-up across the board – in contemporary classical music, nouveau-folk, pop, rock and even urban genres.

Sibelius's project ran rather deeper than Grieg's. It would bring about a significant reimagining of the structure and grammar of notated music and become more fully emblematic of the separatist sound of the north, despite its entanglement with progressive trends in Europe. Sibelius's most interesting music would even disrupt the traditional teacher–pupil relationship that had existed between Germany and the Nordic countries. Using the rune singers, the kantele players, the flat yet lyrical syllabic gabble of the Finnish language and nature's combination of the apparently miraculous and the coldly scientific, Sibelius moved Nordic music away from the Germanic idea of symphonic 'argument' entirely.

◢

I first arrived in Finland in January 2008, landing in the country's second city, Tampere. The next day I took the train to Helsinki where I stayed in a hotel filled with distinctive furniture and textiles: bent laminate wood; bedding and curtains decorated with tight, repeating patterns rooted in natural blacks, browns and greens. The hotel's interior was distinct from any I had stepped foot in elsewhere. Organic-style patterning was everywhere in Finland: on tablecloths and clothes, on trains (outside and inside) and in TV news studios – the same crosshatching, weaving and hazing I heard everywhere in Sibelius's orchestra.

There was no Finnish music on offer on this first visit to Helsinki, but I had a ticket to see Puccini's *La Bohème* at the National Opera. The production by Reto Nickler took the indiscriminate cruelty of winter as its central theme. Nickler imagined the moments of jocular camaraderie Puccini gives the male cast as those in which the characters had simply forgotten how cold they were. Mimì shuddered and died, happy to enter death's embrace where temperatures might just be higher. No opera audience is representative of a city's populace, alas, but I was immediately aware of the distinctive language and looks of the Finns in the theatre. They appeared to have cultivated a fashion all of their own, disconnected from the European mainstream. Their conversation played to different rules. When Finns spoke English, they invested the language with emotions almost entirely new to me.

Helsinki felt like a hostile place in a January with more sleet than snow. Wind-chill pushed temperatures far below those of Tromsø, which only reinforced the Finnish capital's Cold War ambience. The town rivalled Bergen for damp greyness, but Finland didn't really do urban coziness like its Scandinavian neighbours so there was little to take the edge off it. The cold was accepted for what it was: the great leveller, the manifestation of a lifetime's endurance.

Despite its outbreaks of architectural elegance and art-nouveau flair, Helsinki greets new visitors with a stern face. But its expression has softened year on year as it has danced ever more enthusiastically to the tune of the tourism industry. That industry took me back to Finland six months later, now on a reporting assignment. I stayed my first night in the hotel that sits on top of the Sokos department store, in a room with a roof terrace overlooking Helsinki's central railway station. The difference in everyday existence dictated by change in the season was stark. Way past midnight, red-faced revellers stumbled about in T-shirts in the square below, dodging trams in the faint sunlight.

The next morning I flew north to Kajaani, en route to the town of Kuhmo. Well known it may be in musical circles, but Kuhmo is a town you can easily drive through without noticing. It is an unassuming crosshatch of streets, the landscape rising onto hillsides on one side and sloping down towards the lake on the other. The architecture ranges from drab, flat-roofed commercial properties to proud wooden villas, with the odd modernist showpiece thrown in. On the edge of town is the Kuhmo Arts Centre, a typically Finnish marriage of white concrete and glass topped-out with the angled roof of an auditorium. A straight foyer-corridor leads from the front door on one side of the building to the croissant beach that edges the lake on the other.

I spent nearly a week in Kuhmo, listening to all manner of conceptual concerts in that auditorium, courtesy of the Kuhmo Chamber Music Festival. One concert exclusively presented works labelled Opus 1, starting with a performance of Mozart's Op. 1 by a local seven-year-old and ending with Bach's BWV1, performed by one of Sweden's most respected professional choirs and a full baroque orchestra (the next day, the same choir gave a vigorous performance of Grieg's *Four Psalms*). In the Arts Centre's foyer was an exhibition of animalistic sculptures in smooth and unmovable granite. I sought out their creator Jaana Bombin, who described them to me in magical terms but with the deadpan delivery of someone reciting phone numbers: 'This is the mythical deer whose antlers hold up the sky.'

On my last night in town, I was invited to a traditional Finnish sauna party and duly squeezed naked into a steam-filled garden shed with a colleague from London and the entire male membership of the Eric Ericson Chamber Choir. The heat was enough to permanently damage my contact lenses but the whole experience was liberating, as we shuttled from the sauna to the lake, the nuclear energy of the low sun carrying us through to the small hours. An American harpsichordist grilled reindeer sausages on an open fire, while teenage festival volunteers served us sauna beer (a thing in Finland) from the fridge of a nearby house. The light remained all night, but it changed from hour to hour. By 5 a.m., it had taken on a distinctive orange-blue colour.

Everything about Finland seemed exceptional. A prime-time TV show on state television consisted of a group of women discussing a literary classic for thirty minutes with no cutaways. Folk seemed to go about their business with an expectation that the majesty of nature, the wisdom of animals and the spiritual value of classical music be discussed with no grandstanding. Some musicians played concerts in tracksuits, others in tweed suits with bow ties. Every concert at the festival contained something unusual – music brand new, long forgotten or improvised in the moment. Audiences listened in genuine silence, hour after hour, all day. When they emerged from the dark concert hall into the blazing sunlight, it was to counterbalance concentrated sound with the almost-silence of their almost-empty country. I came away with a new understanding of the phrase 'essential listening'.

Earlier in in the week, I escaped from the Kuhmo Chamber Music Festival's intensive concert schedule and walked as far as possible around the lake from the Hotel Kalevala, whose receptionist had scribbled down a phone number and told me to ring it immediately if I encountered a bear (she wouldn't tell me who would answer). The landscape was flat, its lakes interrupted by patches of forest whose ground level rarely rose more than a few metres higher than the water. The silver birch trees had their own respiratory rhythm and stood remarkably tall; look up, and they appeared to twist into the sky, gently rocking your sense of internal balance like the leering, dizzying lilt that takes root in the first bars of *Tapiola*. Individual birds sang without response. The loudest sounds were the occasionally raised voices of the people on the water and the splash of their oars. It was easy to wade across from a headland to a small, isolated island with its own beach.

I couldn't leave Kuhmo without sampling Kalevala World, a theme park across the road from my hotel that took Finland's epic poem as its subject. I was given a tour by Helena, a student spending her summer as a guide there. She showed me traditional traps for catching bears and wolves and the mocked-up lair of the *Kalevala* witch, Pohjola. She demonstrated some traditional cooking methods and we munched on the pasty, fruity results. My tour ended in the park's timbered main hall (less grand than it sounds), where Helena poured a small glass of strong, clear alcohol and invited me to sit on the floor having turned off the electric lights and extinguished the last remaining candle. 'I will be playing some music very dear to Finns, and we will listen,' the 17-year-old sports science student announced with as much solemnity as she could muster. A technological fumbling, and through the darkness came the sounds of Sibelius's most famous work, *Finlandia*.

▲

On 6 December 1917, Finland found itself free after more than a century of Russian rule. What had been strived for over decades of protest and political machinations had come about almost by accident. In the chaos that ensued after the Bolshevik Revolution, the Finnish Government managed to get a draft proposal for independence onto Lenin's desk. It was signed off on the assumption that Finns would rush to join the new Soviet administration once the dust had settled, driven by left-leaning factions from within.

Lenin had called it wrong. Finland was free, and there was no looking back. In the immediate term there was not much looking forward either. The ensuing power vacuum handed Finland its greatest national tragedy, a brief but bloody civil war that killed 36,000 people – the highest rate of slaughter, per capita per day, of any modern conflict before the Rwandan genocide of 1993. The civil war divided the nation and even families. But reconciliation was swift. The new Finland that emerged from the process was tighter, more pragmatic and somehow more unified than its predecessor.

Ever pragmatic, Finns knew their geographical precariousness and cultural isolation required nothing less. Two decades later they were proved right. In the Winter War of 1939–40, Finland's 340,000 troops and 32 tanks succeeded in holding off the might of the Red Army, albeit losing a fair bit of territory in the process. Finland retained its newly drawn borders and its independence after the World War that followed, despite having effectively been caught on the wrong side. No other Nordic nation drew such a character-building experience from the period.

Through all these conflicts, Sibelius's music played. As a Swedish-speaking Finn who had consciously embraced linguistically Finnish elements of the country's culture, the composer had become a unifying figure almost by default, despite his apparent supporting of the German-backed Whites in the civil war (many socialist Reds also believed the composer theirs). *Finlandia*, the piece Helena played for me in Kuhmo, had set the psychological context. It started life as a direct reaction to Russian antagonism towards Finland enacted by the country's Governor General Nikolay Bobrikov, a controversial figure installed by Tsar Nicholas II in 1898.

Bobrikov was unpopular in Finland from the moment he stepped off the train from St Petersburg. His popularity ratings plummeted further when he attempted to cripple the Finnish press by closing two newspapers in 1899, including the influential Swedish-language *Aftenposten*. An event was hastily organized to raise money for the redundant journalists, for which Sibelius wrote seven short musical tableaux evoking Finnish history. They culminated in a rousing finale: 'Finland Awakes'. The piece opens with angry brass, snarling defensively before giving way to a choral hymn of hope and resolve filled with the rhythmic inflections of the Finnish language and the bowed head of Lutheran obedience.

Finlandia, as it came to be known, has never been Finland's official national anthem (that privilege has thus far been reserved for the African state of Biafra). But it might as well be. It was the piece sung from the steps of Helsinki Cathedral in the summer of 2017 when Finns celebrated 100 years of independence, and two years earlier when they marked 150 years since Sibelius's birth. Finns were uncharacteristically self-satisfied when *Finlandia* was used in the movie *Die Hard* and notably touched when it was covered by Joan

Baez. The piece has been used in flash-mobs supporting gay rights and sung at state funerals. For some time, the Finnish metal band Stratovarius opened sets with its own bespoke *Finlandia*.

Unlike Grieg, Sibelius altered the style and base material of his music according to the project and the audience. He was a naturally cosmopolitan artist, but a distinctly Nordic small-mindedness created in him an ambivalent attitude towards European musical developments in parallel to his own personal oscillation between lambasting Finland as a backwater and cleaving to it as a mother. Whatever motivated it, and however uneasily it occasionally sat, Sibelius's proactive attachment to cultural and linguistic Finnishness would prove essential in rendering his music structurally revolutionary and so sonically different to Austro-German ears. However much he occasionally wanted to, Sibelius just couldn't escape his own country – perhaps because he'd proved so adept at helping to define it.

As in Norway, Finnish artists had been encouraged to search for the nation's peasant heart in order to distill some sense of identity and stir nationalist feelings. The process had got underway long before Bobrikov's rule in Finland but the Governor General's presence only accelerated it. In a direct parallel with Norway's artistic interest in its own west coast, a district of eastern Finland, conveniently located close to the Russian border, was held up as representative of Finland's true spirit and identity. The landscape, folklore and musical traditions of Karelia, including the playing of the kantele and the telling of stories through rune songs, were there for the taking by national romantic artists. And taken they were.

The creative fruits of that process were mixed. Many artists and writers set out to engender a collective sense of Finnish stoicism – a combination of Lutheran perseverance, meteorological fortitude and unerring spiritual resolve that were seen as historical virtues worth calling upon once more. All three were united in an illustration by Sibelius's brother-in-law Eero Järnefelt, published in 1893. It was titled *En Saga*, and shows a hunter poised at the foot of a barren tree in a snow-covered landscape. At the top of the tree cowers a lynx, apparently done for.

Some months later, Sibelius wrote a piece for orchestra with the same name. In Sibelius's mother tongue of Swedish the title refers to 'a story' or 'a tale', heavy with emotional and metaphorical implication. For Sibelius and his circle, the music suggested a deep delve into Finland's ancient history for moral and physical strength. The music for *En Saga* sits at the opposite end of Sibelius's orchestral career to that of *Tapiola*, but surely sewed the seeds for its successor in sound and psychology. 'In none of my other works have I revealed myself so completely,' Sibelius would say of *En Saga*, a whole 50 years after he'd written it, referring to the piece not so much as a story as 'a state of mind.'

▲

In 1891, the son of a doctor from Finland's Swedish-speaking elite and by now an emerging composer, Sibelius joined a busload of colleagues on a nationalist-sponsored trip to Karelia. In the town of Porvoo, Sibelius sat and listened, apparently in a semi-hypnotic state, as one of the last of the rune singers demonstrated her traditional methods for the invited audience. Larin Paraske chanted a handful of *Kalevala* myths from memory in cyclic and emotionally strained incantations lasting hours. Sibelius knew that whatever passed through his large ears could prove useful for future work. He jotted quite a bit of it down.

As he worked to refine and characterize his music's expression, Sibelius developed techniques that are clear descendants of those he heard from Paraske: moulding a small musical motif through repetition; forming tunes from strings of the same note; letting rhythmic emphases induce gradual transformation; fuzzing the distinction between background and foreground. All are tentatively explored in *En Saga*, written two years after Sibelius heard Paraske sing but revised a decade later to better reconcile its combination of beauty and brutality, obviousness and subtlety. By now, Finland had already heard Sibelius's First Symphony, a piece the British critic Ernest Newman believed spoke of 'another way of living'.

The revised *En Saga* goes deeper than the symphony. It bewitches right from its opening, which asks divided strings to play rapid up-down patterns in opposite directions, evoking the jangling resonance of the kantele to the ear while, to the eye, resembling the crosshatched patterning that would become so ubiquitous in Finnish design. Like the sweeping glissando of notes that opens Grieg's mystic song-cycle *Haugtussa*, the opening bars of *En Saga* could be said to form a portal – an invitation to pass from everyday life into another time, another space; a welcome proposition in the troubled Finland of the 1890s.

As the music proceeds, these brooding patterns induce a chant-like musical motif founded on repetitions of a single note. The motif recurs throughout the piece, most notably on a solo cello – the closest the symphony orchestra gets to a lone human voice. There is a certain neutrality to the music that stands in direct contrast to the romantic, central European tradition of the narrative symphonic poem. When you listen to *En Saga*, the effect is of a story not being fed into your ears but unfolding, in your own mind, between them.

Whether or not it sounds Finnish, *En Saga* looks Finnish. The opening pages of the score resemble a classic view of the country's landscape: flat lake (cellos and basses), ordered band of forest (middle strings) and horizon (woodwinds and timpani). As the ingredients already laid out start to alter their shape, the piece advances the idea of musical hypnosis so adeptly deployed by Grieg. Static chords and long-held notes in the bass – so-called 'pedal notes' – create their own sense of distance. Where Grieg led his listeners metaphorically up into the mountains, Sibelius draws them into the tall, spindling forest.

In the short term, Sibelius would be subsumed into the national consciousness of his homeland like no other cultural figure; through all the twentieth century's assorted traumas, a culturally isolated and geopolitically threatened Finland found unity in his music. In the long term, the technical significance of the organic, repetitive musical style he developed would arguably have a hand in shaping musical 'isms' born as far away as Paris and San Francisco. In the twenty-first century, Sibelius is at last being recognized as the pivotal musical figure he was. In 2015, Finns marked 150 years since the composer's birth with major festivities. If that proves to be the last such celebration of her greatest musician by an ever more international Finland, so be it. Since 2015, Sibelius has been increasingly regarded as a composer belonging to the world – even, arguably, by Finns.

In the medium term, Finland felt the effects of having a composer as its national hero, rather than a writer, painter or politician. Within three decades of Sibelius's death, the country had established the largest network of professional orchestras, proportionate to population, of any multi-city country on earth. 'We had the famous portrait of Sibelius by Yousuf Karsh hanging in the classroom at grade school,' one Finnish musician told me in 2015 – not a conductor or violinist, but the rapper Paleface. 'We were all taught that the wrinkles on his forehead, seven, equaled the number of symphonies he wrote. You could just make out a faint eighth wrinkle, the symphony that got away!'

▲

Sibelius was doubly lucky to have been born in Finland, a country where European-style music education barely existed, where it was perfectly possible to grow familiar with classical music's Austro-Germanic compositional conventions without having them embedded in your psyche. The great symphonist Carl Nielsen, Sibelius's senior by just six months, came from a country that had been producing composers for centuries and knew its place in the world – or so it thought. Denmark was Scandinavia's original colonial power. Long after the Vikings had conquered Britain and discovered North America, Denmark ruled over Norway, Sweden and Iceland as well as Estonia and swathes of modern Germany. Before it all came tumbling down, Denmark had colonies in the tropics and India.

You can draw a straight line through the history of notated music in Denmark courtesy of a single institution. In 1448, King Christian I established his own band of trumpeters and drummers that assumed the title Det Kongelige Kapel (The Royal Chapel). As it expanded over the years, the ensemble attracted some of the best musicians in northern Europe, among them John Dowland from England and Heinrich Schütz from Germany. Having lived in Copenhagen for a decade from 1810, Mozart's widow Constanze concluded that the orchestra played her late husband's music better than any other. Eventually, the band migrated out of the royal household and into the Royal Theatre, which flourished as Copenhagen enjoyed a golden age of creativity in the 1800s. It became the house orchestra of the Royal Danish Opera and of the ballet troupe founded by August Bournonville, and was the Danish capital's first concert-giving orchestral ensemble.

In 2004, the Royal Chapel moved with its parent opera company into a new glass-fronted opera house that occupies an artificial island opposite the Copenhagen residence of the Danish royal family. In November 2005, I spent my first evening in Scandinavia in this building, listening to the Royal Danish Orchestra, as it's known internationally, playing for a new production of Richard Wagner's opera *Das Rheingold*. Seven years earlier, the orchestra had celebrated its 550th birthday – the oldest musical ensemble in the world by some distance.

Even in Grieg's day, Denmark had a long history of welcoming fine musicians. The legacy of the Hanseatic League and the trauma of the Thirty Years' War pushed seventeenth-century European composers north to wealthy Copenhagen, whose position at the gateway to the Baltic Sea had made it rich enough to employ the best of them. Bang in the middle of Grieg's three-year stint in the city, Denmark experienced its own transformative rite of passage in preparation for the upheavals of the twentieth century. It was the very opposite to that experienced in Norway and Finland.

Having declared itself a democracy in 1849, a disastrous war with Prussia saw Denmark lose not only the remnants of its empire but also a third of its own land mass, acceding the district of Schleswig-Holstein to Germany after a battlefield routing in 1864. Something rather curious happened next. Nationalism blossomed in Denmark, but not the freedom-fighting kind. This was the pragmatic nationalism of a country reborn smaller and weaker, determined to celebrate what was left: hearth and home, self-improvement, understated beauty – fellowship, family, pragmatism and art's capacity to comfort and stimulate. The country seized upon a phrase written 53 years earlier by the author Hans Peter Holst, best translated as 'what is lost on the outside shall be found on the inside'.[5] A distinctly Danish form of creativity took root – interior design included.

A bumpkin fiddle player made good, Carl Nielsen arrived in Copenhagen in 1884, a decade after the city's original bespoke opera house had been inaugurated (he would later get a job in the Royal Danish Orchestra's second violin section). Nielsen found a music scene that was active but anonymous, reflecting a comfortable cosmopolitan capital. This was the focal point of a land with no more battles to fight, where popular music entertained citizens decadent by Nordic standards. The centre of Copenhagen was dominated by a vast amusement park, the Tivoli Pleasure Gardens, which had not long since spawned an orchestra of its own, specializing in waltzes, polkas and tangos.

As the new century loomed, Nielsen considered how he could move Danish concert music away from what he described as the 'gravy and grease' of the German musical tradition, just as Grieg had before him. He began to imagine a new sort of music that would fuse perceptions of the high and low in art. He would present his radical alternative across six symphonies, three concertos, two operas and much more.

Nielsen's music retained a strong regard for Danish nationhood while bursting with vitality, humour and energy in its idiosyncratic celebration of life. It also looked unflinchingly to the future at a time when Denmark had little choice but to do the same. Its composer followed the trajectory of the country's own national hero, the poet and author Hans Christian Andersen. Both Andersen and Nielsen were born poor on Funen, the island separated from Zealand (and therefore Copenhagen) by a stretch of water known as the Great Belt. Nielsen and his violin only made it to Copenhagen after his local MP had organized a whip-round, funding his audition at the Academy of Music. The example set by Andersen was foremost in people's minds: if this spiky-haired young violinist had enough talent, he must be given every opportunity. Andersen, for many years, hadn't been so lucky.

Nielsen's abrupt, forceful and often rough-hewn music had an energizing effect. His musical language never stopped evolving, despite embracing Denmark's own folk-music traditions where it could and conjuring up phantom ones to order where it couldn't. Niels Gade, the former Leipzig bigwig and principal of the conservatory in Copenhagen, was wrong-footed by the assorted ill behaviour in Nielsen's student works but he hadn't seen the half of it. After a *Suite for Strings* described by Gade as 'messy', Nielsen wrote symphonies beginning and ending in the wrong key, in which chaos was apparently given free reign and in which instruments were instructed to improvise freely 'with all possible force'. Nielsen's direct tunefulness disguised the rigour of his music's advanced contrapuntal techniques and ominous tectonics.

It doesn't take a musicologist to trace the basis of the style to Nielsen's formative experiences during childhood. Unlike Grieg, Nielsen had been a folk musician by training. He started out playing the fiddle in his father's touring wedding band, later moving to the bugle which he played in the band of the local army barracks. In his memoir, *My Childhood*, the composer describes the experience of playing with the army band as 'like being thrown into a raging sea inhabited by all sorts of monsters'. Nielsen relished the cacophony, and then made it his own.

I returned to Denmark in 2011, on an assignment from *Gramophone* magazine to investigate the topsy-turvy musical world of Knudåge Riisager, a part-time composer whose witty ballet scores paint a colourful picture of Denmark's inter-war interest in everything French. I travelled this time to Aarhus, the second city and capital of Denmark's biggest landmass, Jutland. At its chic new concert hall lined with grey ash, the Aarhus Symphony Orchestra was coming to the end of three days recording works by Riisager, including two symphonies, a concerto for orchestra and the 'poème mécanique', T-DOXC. It was music full of abruptness, gameplay and pleasure-seeking brilliance, with a certain disdain for the haughty.

The final recording session took place on a Friday morning in June. Afterwards, the players tore open a crate of Carlsbergs in their canteen to mark the start of the traditional Nordic summer holiday. Many would be heading off to summer houses for a month or more. As always at such events in Denmark, there were speeches and 'hoo-rah's. I felt a little like an unwanted guest at the gathering but before long, a friendly percussionist approached me with a gift: a book of cartoons lampooning the various conductors who had led the ensemble over the years. 'We are quite famous for cartoons in this city,' he said, attempting to suppress a grin. Some years previously, the local newspaper had printed a cartoon of the Prophet Muhammad, igniting a global debate on free speech. Many in Denmark still believe the country came out of the affair the picture of democratic nobility. Plenty disagree.

I convinced *Gramophone* to shelve the article on Riisager and print one on Nielsen instead. It felt like good timing. In a speech at the Lincoln Center in New York, the Queen of Denmark had recently announced that the city's Philharmonic was to perform and record Nielsen's complete symphonies and concertos over the course of three years, starting immediately. The focus of the article, I suggested, should be on Nielsen's early symphonies. These works had thrilled me when I first heard them: blazingly impulsive, full of nervous ticks and stuck-out tongues, bouncing off the legacy of Beethoven, Brahms and even Mahler into something highly individual, fresh-faced and spiky-haired – a picture of the ever-young Nielsen himself. I was most taken with the pivotal Symphony No. 3 – the link between Nielsen's early symphonies and his mature ones, and a piece Nielsen himself gave the title *Sinfonia Espansiva*.

The *Sinfonia Espansiva* is also the most overtly Danish of Nielsen's six symphonies. At the time of its first performance in 1912, it must have seemed like the clearest signal yet of the composer's desire to bring stronger rhythms and more advanced harmonies to orchestral music – to combine the vigour of dance with the simplicity of song, giving musical expression to the blustery energies experienced in flat, coastal Denmark.

In a clear echo of Beethoven's own 'heroic' Symphony No. 3, Nielsen's has its own arresting opening gambit. The orchestra punches-out a single note 26 times, each series of thwacks packed slightly closer together than the one before. From this musical particle accelerator a tune is spewed out based on the three fundamental notes of the major chord, the triad – just like the tune that emerges, at the equivalent moment, in Beethoven's symphony. For a time, Nielsen's music rides the crest of the wave: confident, unstoppable, expansive – an unobstructed image of the energies that underpin life itself.

After the drinks party in Aarhus, I took the train to Copenhagen and found a city teeming with life. The train left me at the city's central station, whose vaulted wooden roof, like the upturned hull of a Viking ship, I had first encountered back in 2005. Heinrich Wenck's building was completed in 1911, the year Nielsen finished his symphony. Each appeared to me like an image of the other: built of traditional materials (after the first movement, Nielsen's symphony is driven by 'composed' folk songs), projecting sturdy reliability, celebrating hard graft. I walked past a bustling Tivoli Gardens and crossed Hans Christian Andersens Boulevard, turning right onto

Nansensgade, where I left my bags at a hotel. I then walked the short distance to Queen Louise's Bridge, which crosses the series of ponds known as the Lakes that skirts the western edge of inner Copenhagen.

Every Copenhagener under the age of 40 appeared to be perched or reclined on this low, elegant bridge, soaking up the evening sun. As in Aarhus earlier that day, teenagers wore the traditional white nautical caps that mark recent graduation from high school. Almost every second hand clasped a miniature can of Carlsberg. There was a festival atmosphere made more apparent by Copenhagen's characteristic lack of traffic noise. This, it seemed clear, was the fun-loving city Nielsen depicted in his 1906 opera *Maskarade*, a manifesto for social renewal 'masquerading' as a celebration of nightlife in a land 'where sunshine comes but once a year'. When Nielsen looks back at Denmark's old music and traditions in *Maskarade*, it is without the sadness of Grieg. Nielsen's nostalgia balances affection with gentle mockery, suggesting an eagerness to move forwards more than look backwards.

Nielsen's fresh view of music, what one American academic referred to as his 'homespun philosophy',[6] came in part from the most important upheaval of his life: his move from poor, rural Denmark to its glittering, cosmopolitan, fun-loving capital. Nielsen didn't have to go hunting for his musical roots in folk music, because folk music was all he'd known before he got to Copenhagen. The triad-like tune that emerges in the *Sinfonia Espansiva* is built from the same fundamental ingredients as whole swathes of folk tunes. A short way into the symphony's first movement, it is abruptly confronted by music that appears to hail from the very opposite source: an urbane waltz. One part of the orchestra slams on the breaks (heavy brass) while another charges ahead (strings). The now-elongated triad tune crashes into the waltz in slowed motion, like a combine harvester crunching its way through a mirrored ballroom.

Nielsen sensed the world changing and was determined to embrace that change. Denmark's nineteenth-century humiliation had immunized it to some degree from the shock of the new while

Grieg's fledgling, disorientated Norway could only cleave resolutely to an imagined past. But Europe's industrial destruction was still to come. While the *Sinfonia Espansiva* gives free reign to the energy and optimism of Nielsen's early years in Copenhagen, its successors, written during and after the First World War, would set that energy up against overwhelmingly negative forces or rub it up against itself, sparking fissile internal combustion leading to wholesale collapse. Nielsen was ready to bring the real world into his art – playful but terrifying, challenging but ultimately optimistic, and delivered mostly with a smile.

By the time Nielsen emerged as a composer of note, central Copenhagen had taken the fundamental architectural form that continues to define it today. Denmark had been more ready than any other Nordic land to embrace modernism, unbothered by geopolitical notions of greatness that, ironically, led it to deliver precisely that across the arts. In keeping with the country's new focus on hearth and home, community and well-being, beauty through simplicity, Nielsen combined his work on progressive symphonies with the writing of hundreds of popular songs – crafted, catchy, but often poignant little ditties known and sung by Danes to this day in schools, offices and at 'morgensang' gatherings where anyone can turn up to sing in unison before heading to work. Denmark didn't have a pervasive, unifying folk music tradition equivalent to that raided by Grieg in Norway. So Nielsen gave it one.

◢

After a series of assignments north of the Baltic that always seemed to come and go too quickly, I moved to Copenhagen from London at the end of April in 2015. It was another of those days in which the sun seemed to radiate energy onto the city's streets, canals and beaches long into the night. The allure of the north had proved too strong to resist, and this seemed like the easiest city from which to indulge it fully – equidistant from London and Helsinki and within touching distance of Sweden. After a week, I got the feeling I'd be here far longer than the arranged twelve months.

The plan was to work as a freelance journalist, correspondent and music critic. My patch would include Skåne, the southernmost tip of Sweden that had been a part of Denmark until the Treaty of Roskilde returned it to its geographical motherland in 1658. In 2000, the wounds of old healing at last, a road and rail bridge opened linking Copenhagen with Malmö, Sweden's third city and Skåne's administrative capital. The Øresund Bridge turbocharged Copenhagen's economy and utterly transformed Malmö's long before it spawned its own TV crime series. From a musical perspective, the bridge created a hub-like network of professional opera companies, orchestras, choirs, early music ensembles and conservatoires, all within a 20-kilometre radius.

The playwright August Strindberg wasn't the first to note that Skåne can feel foreign to many Swedes. What he surely meant is that it feels more like flat, arable, brick-built Denmark. The dialect of Swedish spoken there errs towards glottal Danish and the landscape is peppered with medieval churches in the Danish style, with distinctive crow-stepped bell towers in white. Skåne was described by the songwriter Michael Saxell in 'Om himlen och Österlen' ('On Heaven and Österlen') as being 'a little closer to heaven and the big, unending sky'. That sky, its extraordinarily lucid light and the undulating landscape it looks down upon, is captured magnificently in another TV crime series, the interpretation of Henning Mankell's dour sleuth Wallander produced by Kenneth Branagh. It is set and filmed in the port town of Ystad.

On a hot June day, I made my first journey over the bridge to Malmö. The weather had lured half of the city's population onto the beach that stretches out in the shadow of Malmö's most famous landmark, the apartment block known as the Twisting Torso. Immediately, the place seemed less pale than Copenhagen. In the midst of the refugee crisis, platforms at the main railway station had been plastered with floor stickers directing new arrivals to registration points where the smiling, compassionate Swedes of international stereotype stood waiting for them.

At first I thought of Malmö as an annex to Copenhagen, the capital of a flatter, more laid-back patch of Sweden and a city with much the same mix of urban cosmopolitanism and maritime bluntness as its Danish cousin across the water. Soon enough, vital distinctions started to emerge. I noticed one of them during my first reviewing assignment at Malmö Opera a few months later. In Denmark, perhaps the most informal country in Europe where weather forecasters wear shorts and government ministers proudly display their tattoos, nobody really cares what you wear to the opera. At the squat opera house of Sweden's third city, I found myself wholly underdressed, getting my first taste of the country's distinct attachment to formality – albeit one magnified by Malmö's provincial eagerness to do things 'properly'. Swedes have much to be proud of but proud they are – not of some mythic past, but of the situation they have made for themselves right here, right now. At civic institutions like the Malmö Opera, the pride almost radiates off them.

Soon enough a London client sent me to Stockholm, and the experience underlined the city's ennobled position at the top of the Nordic region's urban pecking order. Sweden's is the only Scandinavian capital that feels, when arriving by train, like a city of real global significance. The dominant feature of my hotel was its inner lobby, converted from an outdoor yard into an indoor palm court restaurant aping the art nouveau elegance of Paris. I walked down Strandvägen, a broad avenue lined with lime trees, to the necessarily grander Grand Hotel to conduct an interview with a violinist. This is a huge edifice on the waterfront whose American-style foyer would long since have been modernized and minimalized in Denmark or Norway. The next day I saw another production of *La Bohème*, this one at the Royal Swedish Opera. I had learned my lessons about what to wear from Malmö. When I asked for my press ticket from the concierge-like box office, I was shown to the 'press box' for which no ticket was required. I had never been in a more ornate theatre anywhere in Europe, let alone in Scandinavia.

Stockholm is where you smell Scandinavia's old money, in so far as it ever existed. It feels like the respectable, aristocratic face of an otherwise robust part of the world, a fitting setting for the doling out of Nobel Prizes. Ever-present water lends the city the ambience of a Scandinavian Venice, with imperial stucco architecture to match. Only multiple concrete boxes, dropped like Monopoly houses, sully the image, making parts of Stockholm feel more like Croydon. These dispiriting car parks, flyovers and administrative buildings betray the imperatives of a 1960s Sweden keen to prize pragmatism over display, literally straightening its roads in the process. Still, Stockholm's general air of monarchical responsibility continues to underpin its musical life. When classical music is played here, it is played in buildings with deep carpets and pillars either side of the door, in stark contrast to the rest of Sweden and indeed the entire Nordic region.

The divide was there from the start. While the plaintive strains of the nyckelharpa were buzzing through the scattered, isolated communities where real Swedes lived, Stockholm's royal court incubated a formal musical life along the lines of pre-revolution France, its civic and constitutional model. As in Denmark, the court knew it had to attract musicians from abroad and did so efficiently. In 1778, a 21-year-old German named Joseph Martin Kraus was persuaded to move to Sweden by a friend, and spent three years attempting to attract the attention of the music-loving King Gustav III. When he finally succeeded, Kraus became a celebrated figure and would be referred to as the Swedish Mozart given the brevity of his life (he died in 1792, a year after his Austrian counterpart and just a year older) and the passing resemblance of his music to that of Wolfgang Amadeus.

Nothing much in Kraus's work sounds specifically Swedish. The sudden outbursts and contrasts that are strewn about his music could be interpreted as an affront to the carefulness that characterized so much in Swedish art and behaviour – Kraus staking claim to his German roots, perhaps. As the symphony orchestra matured in the nineteenth century, Sweden delivered copious rich pastorals but few with the edge of Nielsen's or the depth of Grieg's, and frequently with a little too much Vaseline applied to the lens. In 1896 the composer Hugo Alfvén unveiled his Symphony No. 1, describing it as 'the first written in the Swedish language'. At a stretch, you can point to brooding fatalism and lolling, downward-turning phrase shapes as palpably Swedish, but the work makes less of an impression when taken as a whole. The under-productive Wilhelm Stenhammar wrote high-quality music that works itself hard, but its grandeur was out of step with the close-quartered innovations that were sweeping local literature and art at the time. Sweden was moving away from the plush, a shift that would come to colour the way the country and its neighbours would be seen from the outside.

So often, as the writer Michael Booth has wryly observed, the world's collective view of Scandinavia is actually a view of Sweden – the most anthropologically emblematic of the Nordic lands and the most talked-about, from its near-perfect societal structures to its fertile education system, industrial productivity, taste for nudity and distaste for confrontation. And, of course, for IKEA – the home furnishings giant born of a desire to connect unfussy, progressive modernism with traditional Swedish crafts. Functionalism in Swedish creativity became a guiding principle in the twentieth century, prompted by the country's collective recoiling from the status and display of its aristocratic past. As it consciously homogenized in the early 1900s, the largest Nordic nation by population looked to build itself new landscapes in which everyone could be seen to lead a civilized life in a good home filled with beautiful, useful things.

Nordic social democracy came to full fruition in the middle of the twentieth century, even if its roots lay in the Lutheran mindset that had existed long before. Its most obvious ingredients are generous welfare provision and widespread public spending funded by high taxation levied on high wages – all leading, theoretically, to greater government accountability and reciprocal public trust. There were creative and physical manifestations too, among them an emphasis on culture and its associated infrastructure. Soon enough, new forms of architecture and design started to inform ideas of a regional aesthetic. Swedish concert music, meanwhile, was stuck in the previous century. Stenhammar finished his well-upholstered, Brahms-indebted Symphony No. 2 in 1915 – two years after Stravinsky's *The Rite of Spring*, three after the proto-rap of Schoenberg's *Pierrot lunaire* and four after Nielsen's fresh-faced *Sinfonia Espansiva*. Sweden's civic architects were already beginning to rethink the look of their country along pure, clean, Bauhaus-influenced lines.

In Gothenburg, Sweden's second city, town planners would soon be designing whole new districts. These would come replete with large concrete apartment blocks moulded so that every dwelling would have its own private balcony and rubbish chute. Like the structures conceived by the architect Uno Åhrén, these buildings were as much about social engineering as architecture, in which sense they had far more in common with Nielsen's music than with Stenhammar's. For most of Sweden, Stockholm might as well have been a toy town. Everywhere else, the generational proximity to poverty focused the mind; a solid apartment in a town with good job prospects would have sounded like a very nice proposition indeed.

◢

No-nonsense Gothenburg is tucked inside the blustery west coast of Sweden that faces Denmark and Norway. The city remains as proud of its industrial heritage as Stockholm does of its blue blood. A sense of fortitude pervades this wind-battered place. Even its classical architecture seems to foreshadow the modernism that was on the way, with clean lines and minimal fuss. Gothenburg's industrial-chic modern opera house, opened in 1994, sits on the harbour like a merchant ship sliced down the middle, showing its backstage workings through a skin of steel and glass. On my first proper visit to the city in 2015, I stayed in a hotel across the water from the town centre, on the Lundbyvassen side of the wide River Göta. To get there, you'd wait for a water taxi on the old docks just by the opera house, whose architecture offered a playful hint of what lay on the other side: huge hulking ships, rusting cranes, factories and heavy industry. If you didn't get the ferry, you took a rattling old tram over the rudimentary and altitudinous road bridge that spoke of a city not prone to prettifying what it didn't have to. The bridge was later condemned and replaced.

In Gothenburg, one early twentieth-century composer demonstrated a certain ambivalence to the grand orchestral landscapes being presented by composers from further east – even those who had, like Stenhammar, come to Gothenburg to work. Kurt Atterberg was born in the city in 1887, the son of an engineer. He studied electrical engineering himself before taking a job in the Swedish patent office, where he remained in post until the age of 81, all the while indulging a fruitful musical side-hustle that would produce nine symphonies, five operas, two concertos and plenty more. Atterberg became the most popular Swedish composer of his day outside the country, his music taken up by orchestras from Berlin to New York and championed by the conductors Thomas Beecham and Wilhelm Furtwängler. There were only two problems: Atterberg's Swedish peers weren't too keen on his music, and Atterberg was a little too keen on Adolf Hitler.

Was Atterberg so different from Alfvén and Stenhammar? On the surface, perhaps not. He used Swedish folk music. He delivered the occasional pastoral landscape. But a tranche of his music is possessed of something deeper: a certain nervous energy, a rustling unease and a fierce irony that can see the musically regimented veer into the trivial – and back. Atterberg spoke out against 'formless mood pieces', in which comment he could have been referring to any number of colleagues. He may have formally represented the Swedish musical establishment, founding and serving in its official Composers' Society and mixing in the right circles even if he didn't have plenteous friends within them. But a good number of Atterberg's works have more in common with Shostakovich's modernist Russian music than Stenhammar's.

In 1928, the Columbia Phonograph Company in Washington DC organized a competition for new symphonic music to mark 100 years since the death of Franz Schubert. Atterberg reacted with typical strong-headedness. He interpreted the competition's rubric, which suggested Schubert's unfinished Symphony No. 8 might inspire its contestants, as an affront to composers who should be free to write whatever music they desired.

Half in protest, Atterberg wrote a symphony of unusual proportions, industrial strength and extreme changeability that somehow got around the Nordic constituency's judges and made it into the final (perhaps because one of those judges was Carl Nielsen). Against the odds, Atterberg's score then won the competition outright. He bought himself a Ford Model T with the US$10,000 prize money and travelled to Germany to conduct the piece, his Symphony No. 6, with the Berlin Philharmonic Orchestra – a performance captured by the Columbia Phonograph Company's microphones. The following Monday, Atterberg was back at his desk in the patent office.

The composer's nickname for his winning score, the *Dollar Symphony*, suggests how seriously he had taken the entire process. But there is no lack of seriousness in the music, whose outer movements sound unlike anything else written in the Nordic region at the time and are every bit as stark, lucid and unsettling as those of Schubert's own symphony. The first movement locks in to a dark musical production line not unlike that which seizes control of proceedings in Lutosławski's Concerto for Orchestra, written three decades later in Poland. Upward-ratcheting speeds, curious asides, strange accents and wild changes of key ensue – the latter clearly descended from those that crop up in Atterberg's First Symphony, written 18 years previously. The whole orchestral conversation is characterized by juddering crises of confidence, brittle changeability of mood and the rapid adoption of contrasting musical personas. Everything is hard-edged and clear, allowing a direct view into the innards of the composer's musical workings. This was still music based on the raw materials of Swedish folk song. But Atterberg appeared to adapt traditional materials to the new world he saw emerging around him – to the aesthetics of industry and the dance of modern life.

It's little wonder the received wisdom of Atterberg 'the conservative romantic' has stuck. He was reactionary, protectionist and terrified by the many musical innovations of which he didn't approve. But he maintained a strong belief in music's functional, societal responsibilities and filled the *Dollar Symphony* with apparent dissent, not least in those passages where the music sounds in two keys at the same time. The symphony's own excess of regimentation appears to rant at order and consensus. Atterberg against the Columbia Company's rules, sure, but against the pernickety Sweden he experienced every day from his desk, too? The slow movement is often described as a nostalgic pastoral but is anything but. Its whimsical main tune runs into profound harmonic unease, recoiling from its own haughtiness when admonished by the fanfares that return from the opening movement, now all pinched and coy (there are shades of Sibelius here). Rarely in the symphony does a folk song sing out unchanged by new, vital contexts. In its final bars, tuned instruments drop out of the texture altogether; the orchestra's factory-floor percussion is left to freewheel towards the buffers.

The *Dollar Symphony* might just be the most riveting symphony written by a Swede. It proved popular abroad, but its strong rhythmic impulse and multilayered grimace didn't go down nearly as well at home. Besides, Atterberg's associations were about to make the quality of his music as good as irrelevant. He travelled to Nazi Germany in 1934, where he represented Scandinavia at the German Composers' Meeting in Berlin, a symposium-cum-rally in which the Master of Ceremonies, the leading German composer Richard Strauss, was flanked by swastikas as he addressed an invited audience. Atterberg's enthusiastic response to the event saw him embrace all sorts of half-baked Nazi ideologies that reinforced his own suspicion of the fashionable avant-garde. Though he's on record as questioning the Swedishness of Jewish composers, he stopped short of embracing Nazi racism in his reporting from the rally, simply dropping it from his dispatches altogether.

Plenty of ideas concerning a new, folk-based art were doing the rounds in Atterberg's Sweden at the time, even if composers were struggling to realize them progressively rather more than their counterparts in literature, visual art and design. This might have given rise to a basic misunderstanding in Berlin. When the Nazis spoke of 'Volk' (meaning Aryan), Atterberg translated the word into the Swedish 'folklig' – meaning natural, simple, of the people. Was he conscious of the mistake?[7]

From the naïve perspective of an isolated country effectively untouched by immigration, the botched ideologies presented by the Nazis in Berlin may well have resembled a sort of well-meaning conservatism. The idea of a people bound together by tradition, DNA and shared experience was a foundation stone of the social democracy that took root in each of the Nordic countries and has been tweaked, with greater or lesser success, to accommodate the more diverse nations that exist today. Atterberg saw the whole Nazi project through Swedish eyes. He admired the plans to reorganize German musical life outlined at the Berlin meeting, noting how they might be replicated at home. Eventually, thanks to social democracy, he lived to see it happen.

In the end, Atterberg was the scapegoat Sweden's post-war cultural establishment needed. Many others present at the 1934 meeting were exonerated by their home nations, Strauss among them. It was quietly forgotten, in Finland, that Sibelius had sent his personal good wishes to Nazi troops in 1942, though he might be forgiven considering Finland's necessarily anti-Soviet position during the war. Unpleasant, naïve and prejudiced Atterberg may have been, but few composers brought 'folklig' to their music with the strong accents he did. His music remains more instantly recognizable as 'his' than that of any composer who breathed the same air before Abba's Björn Ulvaeus (another Gothenburger). There is nothing inflated, magisterial, ostentatious or ennobled in the *Dollar Symphony* unless it is so for satirical sake. There is still less politically correct.

◢

Insular, thoroughbred, riven with romantic folklore and stoked with national pride – the Nordic countries seemed as much a utopia to Nazis of the 1930s as they appear to left-leaning intellectuals nearly a century later. Ironically, not a great deal has changed beyond the collective desire to address those 'insular' and 'thoroughbred' labels. Sweden's tolerance, openness and willingness to accept high numbers of immigrants and refugees is surely related to the very concept of 'folklig' that Atterberg thought he'd heard discussed in Berlin.

The concept places a regard for fellow man above ideas of individual ownership. But it also allows anyone who wants to learn the tunes and the moves the right to join the idiosyncratic clubs that are homogenous Nordic societies, whatever the colour of their skin or passport. One way for immigrants to get a foot in the door of the Nordic region's tightly bound and frequently frosty communities is to learn the respective nations' various songs and games, proving we're not all that different. Atterberg placed his chosen Swedish folk tunes in a vital, cosmopolitan and broad musical context whose modal inflections even glance towards the Middle East. He may have failed to see the parallels in a diverse Swedish society, but that doesn't prevent us from hearing them in his music.

In late June 2019, with two other immigrant friends from my state language school, I sailed out of Sydhavn, a down-at-heel harbour in south Copenhagen where the real sailors moor their boats. We were on a small yacht bound for Sweden, which was celebrating midsummer that night. In fair winds, we edged our way across the Øresund in the shadow of its bridge, tacking to avoid the huge ferries and oil tankers motoring along the Baltic's busiest shipping lane. What takes around four minutes when you fly in a south-easterly direction out of Copenhagen Airport took us around four hours. We arrived at Skanör, a spit of land surrounded by white beaches whose far more rigorously policed Swedish harbour was populated by far more expensive boats.

It was an unusually hot day. We found a mooring and walked into the village to buy some cold beers, encountering hordes of Swedes, many with flowers in their hair, walking in the other direction. They were returning from the supermarket we were heading towards, ferrying schnapps, herring, cheese and pork back to the town's wide common to eat from paper plates. We made it back from the supermarket just in time to see the hoisting-up of a large green maypole. It was formed of a cross with two circles hanging from each arm, themselves linked to the peak to form triangles (sketch it out and you'll see the fertility symbolism). It was decorated with fresh birch branches and flowers of all colours, gathered by young women, according to tradition. A group of men and women in yellow breeches and white socks then poked the structure into an upright position with giant sticks, to the accompaniment of traditional music. There was no nyckelharpa, but a few fiddles had gathered in one corner of the small field, playing in unison with an accordion for accompaniment.

Swedish midsummer parties are usually private affairs but this one was communal, open to all. Some picnicked on the large traditional midsummer cakes decorated with strawberries, alternating schnapps with black coffee to wash it down (pockets of visitors from Denmark proudly defied the tradition, sticking to fizzy lager). A hundred or so stood in a broad approximate circle, cheering when the maypole became vertical. There were Swedes of all kinds, but fewer than usual of the moneyed Stockholm and Gothenburg types identifiable from the sort of regatta-wear beloved of 1980s British aristocrats. Perhaps they'd decided to dress like everyone else for a change.

People sang and danced to 'The Little Frog', a Swedish Midsummer staple, after which smaller groups sang more unusual songs I presumed to be native to Skåne. I thought I made out the folk song 'We Are Musicians' and one violin tune bore some resemblance to the main theme of the final movement in Atterberg's *Dollar Symphony*. The drinking songs were yet to come. Most faces were white but a good proportion were not. There were men, women and children of Balkan, African, Indian, Middle Eastern and Far Eastern extraction, the majority of whom probably held Swedish passports. Some joined in with the singing and one, on an accordion, with the playing.

It was tempting to wonder what the reactionary Atterberg would have made of all this. After all, it was his assertion of the importance of folk music that had helped create the scene, as near to a socially level playing field as Europe gets. The music we heard in Skanör was free from hierarchies of fashion, age, lineage and commercial success, while its central importance at strategic points in the Swedish calendar means it can be offered to new Swedes as a means of orientation and, that troublesome word, integration. For the wider population of pale-faced Swedes, the music appeared to celebrate something current and evolving, more than something lost. We returned to the boat to drink our beers on its stern deck, listening to the singing that continued long into the night. Above us, Skåne's big, unending sky turned from blue to grey to orange, and then back to blue again.

2

Performance

"After Sibelius, people began to understand that it was possible to create internationally important music in a small place like this."

Pekka Kuusisto

The paradox of isolated, rustic, small-town Bergen is that it has a symphony orchestra older than any in the United Kingdom or the United States. The Bergen Philharmonic can trace its roots back to 1765, when the city was rather more pivotal to European trade than it is today.

That chocolate-box wooden terrace on Bergen's harbour was built not for the enchantment of tourists but for the cut and thrust of hard-nosed business. It housed one of four satellite hubs established by the Hanseatic League, the trading network headquartered in Lübeck on Germany's Baltic coast. Stripped of capital city status from the 1300s, Bergen was compensated by an influx of German merchants who had clocked its advantageous position, facing England, Scotland and the North Sea on one side while offering plenteous routes into Scandinavia and Europe on the other. Norwegians finally seized control of trading in the mid 1500s and by 1754 they outnumbered their German counterparts ten to one. That year, a Norwegian flag was raised above the trading office for the first time. The ensuing flush of civic pride brought forth a new association: Musikselskabet Harmonien.

The title, referring to 'the harmonic music society', was eventually shortened to 'Harmonien', the name surviving now in an unlikely capacity as the web address of the Bergen Philharmonic Orchestra. Some locals still refer to the orchestra as Harmonien (literally 'the harmony'). Its special position in Norway's music life reflects its city's equally exceptional place in the nation's psyche. Even after replacing Bergen as the nation's capital, Oslo was seen by many as contaminated, the town from which the Danes and Swedes had meted out colonial rule. Plenty of Norwegians looked to Bergen as the country's spiritual hearth and many still do. Its orchestra's geographical ties with Norway's musical bigwigs, Bergen locals Edvard Grieg and Leif Ove Andsnes in particular, continue to consolidate its special artistic status whatever happens in Oslo, Trondheim or elsewhere. 'Bergen has much to be proud of,' a pianist from slightly further down Norway's west coast once told me. 'It's a little bit chauvinist – in the good sense of the word.'

When Grieg came home to Norway in 1866, Oslo had no permanent orchestra at all. The ensemble in Bergen had gathered enough musicians to play his piano concerto and Mendelssohn's oratorio *Elijah*, the latter featuring the composer's Danish wife Nina Hagerup as soprano soloist. Grieg took over as artistic director for a two-year stretch starting in 1880 but it wasn't a good fit. Perhaps the biggest favour he did the organization was that of dying. When his will was read in 1907, he had bequeathed it much of his estate.

A string of Norwegians followed Grieg at the helm of the orchestra. But in this former Hanseatic city with a taste for foreign labour, it wasn't long before Hungarians, Italians, Russians, Australians and Americans came to play in the ensemble and lead it as conductor. In 2015, a new boss arrived in low-tempo Bergen straight from the high-tempo streets of London's West End. Edward Gardner had spent eight years as music director at the English National Opera. For Gardner, it was a paradigm shift: trading a taste-making institution in a major world city with a permanent staff in the hundreds for a regional orchestra with a strong local remit in a small town on the edge of the continent.

Gardner's move was a pragmatic one. Looking for his first orchestral chief conductorship, a job that brings overall responsibility for an ensemble's sound culture and pivots on the cultivation of a deep, workable musical partnership, Gardner was aware of the benefits presented by an institution like the Bergen Philharmonic Orchestra. 'As chief conductor, you build up a shorthand for what you're looking for that allows you to work at a much higher level,' he told me in May 2018, as we both gazed at a chunk of mountainside framed by the glass walls of the Philharmonic's boardroom. 'It's different with an opera company, where it's not just about how the orchestra plays but about tying bigger things together.' The Bergen Philharmonic afforded Gardner the oxygen of time, space and a comparative lack of forensic critical attention – the room to experiment, even to make mistakes. As an orchestra with an institutional legacy and a distinct sound tradition, it also offered Gardner exceptional tools to work with and the chance to exert an influence on Norwegian musical history.

Nordic symphony orchestras have a reputation for their relaxed modus operandi, an existence that can appear as unhurried as life in Bergen seems to be. Most work to a weekly schedule that starts with rehearsals on a Monday and ends with concerts on a Thursday, perhaps repeated on Friday. Rehearsal time is generous, particularly in comparison to the UK, where orchestras might present multiple sets of repertoire in a week. Opera houses in the region can appear like ghost ships at weekends, which start on Friday lunchtime. 'Everybody's gone at 3 p.m.,' the late British opera director Graham Vick exclaimed to me, flabbergasted, during rehearsals for a production in Copenhagen. 'That's why Graham's so marvellous and it's also why he's not running a Scandinavian opera house,' the British artistic director of the Gothenburg Opera, Stephen Langridge, responded when I put that comment to him a few weeks later. 'Of course, there is a frustration,' Langridge continued. 'But this [Gothenburg] is not a lazy place. People want to have a sustainable and balanced working life and I think that's pretty valid.'

In provincial cities across the Nordic region, there are fewer critics at operas and orchestral concerts but a significant core of trusting subscribers likely to suck up whatever repertoire they are offered. Empty weeks are set aside for orchestral recording projects, made economically viable given salaries cover the whole year but performances don't. In my time on the reviews desk at *Gramophone*, it became abundantly clear that orchestras from the Nordic countries were those with the time and money to make recordings in an age when major record labels no longer held the cards.

Whatever picture those tendencies paint, these are advantageous conditions in which a young musician can learn the trade of the chief conductor or music director. Gustavo Dudamel, Daniel Harding, Krzysztof Urbański, Robin Ticciati, Neeme Järvi, Christian Vásquez, Simone Young, Andrew Manze, Nathalie Stutzmann, Franz Welser-Möst, Susanna Mälkki, John Storgårds, Hannu Lintu and Gardner himself are all front-rank musicians who took their first chief conductorships at provincial Nordic orchestras, away from capital cities. In most cases, they were blessed with technically solid, well-remunerated musicians residing in fit-for-purpose concert halls.

◢

You know you're heading against the prevailing direction of travel when your train gets progressively shorter. The further the 13.52 from Copenhagen trundled from the capital, the more carriages it shed. When it arrived in the South Jutland town of Sønderborg nearly four hours later, just three cars long, it had crossed the Great

Belt linking Zealand with Funen and the Little Belt linking Funen with Jutland. Along the way, the train windows had framed landscape views of Denmark that might have been dreamed up by the romantic painters. Danish soil spread out curvaceously in satisfying browns and bountiful greens; Danish sea stared up in dull, menacing greys.

Even under a starlit November sky, arriving in Sønderborg was underwhelming. The terminus station has no structural feature beyond a single platform and its functional canopy. It is a tram-stop with buffers, bereft even of a vending machine. The one building you do see when disembarking the train is that which houses the town's resident orchestra, the South Jutland Symphony. On the other side of that building, Sønderborg lays itself elegantly out over the hills that surround the Alssund straight, resembling the backs of gigantic, grass-covered whales. It's Bergen without the topographical drama or whiff of metropolitan significance, but with the charm – multicoloured harbour terrace included.

Sønderborg, population 28,000, skirts a fjord almost within touching distance of northern Germany. It doesn't feel like a town that should have a symphony orchestra. But a symphony orchestra it has, and because of that fact it has Alsion, a chic concert hall in pale ash opened in 2007 whose statement glass foyers overlook the sound that splits the town in two. Some private and foundation money was channeled into the building project, which piggybacked the construction of a new home for the local university. Otherwise, the orchestra and its hall are products of the distinct form of social democracy that makes the Nordic region an aspirational, egalitarian utopia or an incubator of stifling, crushing conformity destined for economic ruin – depending who you ask.

Unlike the Bergen Philharmonic, the vast majority of the 37 full-time concert-giving symphony orchestras in the Nordic region were established between 1910 and 1965, when their respective governments became the architects of cultural policy and infrastructure rather than its patrons. Norwegian cultural policy of the time (Norway was the only country to actually write it down) decreed that government action must strengthen a common national culture that would embrace as many citizens as possible and traverse the length and breadth of a very long land. Across Scandinavia, the role of culture minister was elevated to cabinet level. Culture literally became a building project.

Sibelius's life straddled the exact period in which Finland's music-making started to migrate from private homes and clubs and into purpose-built concert halls. More than anyone, Sibelius had personified the idea that in this part of the world, orchestral music could serve a broad and useful societal purpose. Social democrats in mid-century Sweden and Denmark latched onto the idea. They saw themselves as harbingers of a new future whose prosperity would be rooted in egalitarianism, feminism and some semblance of a Lutheran work ethic. With state churches, they would eradicate poverty. With state schools, they would form functional and curious minds. With libraries, orchestras, galleries, theatres and a thriving press, they would ensure those minds remained irrigated for life.

In practical terms, this called for the formalizing of military bands and small, ad hoc ensembles into full symphony orchestras. The new institutions found their personnel increasing and their operational costs being met almost entirely by local and national authorities or newfangled state broadcasters. Those funding arrangements have survived. In 2019, almost every civic symphony orchestra in the Nordic region received between 80 per cent and 90 per cent of its annual income directly from local or regional government, with conspicuously few accepting corporate or private sponsorship. The equivalent figure for UK orchestras, with the exception of the BBC's ensembles, was less than half that amount while public funding for orchestral music in the United States barely exists. Orchestras, even more than theatres, became flagships of the Nordic region's new cultural networks as the prominent role composers had played in national awakening lingered still. Besides, orchestras weren't just the perfect operational metaphors for democracy, they actively lubricated it: democracy starts with listening.

There was a bourgeois element to all this, a longing gaze south to German civilization and orchestral music's perceived nobility, even if the Scandinavians were quick to foreground its more embracing, egalitarian qualities and had their own repertoire with which to do so. The idea was as laudable as its legacy has proved phenomenal. When Sibelius wrote *Tapiola*, Finland had one orchestra. In 2020, it had fifteen full-time, professional, symphony-sized orchestras, twelve of them located outside Helsinki. Beyond the confines of London, the United Kingdom had ten, for ten times Finland's population.

There is more to the classical music life of the Nordic countries than orchestras. Scandinavia and Finland spill over with chamber groups, freelance ensembles and music festivals while the Nordic region operates seven full-time opera companies with orchestras and choirs of their own. But the proliferation of high-maintenance, high-performance instrumental ensembles and their architecturally demanding homes gives the region the strongest of musical backbones, which is undoubtedly linked to its proliferation of conductors and composers. These orchestras play far more than 'classical' music, too.

In cutesy Sønderborg, determined locals ensured the establishment of the orchestra proper in 1963. The real reason the orchestra exists is prosaically geographical. If the South Jutland Symphony Orchestra wasn't here, the nearest comparable outfit would be found in Denmark's second city, Aarhus, 190 kilometres north and all but inaccessible to those in the country's southern-most reaches (not insignificantly, the area historically disputed with Germany). When the salaries of orchestral musicians are drawn from the public purse, location matters. You wouldn't deny citizens access to a library or hospital, so you wouldn't, within reason, deny them access to a professional classical music ensemble when they have paid for it.

Sønderborg was all but deserted as I made my way to Alsion to hear the South Jutland Symphony Orchestra in November 2019. But the concert hall was almost full, and even in pale Denmark there was hardly a demographic not represented (though the white-skinned and grey-haired dominated). Between big chunks of Tchaikovsky and Mendelssohn, the audience spread into the glass-box foyer by architects Nielsen, Nielsen & Nielsen. Its central feature is a set of oversized wooden steps that invites concertgoers to lounge informally, looking out at the water. At ground level, visitors played table football and queued at the canteen to buy chocolate and fizzy lager. Only a handful were dressed for a night out. There was a relaxed energy about the space, incubated by the architecture but also by the fact that the concert apparently wasn't a special occasion for anyone except me. The prevailing air was one of satisfaction, as if Sønderborgers expected nothing less of the working week than a dose of orchestral music, in an acoustically perfect modern concert hall, at the end of it.

This semi-contractual coupling of expectation to satisfaction helps explain the paradox of Scandinavian 'happiness'. Nordic societies are consistently rated the happiest in the world, which will surprise anyone who has shopped in Denmark (where the customer is always wrong), joined a cloakroom queue in Sweden (rugby without a referee), dined in a Finnish restaurant or taken a cursory glance at global indices pertaining to suicide and divorce. It can be explained, says an emerging school of psychology, by the cool rationalism with which the Nordic folk respond to such surveys in the first place: of course we're happy, we live privileged lives in wealthy countries that are constantly rated happy.

The sort of happiness I saw around me in Sønderborg was less that of radiant smiles than that of contented satisfaction, one that stems from a deep sense of trust in the apparatus of the state and in fellow citizens. At the general election of 2019, 85 per cent of Danes cast a ballot (before eating the celebratory election night dish of 'stegt flæsk' – fried pork belly) while recent polls suggest they believe in the function and legitimacy of their democracy more than any other populace on earth – possibly because that very word 'democracy' denotes an expression of human solidarity more than it does a voting system. Reservoirs of trust are a prerequisite when you're asked to surrender half your income in tax. But the sense of responsibility that weather-beaten Nordic folk feel towards one other also engenders collective purpose, which itself tends to underpin feelings of individual fulfillment. Cultural Lutheranism often steps in to ensure those feelings rarely stray into the domain of the priggish or smug.

The social contract that binds all of this into a remarkable fiscal–cultural union extends to the Nordic region's arts institutions, especially those situated outside capital cities. The orchestral network was established at a time that seems socially and economically unrecognizable today. And yet these ensembles cling stubbornly to their roles at the heart of societal living – at once curiously outdated and inspiringly idealistic, aesthetically specialized yet reaching a variety of demographics few other performing troupes could hope to match. In Norway, the Bergen Philharmonic plays annual concerts celebrating the local newspaper and the local university. It appears on National Day. It broadcasts on television. It is a staple of Christmas and summer rituals and is sent abroad on soft-power diplomatic missions.

Week in week out, local subscribers support the orchestra, as in Sønderborg. Folk have paid for their local symphony orchestra to exist and when they reach a certain age, a significant proportion of them subscribe to its concerts as if it were the done thing. Woven into the reasons for doing so are telling local nuances: national unity in a Finland divided by language and a Norway bound by tradition; intellectual and cultural aspiration in Sweden; and in Denmark the particular and persistent idea that to engage with art is to better one's self, no bourgeois strings attached. The Danish language even has a word for it, 'dannelse'. It translates roughly as 'cultivation' but means something more: that education never ends, and is fuelled by a person's continued interaction and discussion with the world around them, from the biggest to the smallest of its ideas.

I got a sharper definition of 'dannelse' from Jens Nielsen, an arts consultant and former orchestra boss who co-authored a report into the state of Denmark's professional orchestras in 2017.[1] 'The word suggests springing into life through an awareness of art and culture,' Nielsen told me. 'It is connected to the pursuit of happiness and leading a good, meaningful life. We know, not only from the obvious, but also from scientific research, that people feel those things from participating in cultural activities in particular, but that they also feed into democracy and free speech.' As always in the Nordic region, the state shoulders a portion of the responsibility. It's one thing that the orchestras exist. It's another that ticket prices are kept low, that their municipalities use them fully and that they play an increasingly broad range of music.

And, vitally, that they are seen and heard even by those who don't turn up in person. Across the Nordic region, broadsheet newspapers still carry pages of classical music reviews and features while the broadcasting orchestras in Denmark, Sweden and Finland all fill weekly television slots. For half an hour before its weekly concert on DR2 television, Denmark's DR Symphony Orchestra also appears on the televised panel show *Den Klassiske Musikquiz* ('The Classical Music Quiz'), a ratings success story since it was inaugurated in 2018. Sweden's SVT is so sure of its public service mission that it frequently gives Saturday nights and Sunday afternoons on SVT2 television over to classical music, including whichever full-length Wagner and Strauss operas it can access via the European Broadcasting Union (SVT has also recently revived its own TV classical music quiz, *Kontrapunkt*). Residents of all three Scandinavian nations have access to each other's public broadcasting channels, delivering a wealth of new broadcast performances every week. A favourite anecdote in Denmark is that the idealistic Swedes running SVT don't even collect viewing figures for their classical music and opera broadcasts. SVT viewing figures are in fact collected, by an external agency that dutifully files the results away. But SVT sees no need to routinely publish them and, one source told me, even less to let them dictate programming.

Finland's state broadcasting corporation YLE, meanwhile, has steadily increased the amount of classical music it televises over the last decade while the legacy of the Covid-19 pandemic now sees it transmit every concert by its own orchestra on screen. When that orchestra plays a piece of new music on TV, the piece in question is often chewed over for another thirty minutes by critics back in the studio, *Match of the Day*-style. 'We are not focusing on the size of the audience,' YLE producer Miikka Maunula explained to me when the corporation started to ramp-up its classical music offering in the mid 2010s. 'We are focusing on what sort of value we bring to society, which has been a strategic goal since the introduction of the media tax.'

The media tax, paid by every Finn, replaced the antiquated licence fee in 2013 on the principle that public service broadcasting, like healthcare, should be paid for by every citizen in a democracy including those who claim to have no need of it (the same system has since been adopted in Denmark). But there was another reason for YLE wanting to broadcast more concerts on screen: the photogenic new concert hall in Helsinki it had just helped to build.

◢

On the waterfront in Aalborg, Denmark's northernmost major city, stands a very un-Scandinavian looking edifice in aluminum and concrete. The House of Music (Musikkens Hus) looks proudly out over the Limfjord, its gaze brutishly returned by the cranes of heavy industry. More garish and angular than the glass box that is Alsion, the House of Music is north Jutland's answer to the Walt Disney

Concert Hall in downtown Los Angeles. Underneath a billowing aluminum roof that harvests sunlight for energy are four auditoria and a foyer in phantasmagorical concrete. The centrepiece is a cello-shaped concert hall in the white and red of the Danish flag, complete with a hydraulically rising stage and showpiece four-manual organ. The principal resident of this Austrian-designed rhapsody on architectural deconstructivism is the Aalborg Symphony Orchestra. When the building opened in 2014, all three symphony orchestras in Jutland found themselves playing in sleek new concert halls opened within a decade.

Nothing has transformed the operational realities of its culture sector like the Nordic region's predilection for beautiful new performing arts buildings, preferably overlooking water. The new concert halls in Aalborg and Sønderborg quickly became beacons of local pride despite the inevitable handwringing over cost, an essential part of the democratic process and much-needed tucker for the local press. What some labelled a manifestation of city hall hubris was arguably more a vote of confidence in the public sector. More than half of the House of Music's 703 million Danish kroner price tag was coughed up by Realdania, an architecturally minded charitable foundation built on mortgage investments. The bulk of the rest came from the local council, aware that a structure like this would turbocharge the investment it already makes in the occupying orchestra – improving musical standards, increasing attendance and transforming every part of the concert-going experience.

As a building, the House of Music turns an operating profit. Plenty of intellectual Danes like to claim that their wider 'nation of farmers' cares little for bold cultural infrastructure projects like these, a dubious standpoint when you see, statistically, how many citizens actively attend cultural events. Either way, when a landmark building like the House of Music becomes the symbol of a city as it has in Aalborg, we're into the more penetrating domain of civic pride. Few in Denmark would dare trample on that.

Denmark quite possibly has the most architecturally discerning population on earth, which helps explain the relish with which projects like these are discussed and criticized. At the turn of the century, the Danish Broadcasting Corporation (DR) took the decision to move its physically separated television and radio operations to a single, purpose-built Broadcasting City (DR Byen) in a newly developing district of the capital. At the heart of the complex would be a vineyard-style concert hall designed by the French architect Jean Nouvel, then the most expensive venue of its kind ever built, even before it soared over budget. Soon the selection of Nouvel as the architect and the high-spec nature of his design started to ruffle feathers. The press labelled the concert hall a vanity project, the plaything of DR executives who had been faced with cheaper alternatives but were set on making a statement. As the price tag rocketed even higher, DR was forced to sell its rights to broadcast the Olympic Games. Politicians of various colours demanded the concert hall be sold off. Some DR employees joined them on a picket line.

The fuss was soon forgotten when Copenhageners settled into the hall's comfortable teak and velvet seats following its opening in 2008. Twelve years later, the DR Concert Hall was being credited with creating an almost entirely new, more diverse and rapidly growing audience for its resident DR Symphony Orchestra. In 2018 the venue's success motivated further calls for it to be removed from the auspices of DR and made independent. Meanwhile, many who subscribed to the DR Symphony Orchestra's concerts at the old 'radio house' across the city in Frederiksberg before 2008 simply transferred their subscriptions to that hall's new occupant, the Copenhagen Philharmonic. Plenty of them couldn't face losing their relationship with the beautiful 1945 concert hall by Vilhelm Lauritzen, whose design clearly influenced Nouvel's. In the years leading up to the Covid-19 pandemic, Copenhagen had its biggest ever audience for orchestral music, a triumph in which the city's regard for quality architecture played a significant part (the process was almost immediately replicated in Helsinki, whose Musiikkitalo concert hall complex opened in 2011).

The Danish capital's harbour-side opera house, inaugurated in 2004, hasn't slipped so easily from controversy's clutches. The fuss is largely connected to the social faux pas that was the building's genesis. It was bankrolled by the late Mærsk Mc-Kinney Møller, patriarch of Europe's biggest shipping firm Mærsk, who styled the building as a gift to the people of Denmark. Given the country's tax rules, Møller effectively forced the state to pay for half the building in tax relief (the total cost was 2.5 billion Danish kroner), a gesture that went down like the proverbial lead balloon and aroused the fury of the Social Democrat-controlled Copenhagen Council, which for years resisted funding the construction of a bridge to link the building to the city centre. It soon emerged that the institution charged with running it, the Royal Danish Theatre, had begged the state not for a new opera house, but for a badly needed new playhouse.[2] Not only that: Møller apparently strong-armed Denmark's most distinguished architect into accepting certain design features of his own.

Only in Scandinavia could a new opera house attract controversy because it wasn't being paid for by the state. But as a symbol of personal wealth, Møller's gesture kicked against the traditional Scandinavian social code known as Jantelov (The Law of Jante). It originated in an oddball novella on the subject of inverted snobbery by a misfit Danish-Norwegian named Aksel Sandemose, and lays out a sort of Ten Commandments for good civic behaviour. The strongest proof of Jantelov's continued relevance can be found in the regularity with which Nordic folk pause to analyse its dictates. The gist is that no citizen should believe themselves better or more successful than any other, a point of etiquette which sees the comparatively few millionaires in the region keep a low profile (Denmark's incarnation of the TV quiz show *Who Wants to Be a Millionaire* retains the same format as the UK and US versions, including the cash figure won: a million Danish kroner – around £120,000).

Nothing tickles Nordic folk quite like an act of fiscal arrogance backfiring. A notable example came in 2002 when one of Finland's richest men, a Nokia executive, was caught speeding on his Harley-Davidson motorbike. As is standard in Finland, his fine was calculated against his income and was set at €116,000.

In 2018, the Royal Danish Theatre staged a play depicting the power struggle between Mærsk Mc-Kinney Møller and the opera house's architect Henning Larsen, two of the biggest fish that ever swam in the small pond that is Denmark. Though both men were dead, it was a bold move considering the foundation Mærsk established, the AP Møller Foundation, remains one of the theatre's biggest donors and pumps enough money into the country's arts institutions to be known in the press as the Second Culture Ministry.

The play was a fascinating study of two egos that painted the opera house itself in rather pale terms by default, a reminder that it's not such an extravagant structure after all. Yes, it was built within view of Møller's office across the water and forms a grand schematic triptych with the four buildings of the Amalienborg Palace and the Florentine dome of the Marble Church. But in the context of architectural history outside the former Eastern bloc, it is a softly spoken building given its function and size. Its sleek auditorium raises a twenty-first-century eyebrow at the traditional operatic horseshoe. It has no boxes and no private rooms whatsoever front-of-house, save one reserved for the monarch, who must enter via one of the three revolving front doors like everybody else. You never queue for the toilet and the auditorium empties quickly, the back wall of the stalls doubling as a huge sliding door. Views across the city from the foyers are universally rewarding but get better the higher up (and therefore cheaper) your seats.

The biggest single architectural sticking point, beyond the fact that many Copenhageners consider the building dull, is the series of steel slats that slice horizontally across its façade – Møller's idea, not Larsen's. A newspaper columnist recently argued for the refashioning of the façade in the plate glass of Larsen's original scheme. If that were done, and it won't be, operagoers would be seen more clearly enjoying their interval drinks from across the water. Perhaps Møller's one concession to Jantelov was that, as it stands, the building lets its occupants look out but obscures their presence from those looking in. In Denmark, you don't go to the opera to be seen.

Over in Norway, the capital's new opera house doesn't so much sit on the water as emerge from it, an amphibious marble iceberg that leers upwards from the waterline of the Oslofjord. Similarly obscured is the building's financial provenance, which wasn't so different from that of its equivalent in Copenhagen, despite taking a more circuitous route. Much of the Mærsk Corporation's money came not from shipping but from drilling, during Denmark's stretch as the European Union's largest oil exporter. Mærsk had access to those limited parts of the North Sea fields that the Norwegians hadn't snapped-up already. The difference, in Denmark, was that the company responsible for drilling it lay in private hands, not the state's.

Before huge oil reserves were discovered in the North Sea in 1969, Norway was Scandinavia's poor relation. The black gold brought floods of cash into the country via state-owned drilling firms. With the memory of poverty lingering still, Norway invested most of the proceeds in the so-called Sovereign Wealth Fund. In 2020, the Fund was worth nearly US$200,000 per Norwegian citizen, delivering an astonishing yield in interest alone – Lutheran self-discipline writ large on the stock market. Norway remains frugal with its oceanic wealth, limiting annual domestic investment to around 4 per cent of the balance and with a particular fondness for capital projects that won't spark inflation. One result has been a rebalancing of the already-awkward sibling relationship between Norway and its former colonial masters Denmark and Sweden. Another has been the spectacular growth of Norway's cultural infrastructure.

To build the Oslo Opera House, the new home for the national opera company that gave Antonio Pappano his first conducting job, cost the Norwegian Government 300 million Norwegian kroner less than the projected 4.4 billion budgeted. In January 2012, four years after the building's inauguration, a new theatre and concert hall complex opened overlooking the Skagerrak Strait in the town of Kristiansand. Eight months later, on the other side of Norway's southernmost tip, perhaps the most beautiful concert hall in all of Norway was opened: a new waterside home for the symphony orchestra in Stavanger, the seat of Norway's oil industry.

It was always about more than the buildings. In the Oslo opera's first season, over a fifth of Norwegians attended a performance at the building and tens of thousands visited the capital to see it. Norway has become a country in which 'people are interested in opera in a way I have never come across', according to the Norwegian Opera's artistic director until 2020, Annilese Miskimmon. To coincide with the opening of the Kristiansand concert hall, the town's orchestra was upgraded from chamber status to become the Kristiansand Symphony Orchestra.

◢

If landing at Haugesund Airport is tricky, touching down at Sandane is a veritable stunt. The runway sits on a plateau between two mountainous peaks, perpendicularly straddling the Anda peninsula between the Nordfjord and the Gloppefjord, 250 kilometres north-east of Bergen. On approach, the turboprop plane flew so close to the mountaintops and glaciers that I could see down cracks in the ice. It seemed unfathomable that there could be a functioning runway anywhere near terrain like this. The plane sank suddenly into a valley bottomed-out with water, heading for a sheer wall of rock. It then banked sharply into a U-turn and had barely straightened up when it hit a runway, hard. The three passengers making the journey for the first time were easily identifiable from the involuntary noises they made.

It turned out we were all heading for the same place, the sleepy village of Nordfjord. From the airstrip at Sandane, a minibus took us through a tunnel bored under the runway and emerged in dazzling sunshine on the opposite hillside, sloping down towards a fjord. It was one of those September days on which the Norwegian sun seems to radiate an all-seeing strength, its last hurrah before a six-month hibernation. The sky appeared as a cupola of Yves Klein blue, the fjord as a flat mirror, spread out in the cool shadow of the pine-forested hills on each side. On the ferry crossing the fjord, Norwegians partook of their hotdogs and coffee as we chugged for a heart-slowing ten minutes to the opposite shore and then continued to the town of Nordfjord itself, a sprawling village, population 5,900, spread over one of the fjord's bays. Nordfjord had a post office, an abundance of hairdressers, the obligatory branch of Intersport and a hotel that time forgot. The expiry date on the minibar's orange juice read 30 September 2012, a year to the day before I checked-in.

Only one building dominates Nordfjord, though. And yes, it's a modern opera house. In 1989, a Norwegian violinist named Kari Standal returned to Norway after studying in Michigan, where she had met and married an American tenor. Kari and her husband Michael Pavelich set about re-energizing community music-making in the municipality of Eid, and, in 1996, Kari took a freelance job substituting in the pit for the opera company in Kristiansund further up the coast. 'The day I came home, I contacted Eid Municipality and presented my plans,' she explained to me in her car, as we drove down Nordfjord's one commercially significant street. 'I wanted to make an opera company here.' A week later, her idea was approved by the board.

From scratch, Kari and her husband built an opera company with a fundamentally professional operating model. It would combine professional orchestral musicians, vocal principals, creative teams and technical leads with a volunteer chorus and crew, inviting everyone here and nearby to participate on their own terms. Eleven years after the company's debut performance, of Johann Strauss II's *Die Fledermaus*, the Norwegian Government offered to build it a bespoke theatre and workshop suite. Opera Nordfjord is now the single most unifying organization in this tiny town and its surrounding hamlets, an echo of the Lutheran church in pre-secular times.

'Nordfjord was an unlikely place to start an opera company,' conceded Kari, reversing into a parking space in the shadow of her opera house's slate-clad fly-tower. It overlooks the town from a privileged position on the side of a modest hillock, a colossal snowcapped mountain rearing up behind it. Kari struck me as a Scandinavian straight from central casting, her outward charm concealing inner steel and a quick disregard for the frivolous or irrelevant. Her smiles blazed suddenly but lasted a few seconds at best, fizzling out into a look of simmering determination. 'It worked partly because we got enough people to feel like they were on a team,' she explained. 'And that only worked because of what Michael and I had been doing with community music in the seven years before. People trusted us.'

From day one, Opera Nordfjord was about more than opera, a concept that becomes more apparent the longer you spend here. The opera house doesn't stand isolated and unused for months on end, despite the company's annual schedule of just two main-stage productions and one fringe show. Architecturally and operationally, the house is indistinguishable from the local high school. The theatre's well-equipped workshops double as the school's craft and design department. Its rehearsal spaces and stages are used as the school's performing arts faculty. The whole concept insulated the company and its new home from accusations of elitism and the whiff of irrelevance, future-proofing it in the face of many funding decisions still to come.

Fifteen years after the launch production of *Die Fledermaus*, I was in Nordfjord to see the company's new staging of the operetta, its first at the new theatre. Exploring the backstage areas guided by Kari, I met Kristian Myksvoll Sætren from the lighting crew. He had started out assisting on the opera's electronics team while a student at the high school and had stuck at it, now working frequently alongside the renowned lighting designer Hans-Åke Sjöqvist. It was his plan, he told me, to pursue a career in theatrical lighting. The coursework for the Design and Handicraft students at his old school is the same every year: build the set and props for the autumn opera production. The entire school is present for the dress rehearsal, whether on the stage, behind the stage or watching from the auditorium. The performers in *Die Fledermaus* ranged in age from 14 to 76. The production scored highly on relevance, imagination and clarity and was fluently sung. But the heart of the enterprise was its amateur chorus and its army of backstage volunteers. During the post-show buffet dinner, they literally queued up to talk to me about the company's significance to the region.

Nobody encapsulated that significance quite like Magni Flyum, an apparently fearless, direct woman with dark hair and a fondness for Nordic knitwear who ran Nordfjord's Academy for Culture and Business (VAKN). Her children all passed through the Opera Nordfjord system, which doesn't so much set people on paths to La Scala as awaken them to the lifelong potential of engagement with the arts. One afternoon, Magni took me down to a rehearsal studio where her teenage daughter was preparing for a gig with her own band. We then drove up into the mountain range that looms over the village, along increasingly snowy tracks and over nineteenth-century stone bridges, one of Magni's hands on the steering wheel while the other massaged the gearstick. She wanted to show me a view of the village and fjord from above, and eventually we found one, stepping out of the car to gaze down on it and pick out the opera house below. 'Growing up here you tend to think anything is possible,' Magni said. 'After all, we made an opera company.'

Education is often cited as a principle reason for the Nordic region's thriving music life, but the word encapsulates rather more than formal instruction. The region has a sporadic but rich network of ad hoc institutions that lubricate performance and participation, some every bit as idealistic as Opera Nordfjord. Pious Sweden, afraid of the corrupting influence of American pop music on its youth, set up a network of music schools in the post-war years. These went on to provide Sweden with competent musicians in every genre while ironically, given the objectives, also giving the world Abba and the handful of Swedish producers who have taken control of the worldwide pop music industry. The same policy saw the creation of 'study circles', through which any group of organized young adults could request instruments with which to make music and a space in which to do so. The idea was spun off the Danish concept of the Folk High School, a non-academic, creative alternative to higher education with no age restrictions.

These underlying networks fostered a vast array of creativity and a huge amount of talent. In many cases, they still do. One area in which they blossom most obviously is in the Nordic region's thriving amateur music scene, particularly its proliferation of volunteer choirs. It is estimated that 600,000 Swedes sing in choirs, many of them technically accomplished ensembles stylistically modelled on the Swedish Radio Choir, reckoned by some to be the finest a cappella choral ensemble in existence. Churches across the Nordic region are fitted out with striking neo-classical organs built mostly in the last half-century, the majority paid for by the church tax. Their organists, like orchestral musicians, are well-remunerated, highly qualified civil servants.

▲

At Sandane airport the morning after *Die Fledermaus*, the then artistic director of the Norwegian Opera in Oslo, Per Boye Hansen, was interviewed by a local TV news crew outside the terminal building. Eavesdropping as I tried to negotiate an al fresco vending machine, I got the gist of what he told the reporter: that the reach, relevance and sense of ownership achieved by Opera Nordfjord were worthy objectives of any opera company, even his own. Nobody ever mentioned the fringe economic benefits, though in Norway, they rarely do.

For the time being, anyway. On my first night in Nordfjord, Norway had found itself with a new government after 21 days of post-election horse-trading. A coalition was formed between the centre right Conservative party and hard right Progress party, with support in a confidence-and-supply arrangement from the centre-right Liberals and Christian Democrats (eight major parties contested the election). Anders Breivik's 2011 terrorist attack on Norway and its Labour party had been conspicuously absent from the election campaign, even from those 33 survivors of the Utøya island massacre who stood as candidates. Yet it was difficult not to sense a significant shift in Norwegian politics, in tandem with the rise of nativist parties across the Nordic region. Most of them believe wholeheartedly in a version of the region's traditional social democracy, but one ring-fenced for people with the right colour skin.

As the news dripped through, I was eating a dinner cooked by Trond Aarre, Opera Nordfjord's Chairman, a tenor in its chorus and a psychiatrist at the local hospital. His two daughters, both keen students of politics and public affairs, were visiting from Oslo and relayed updates on the ensuing negotiations from the living room until the outcome became clear. At that point, they joined us and opened a bottle of wine.

The family soon declared its political allegiance: it had voted unanimously for a party one shade redder than the incumbent Prime Minister Jens Stoltenberg's Labour. In consensus-based Scandinavia where Conservative administrations have tended to conserve broadly socially democratic policies, I asked the family how the new administration might impact spending on culture. 'I can't see too many problems there,' said Trond, a stern but generous man with a look of the mature Sibelius about him. 'Most parties have strong supporters of the arts.'

Three years earlier, the Norwegian Labour party's culture minister, who would become deputy leader after the 2013 election defeat, had made a speech in Bodø in the north of Norway, 530 kilometres south-west of Tromsø. 'Music and culture are influenced by the places they come from,' said Trond Giske. 'Culture provides a sense of identity, roots and belonging.' Textbook ministerial rhetoric, were it not for the occasion on which he spoke: the launch of the newest full-time, state-funded symphony orchestra in Europe, the Arctic Philharmonic. The new ensemble would straddle the towns of Bodø and Tromsø and have an annual operating budget of 55 million Norwegian kroner (£4.6 million). As he promised yet another new Norwegian concert hall to house the ensemble, Giske proclaimed his determination to enrich the lives of those in the far north of Norway, and with little mention of economic payback. In Norway, the oil fund takes care of that.

As in Sønderborg, it was geography that saw the Norwegian Arctic get its own symphony orchestra, with the remote location a clear source of pride to Giske. The ensemble's nearest equivalent in latitudinal terms is the Lapland Chamber Orchestra (LCO) in Rovaniemi. The town is the capital of Finnish Lapland, part of the huge wilderness to the north of the Scandinavian peninsula and Russia that is home to Europe's only indigenous people. The Sámi are the Nordic region's seventh race – or rather, its first. The LCO's music director of more than two decades is John Storgårds, also a contracted conductor with the BBC Philharmonic and a regular guest at orchestras throughout Europe and America. But Storgårds is first and foremost a Laplander, and a man whose proudest achievement is his stewardship of this orchestra in his homeland's hinterland. The LCO has been nominated for a *Gramophone* Classical Music Award and in 2011 moved into its own new concert hall, the Korundi House.

Like Opera Nordfjord, the Lapland Chamber Orchestra suggests that isolated communities can be conditioned to normalize tastes that might be considered rarefied anywhere else. Even more significantly, the LCO demonstrates, via the impressionability of a captive audience, that the artistic conservatism ingrained in the majority of

European symphony orchestras is arguably self-fulfilling. Storgårds has weaned concertgoers in Lapland off the orchestral sector's generally cautious diet of music written by a list of 30 dead composers, creating in it a convention-defying hunger for the new, the unusual and the unheard.

Audiences at the Korundi House in Rovaniemi readily subscribe to concerts featuring music by Cage, Maderna, Kokkonen, Zebeljan, Valtaoja, Schnittke, Räisänen, Sørensen and other rare, living and young composers – and yes, with a bit of Beethoven and Tchaikovsky thrown in.[3] 'They [the audience] expect that our programmes will be quite wild, that there will be something they have never heard before. If we don't do things like that, they get a bit angry,' Storgårds told me when we met in Helsinki in 2012. Since then, his orchestra's taste has only matured further. 'If you really believe in what you're doing and you do it well, the audience will come with you.'

Maybe. But it might have been harder for Storgårds if his orchestra wasn't the only show in town. His audience's unprejudiced creative hunger has been engendered by its tendency to attend a concert simply because that concert is happening. Some more conservative Nordic orchestras have proved as pragmatic as could be expected in balancing the needs of their communities with a determination to expose them to the miracle of orchestral music in the best possible way. If the Lapland Chamber Orchestra has used its isolation to its advantage, other ensembles have let their fiscal privilege incubate complacency and entitlement, dialling-down imagination and tending not to look beyond the subscriber base – potentially fatal in the long-term as once-homogenous societies begin to change and the social contract shows signs of weakening. Besides, when public funds cover 85 per cent of an orchestra's entire expenditure, it's easy for a politician to convene a meeting and close that orchestra down.

◢

If seventeenth-century organist composers could make a place famous, then the Swedish city of Helsingborg would be famous as the hometown of Dietrich Buxtehude, the man who inspired Johann Sebastian Bach. Helsingborg hugs the Swedish coast at the point where it gets physically closest to Denmark. In Buxtehude's day, the town was Danish.

The region is worth a few hours of anybody's time. Three big, battery-powered car ferries shuttle passengers and traffic across the strait that divides Denmark and Sweden. Ten minutes into the twenty-minute voyage, a claxon sounds to signal the vessel is crossing territorial waters, leading passengers to either reluctantly stop buying alcohol (on the Swedish side) or frantically start (on the Danish). In Danish Helsingør, you can visit the castle palace where Buxtehude was employed as an organist, Shakespeare's Elsinore. In Swedish Helsingborg, you can take in the church where he started his career. At the end of the 2010s, you could also drop in on one of the most restlessly innovative symphony orchestras in all of Scandinavia.

Until 2016, the Helsingborg Symphony Orchestra (HSO) was typical of its kind, its white art-deco concert hall coming to life on Thursday nights for concerts played to a loyal, educated and mostly grey-haired audience. That year, a new artistic director arrived at the orchestra from Stockholm, a man named Fredrik Österling. He was appointed, presciently perhaps, on his commitment to address a problem he saw coming down the tracks. 'Increasingly, the culture sector is being questioned in Sweden,' he explained to me in his office, where a narrow slither of high windows offered a glimpse of the water that separates his country from Denmark.

That water glistened blindingly as we spoke. It was 6 June, Sweden's National Day and one of the hottest of 2019. Österling was possessed of an assurance particular to powerful Swedes and which shines that bit brighter in the middle months of the year. He was dressed in shorts and a loose linen shirt, with architect-style glasses clamped around the centre point of his bald head. He looked as though he was on his way to a jamboree, which indeed he was: his orchestra was preparing to play its traditional National Day concert in an outdoor park.

The outlook for Sweden's orchestral life, according to Österling, wasn't so sunny. Despite oscillating surges of optimism and uncertainty, it would be difficult to argue the long-term situation is any different in Denmark, Finland or even in Norway. 'If you are an orchestra with a handful of subscribers and you are the biggest cost that a city has for culture, it would be a fairly easy decision for the politicians to shut the orchestra down and use the money to buy shows that are touring Sweden,' Österling began, with a matter of fact equality of vocal tone. 'That way, they get diversity, they get different flavours every week and if they want they can even hire a symphony orchestra from Stockholm from time to time.'

When he arrived in Helsingborg, Österling claimed, he found an institution wilfully sealed off from reality. 'We perceived ourselves as being at the top of some sort of cultural hierarchy, but in the view of most people and most politicians, we were expensive and weird – plain weird.' He laid out his prognosis with ruthless clarity: politics, society and the culture sector in Sweden have all changed but the country's symphony orchestras have not. Traditionally, HSO subscribers have been a particular breed: educated citizens who had been weaned on classical music since childhood and probably played an instrument or sang in one of Sweden's many choirs. For the first time since Europe's network of orchestras was firmly established, that group has started to decrease in number. According to Österling, too many Swedish citizens are now reaching the age of 55 and not feeling the urge to subscribe to their local symphony orchestra's season.

Österling's fix was to radically reshape his orchestra's programme. In the spacious, calming foyers of its concert hall, it would accompany yoga sessions during the day. A portion of its Thursday subscription concerts would be played for an hour on Wednesdays, just as every working Swede was clocking off. The subscription concerts themselves would be freed entirely from the homogeneity that rules the orchestral sector from Toronto to Taipei. Rather than the standard overture–concerto–symphony model calling on the same list of 30 composers, every subscription concert in Helsingborg would include a world premiere and the vast majority would include music by a woman. A broad, abstract theme would contextualize all the music played in a single season and provide a starting point for discussion. Space would be left in the schedules for works to be dropped in or written to order in response to local events. When a subscriber wrote to the orchestra lampooning it for giving a platform to homosexuals, Österling, who trained as a composer, set the letter to music and had a gay tenor sing the result in concert a few weeks later.

I have attended some refreshing concerts in Helsingborg, even if comparatively few of them have got my blood racing and none have been anywhere near full. In one, a solo viola weaved its way through every piece on the menu from a world premiere by Emmy Lindström to Berlioz's imposing *Harold in Italy* via Bernard Hermann's music for the movie *Psycho*. Another concert in 2019 titled 'Death' included music by Michael Nyman, John Cage, Lennon and McCartney, Thelonius Monk, Astor Piazzolla, Lukas Foss, Franz Schubert and Galina Ustvolskaya.

Plenty believed the Helsingborg Symphony Orchestra's reinvention a gimmick and were handed potent ammunition when Österling announced his orchestra would no longer be booking soloists and conductors who couldn't travel to the city by land or sea. But there was something more to that decision than the obvious environmental concern. Österling railed against the peripatetic merry-go-round of orchestral life, in which the same soloists appear with orchestras all over the world, playing the same pieces and with the same agents pocketing a fee (in many cases, at the taxpayer's expense). He seemed keen to make his orchestra more relevant to the municipality that pays for it. 'The industry leads us to believe that flying someone in somehow adds to the experience. But there's no artistic reason to do that, it just draws everyone into the same view of what's good or bad,' Österling told me. 'We need more difference between orchestras.'

Österling didn't even mention climate change when we discussed his travel ban. Instead, he returned to the notion of relevance. A colleague in Denmark described the Helsingborg travel policy to me as 'nonsense, bullshit ... simply branding'. But on the latter point, Österling didn't necessarily disagree. 'It is part of our long-term plan to create debate around the orchestra and sustain a way of communicating about it,' he said without a hint of apology. 'Politicians like the fact that we create conversations and win awards for doing so. And instead of a zombie-like audience coming here because it's just what they do, we now have an audience which is alive, and which expresses things. Even when someone leaves the hall in anger it shows we are invoking emotion. That is pretty much the point with art.'

There was no lack of anger stirred up by Österling's tenure in Helsingborg, which concluded not entirely happily in the summer of 2021. The extent to which his artistic upheavals chimed with his state employers were noticeable in the advertisement for a successor who would 'continue to modernize'.[4] What were the effects of Österling's changes where it really matters – at the box office? In 2019, he pointed to a slowing in the drop-off of subscriptions, but a drop-off nonetheless. Single ticket sales, he said, were up 30 per cent which 'proves people are coming here who wouldn't normally'. As for concerns about alienating his existing audience base, he was unapologetic: 'The previous management succeeded in decreasing the subscriber base by nearly a third over 15 years, just by playing Beethoven, Brahms and Tchaikovsky. It would be hard to do worse.' Österling had to try something, not least as his tenure followed the departure of a hugely popular, charismatic and renowned chief conductor.[5]

It's a cliché that there are no such things as good and bad orchestras, only good and bad conductors. You feel its validity in Scandinavia, where not even orchestras are immune from a general air of emotional indifference. Listen to the Trondheim Symphony Orchestra playing under a run-of-the-mill conductor and it will sound perfectly adequate. Its bosses signed chief conductors Daniel Harding, Krzysztof Urbański and Han-na Chang because they wanted it to achieve more than that, to be forced now and then to play the odd concert as though life itself depended on it.

The dynamic is more pronounced in the Nordic region given the municipal nature of most orchestras and the limited budgets with which they can hire the week's conductor – one reason they're so willing to offer permanent contracts to promising youngsters. The sort of reactive, adrenaline-fuelled engagement that can elevate a midweek concert to the level of a life-changing experience demands that salaried, unionized musicians shake off the veneer of comfort and give something of themselves – that they step beyond the confines of Jantelov.

The Finnish conductor Santtu-Matias Rouvali put it in stark terms when I met him one wet March day in 2017. He was preparing to lead his last concert as principal guest conductor of the Copenhagen Philharmonic, an orchestra facing precisely the sort of political problems that so worried Österling. A succession of politicians had called for its closure, for the money it received from central government to be diverted towards musical projects elsewhere. The Copenhagen Philharmonic had pursued Rouvali to be its new chief conductor, but was too late and probably too ambitious. He had already been nominated to the top job at the Gothenburg Symphony Orchestra. In the week we met, he was announced as the new chief conductor of the Philharmonia Orchestra in London, starting autumn 2021.

Rouvali was a bag of nervous energy but a game, honest interviewee, prone to exploding with torrents of cascading laughter. Our paths had crossed in London once before, and, with a view to his forthcoming job in the city, he was keen to discuss the strange operating model of the UK capital's orchestras. In contrast to salaried orchestras elsewhere, at the Philharmonia and London's three other independent symphony orchestras, musicians are booked for each performance from an approved list and only paid for the concerts and rehearsals they attend. '[in the Philharmonia] . . . they are basically all substitutes, they know they'll not be invited back if they don't pay attention [to what the conductor is doing],' Rouvali told me. 'Nordic orchestras can take more advice, but that's because there's more rehearsal time, so musicians are more likely to come unprepared. Up here [Finland and Scandinavia], the musicians know they have four days [of rehearsal].'

At this point, I led him on: so they're lazy? 'Yes, that's the word,' Rouvali said with a coy giggle to indicate jest. 'But I would say that if you reduced the rehearsal time, it wouldn't necessarily make for better results.' Rouvali qualified his statements by heaping genuine praise on the three Nordic orchestras with which he held contracts at the time: the Tampere Philharmonic, Copenhagen Philharmonic and Gothenburg Symphony. I have seen him conduct electrifying concerts with all three. Still, I was eager to compare notes with a conductor whose career, geographically speaking, had gone the other way – Edward Gardner. 'With this orchestra [Bergen Philharmonic], you get to the highest level by gestating rather than pushing for things quickly,' Gardner said, while pointing to the 'massive benefit' of repeating Thursday concerts on Fridays and on tour.

I put to Gardner the creative implications of the entire Nordic orchestral setup: does the relative comfort induce complacency or engender deeper engagement with the music? 'I have to be honest and say both arguments are true, in a way. I push the orchestra very hard. Sometimes, as on a day like today, I'm fighting for it.[6] But the positives are unbelievable. Serious, deep thought goes into how a piece should sound here. A back desk violinist will approach me over lunch and tell me they've spent four days thinking about a particular phrase in Tchaikovsky's Fourth Symphony. In London people don't remember if they played Tchaikovsky's Fourth Symphony yesterday. So you could say the temperature is slightly lower, and that it's my job to keep the energy up.'

▲

For much of the 2010s, Norway's determination to prove its musical worth to the world saw it ferry foreign reporters back and forth to its unparalleled network of music festivals. These festivals resemble a cycle of their own, tracking the grand theatre of seasonal change. Some mark the loosening of winter's grip while others provide sustenance in the midst of it. Many celebrate the lucid light and long days of high summer. Like Opera Nordfjord, they engage entire communities in the organization and presentation of esoteric, niche-interest music.

In August 2013, one such festival took me to Stavanger, the on-shore epicentre of Norway's oil industry situated just down the coast from Haugesund. For a time, a specially modified all-business-class Boeing 737 shuttled across the Atlantic from Stavanger to Houston, carrying oil executives to meetings and home again. You could safely assume that any T-shirted Stavanger Chamber Music Festival volunteer over the age of 40 had family involved in the oil industry, probably a spouse.

I spent time with one of them on my visit, an exhibitionist from Delaware named Gaye who has popped up on social media every 17 May since dressed in her bunad, the traditional costume worn on Norway's National Day. Gaye's domain was the festival's office, situated inside a mid-century bank building on Stavanger's main square. After a robbery, the building had been adopted by the local council and given over to cultural organizations. It was now known as the Culture Bank, one of a handful of stern financial buildings across Norway now commandeered for creativity.

The symbolism of converting banks into arts hubs is obvious enough: a Norway freed from pressing financial concerns looking to cultivate something deeper in its population for long-term benefit. But the oil money that has been pumped into the country has created economic problems as well as solving them, not least in suppressing the 'real' post-oil economy that in the 2020s showed signs of struggling. Of an evening in Stavanger, Gaye and her colleagues were prone to mulling over the corrupting influence of Norway's newfound wealth. Had it made Norwegians more possessive and less tolerant? Had it corroded the sanctity of their relationship with the nature that surrounds them? Had it undermined their belief in wage compression, high tax and the welfare state?

They all believed so, to varying degrees. But Stavanger probably wasn't the place in which to ask the question, still less the best one in which to hear it representatively answered. Walk through the cobbled streets of the city's cutesy Old Town to where the harbour opens up into the fjord, and you arrive at the glass edifice that is the Stavanger Concert House, probably the most exceptional performing arts building in Norway if judged by specification in relation to population (around 130,000). Front of house are sweeping foyers punctuated by a giant spiral staircase, a restaurant and three auditoria. Back of house are individual practice rooms for members of the Stavanger Symphony Orchestra, a gym and a canteen serving fish hooked straight from the fjord. It is perhaps the most overt symbol of oil wealth in Stavanger, along with the Tesla tailbacks that form around its pond-like central lake.

The Concert House's impressive principal auditorium carries the name of a local composer. Olav Fartein Valen was born in Stavanger in August 1887 to Christian missionaries who took their toddler son off to Madagascar for five years. Back in Europe, Valen studied composition with Max Bruch in Berlin and became intensely interested in the expressionistic world of Arnold Schoenberg. Specifically, he alighted upon the radical new view of harmony propagated by Schoenberg that elevated all twelve notes of the chromatic scale to equal status, thus avoiding any hint of allegiance to a particular key

– a technique known as twelve-tone serialism that had the potential to deliver dissonant, disorientating and wholly new music.

Valen's take on Schoenberg's non-tonal style was refracted through the prisms of the baroque German music he loved and the piercing solitude of a life lived in retreat from the world. His functional, beautiful works stoked countless Oslo-based controversies that the composer had no interest in facing down. He retreated to his sister's farmhouse near Haugesund and for nine years hardly left it. Supported by a government stipend, Valen immersed himself in the writing of music as if the act itself were a sacred ritual. He was mostly uninterested in that music's eventual performance, which explains its illegibility.

Valen's self-imposed isolation on Norway's west coast yielded some astonishing fruits, some of which were eagerly devoured by the Canadian pianist Glenn Gould. 'I can think of few composers who disciplined with such monkish regularity their linear environment,' commented Gould in 1972 with his characteristically obtuse turn of phrase, introducing his own broadcast performance of Valen's Piano Sonata No 2 ('one of the great piano sonatas of the twentieth century' for Gould). The pianist's point concerned Valen's insistence on working out all his ideas contrapuntally – with strict, baroque-derived linear counterpoint.

In 1940, an imposing symphony already under his belt, Valen wrote a scented violin concerto in memory of his deceased godson in which sculpted lyricism is spiked by the naturally angular, citric feel of disloyal melodies and pungent harmonies. Eventually, the music finds its way to the Lutheran chorale tune 'Jesu, meine Zuversicht', traced-out like a silhouette by a ghostly trumpet, the shadow of a harmonic chassis only just discernable underneath. Five years earlier, Schoenberg's best pupil Alban Berg had written a violin concerto, also in memory of a dead child, and also arriving at the reassurance of a Lutheran chorale. But Valen hadn't heard Berg's piece.

I listened to Valen's symphonies and string quartets on my journey to Stavanger in 2013 and the city was gracious enough to greet me with a performance that helped contextualize them. In the darkness of the Stavanger Concert Hall's second auditorium, Zetlitz-Salen, an ensemble played arrangements of Johann Strauss II waltzes by Berg, Schoenberg and their colleague Anton Webern. Next came a performance of *Pierrot lunaire*, Schoenberg's wacky cabaret that charts the demise of the sadistic clown-puppet transfixed by the moon.

Pierrot is a touchstone of twentieth-century modernism, a work for a hybrid vocalist-actor and a small ensemble of musicians that blurs the boundaries between performer and creator while looking backwards to the baroque and forwards to rap. It speaks the unspeakable through a mash-up of surrealism, symbolism and Dadaism that takes in a black mass and an erotic asphyxiation. Despite notating the score with absolute precision, Schoenberg was adamant that it should be spoken rhythmically, not sung. The performer in Stavanger was Tora Augestad, a mezzo-soprano from Bergen whose way through Pierrot's tumble towards nightmarish disintegration was as distinctive as it was captivating.

I spent some time considering what it was about Augestad's imperfect performance that felt so perfectly judged, even though it shunned the particular sort of flamboyance on which *Pierrot* usually lives or dies. Augestad had let herself be carried along by Schoenberg's narrative rollercoaster and made little attempt to conceal how technically difficult it is to cling onto, constantly striking a tuning fork and holding it to her ear to level her pitch horizon as the band spluttered and soared behind her. She read the music from a score, even following it from left to right with an index finger. She clutched the music stand in resolve and in panic, crouching down behind it one moment and leering over it towards the audience the next.

Evidently, this was not how some other journalists present liked their *Pierrot*. But the performance said something about the fast-tracking of Norway's music scene, its leap-frogging of tradition with infrastructure. Augestad's execution of Schoenberg's instructions, accomplished and distinctive as it was, seemed to acknowledge that

Norway hasn't been doing this sort of thing for long; that in Stavanger, even in a building partially named after a local serialist composer, *Pierrot* can be possessed of an edge that it has inevitably lost in central Europe. This seemed to me a performance with little cultural baggage. That is not so easily achieved.

There was also a sense of the functional to it – of the musician as storyteller – which reminded me of performances I had encountered from Nordic musicians in London over the course of the previous decade. I remembered one in particular, in which a Finnish soprano had walked onto the stage of the Royal Festival Hall to sing a set of orchestral songs by Sibelius. Finding her position to the left of the conductor's podium, she rolled her head on her shoulders to loosen her neck before linking the fingers of both hands and stretching out her arms. It was, really, an athlete's preparation: an acknowledgement that what she was about to do demanded considerable physical poise and control while necessitating some degree of limbering up. Some in the concert hall probably thought it inappropriate, believing a soloist should display aristocratic grace from the moment they appear. I felt it cleansed and levelled the room, and brought extra realism to the savage songs she then sang, with tremendous beauty.

A trickle of Nordic musicians has long made its way onto international stages in mainland Europe, the United Kingdom, the United States and beyond. In the last decade that trickle has grown into a stream, and might just be on the way to becoming a torrent. None of the British Broadcasting Corporation's five orchestras had counted a Nordic conductor among their staff until 1996, when Osmo Vänskä from Finland became chief conductor of the BBC Scottish Symphony Orchestra in Glasgow. In 2018, all five of the Corporation's orchestras, together with its professional chamber choir, had either a chief conductor or principal guest conductor from the Nordic region or had announced the imminent arrival of one. Nordic musicians play and conduct far more than Nordic music, but the situation couldn't help but shape the repertoire being fed into the BBC's output via its main classical music radio station, Radio 3. 'There was a time in 2015 when we had 14 performances of the Sibelius violin concerto recorded and ready for broadcast,' the station's controller, Alan Davey, told me the year after. The BBC's own New Generation Artists Scheme has advanced the careers of Finnish and Danish string quartets as well as violinists, violists, clarinetists, pianists and singers from Norway and Sweden.

The talent spreads far beyond the BBC. In 2020, Nordic conductors held titles at two other orchestras in the UK and at symphony orchestras and opera companies in four US states, Canada, Colombia, Japan, Italy, France, Germany, the Czech Republic and New Zealand. Leif Ove Andsnes, Martin Fröst, Truls Mørk, Vilde Frang, Henning Kraggerud, Tine Thing Helseth, Anne Sofie von Otter, Nina Stemme, Pekka Kuusisto, Nikolaj Szeps Znaider, Andreas Brantelid, Karita Mattila, Lise Davidsen, Elsa Dreisig, Víkingur Ólafsson and the Danish String Quartet are among the major Nordic soloists touring the world. There are many more without the same PR clout, and still more who operate almost exclusively at home – too grounded to crave the logistical insanity of an international career.

The conductors, to a point, can be explained. The region's network of orchestras solves the Catch-22 of young conductors being insufficiently experienced to be booked by professional orchestras because they have insufficient experience conducting professional orchestras. In Finland, that problem is mitigated further as the ratio of orchestras to people is so much higher. The country's flagship conservatory, the Sibelius Academy, hires an entire orchestra for every class on its outstandingly successful conducting programme. But the country has also benefitted from the wisdom of one the profession's most potent pedagogical figures, a conductor named Jorma Panula.

The vast majority of Finnish conductors working internationally have passed through Panula's tutelage. More importantly, most of them were talent-spotted by him in the first place while playing instruments in orchestras. 'That's his gift,' the Estonian conductor

Paavo Järvi told me in 2020. 'He is so successful because he identifies the right person. It's unfortunately true that conductors are born. You can't make them but you do have to nurture them.' A background of playing in orchestras, rather than training singers in the rehearsal room of an opera house – the traditional route into the conducting profession – never does a rookie conductor any harm when meeting an orchestra for the first time.

In that regard, at least everyone gets equal chance. Instrumental tuition is free in Finland and heavily subsidized in Scandinavia. Music education in schools, conservatoires and universities across the region is entirely free no matter how far it is taken. The city of Helsinki saw a 250 per cent spike in the number of children taking up musical instruments among the cohort born in 2012, half of whose parents accepted the Helsinki Philharmonic Orchestra's offer of institutional god-parenthood to every newborn in the city that year. Finland's huge network of 100 music institutes catches children early and provides comprehensive instrumental and vocal tuition; the country's 2018 redrawing of the so-called National Core Curriculum for Basic Education in the Arts has further cemented the central place creative skills occupy in general education. Within that curriculum, music dominates.

Hardened orchestras don't care about nationality. They care whether or not a conductor has a vision and can communicate it. But any journalist faced with the sorts of numbers outlined above is obliged to ask if there's something beyond those advantageous educational and infrastructural reasons – something cultural, perhaps, that lies behind Finland's disproportionate productivity in particular. 'If a Finnish "school" of conducting exists, it comes from practicality: from the idea that we have to put something together technically first, and will make music afterwards,' the conductor Hannu Lintu posited as we chewed over the subject in 2021. 'That was the case even before Panula's time and we're now living in a world where orchestras everywhere appreciate that practicality more than ever.'

'When a Finnish conductor stands in front of the orchestra, you get a clear message: this is what we're going to do,' Leif Ove Andsnes told me in 2017. 'It's honest and sincere and the musicians respect it.'

Communication is a vital differential. In the last few decades, the culture of orchestral leadership has moved away from the twentieth-century norm of a dictatorial maestro imposing his (and it was invariably 'his') will on a group of musicians, deploying the stick rather more than the carrot and using charisma to mask bullying. Twenty-first-century orchestral life is more collaborative, consensual, empowering and far more female. In other words, it's far more Nordic. Finland's globetrotting conductors, Lintu tells me, frequently share tips on effective working methods for particular orchestras – what works and what doesn't. 'That's valuable, especially when you're going somewhere for the first time and you have a colleague who has already been there,' he says. 'Our international colleagues don't have that.'

In 2018, the American businessman Chris Shern released his book *Return of the Vikings: Nordic Leadership in Times of Extreme Change*. The focus was resolutely on enterprise, but there was a conspicuous exception among the ranks of CEOs and start-up gurus Shern interviewed. It came in the form of Sakari Oramo, the Finnish chief conductor of the BBC Symphony Orchestra. 'My ideal orchestra is a collection of informed, active and motivated musicians where everyone knows their place and function, and can feel free to have an influence on the whole,' Oramo told Shern. It sounded like a description of consensual, responsive Nordic democracy, in which authority is played down and transparency is sacrosanct. In his time as General Manager of the BBC National Orchestra of Wales, Michael Garvey referred to his own Danish chief conductor Thomas Søndergård's 'quiet leadership style'. Ask orchestral musicians what they look for in a conductor and a fair proportion will revert to what they don't look for, with 'talking too much' frequently topping the list.

This all sounds like a recipe for mediocrity, for interpretations lacking focus and performances low on fire. Critical consensus would suggest the opposite is true, and that playing standards in the ensembles in question have risen in tandem. Besides, however dangerous it is to generalize about musicians with individual musical personalities, the critical fraternity has never resisted the urge to do so. For years, critics in the United Kingdom, the United States and even Europe have written of 'cool' interpretations from Nordic conductors. The idea, like the adjective, has proved stubbornly persistent.

Perhaps I have played a part in the propagation of these ideas. In regularly writing comparative record reviews, I have been intrigued by the way in which Nordic conductors appear to handle the guarding and releasing of emotion in long-form music, particularly when that music comes from their own part of the world. Many of them seem to find a different temperament in it to their European, American, Australasian and Asian counterparts – one that can sometimes feel standoffish but can just as often feel intensely patient, all the while overriding the huge and divergent range of actual physical techniques these same conductors (male and female) display.

There's a useful parallel in the slow hand-clap used by Icelandic fans during the 2016 European soccer championship – the so-called Viking Thunder Clap. It started almost impossibly slowly, while gradually increasing speed by increments. When other nations' fans tried to replicate the clap, they inevitably failed to grasp the slow burn that is essential to its structure. They simply got too passionate, too fast, too quickly. That climactic moment when the clap could get no faster would always arrive too soon, robbing the whole gesture of impact. It was as if, for the Icelandic fans, seconds and minutes passed more slowly.

That year, I raised the idea of a Nordic interpretative style with Alan Davey, who has overall responsibility for each of the BBC's performing groups as Controller of BBC Radio 3. He drew a comparison with the Nordic literature he studied at university. 'Scandinavian [sic] conductors have been popular in Britain because they bring with them an analytical approach that can allow big moments to blossom while at the same time they're not entirely driven by emotion,' he said. 'In other words, there's a certain rationality there, on the surface at least. Thinking back to the Icelandic sagas or the dramas of Jón Thoroddsen, it's rather the same: there's something buttoned within.'

Later the same year, the Edinburgh-based journalist Kate Molleson shared her own take on the interpretative nuances of Thomas Søndergård, newly earmarked as the next chief conductor of the Royal Scottish National Orchestra but already a regular with the ensemble. She referred to 'that sort of stormy, stern, northern type of passion', continuing: 'it's almost po-faced, but then something will erupt, and it's ferocious. Draw all the weather analogies you like, but I think that really works with Scottish orchestras and the proof is there in the long connection they have with Nordic conductors.'[7] The Icelandic pianist Víkingur Ólafsson talked to me in 2017 of the very distinct combination of discipline and wildness that seemed to him a characteristic of Nordic conductors. 'There are some conductors who only have the discipline and some who only have the wildness,' he said; 'but there certainly could be a higher percentage of conductors from the north, particularly from Finland, who have both. I can think of a few, for sure.'

When I broached the subject with Santtu-Matias Rouvali – whose conducting technique contrasts markedly to that of his colleague, compatriot and fellow millennial Klaus Mäkelä – his response was to describe hard technical measures he had taken to achieve precisely those ends, including toning-down warmth-inducing vibrato with the express purpose of outlining a work's eruptions more starkly. It could well be endemic. The Norwegian violinist Eldbjørg Hemsing described the characteristic 'white' Nordic orchestral sound to me in 2018. 'It's not too wobbly, it's clear, to the point and pure.' Similar words have been uttered in reference to the much-discussed 'Nordic sound' in choral singing – a clean, lucid, ultra-precise but notably open ensemble singing style.

Much of this is linked to the aesthetics of canonic Nordic music itself, its tendency towards restrained, obsessive, introspective emotional turmoil and ambiguous, crisis-ridden climaxes – and its connection to ritualistic storytelling. 'I have tried to distance myself a little bit from the Romantic idea of "this is my story and I want to tell you about my heroic deeds",' the Finnish musician Pekka Kuusisto told me in 2017 when discussing his approach to interpreting Sibelius's music, as both a violinist and an ensemble leader. 'Sibelius's music feels more about things that have always happened; I am just the person who happens to be channelling them at that moment.' Davey, meanwhile, cited Sakari Oramo's particular way with a composer from an entirely different tradition, the Englishman Edward Elgar. 'Sakari brings a more analytical approach [to Elgar] so when the tunes emerge, they're more foregrounded. It's that rationality again – it's very effective and it's extremely interesting.'

◢

You wouldn't want to live in Copenhagen without a bicycle. When I moved to the city in 2015, I arranged with a bike shop in London to have my steel steed disassembled, packed and sent to an equivalent shop on Nyhavn, the colourful harbour that adorns many a postcard from the Danish capital. Soon enough the shop on Nyhavn notified me that the bike had arrived, and I went there to collect it: a Swedish-built Pilen Lyx purchased at quite some expense the year before from a specialist dealer in Chiswick. The man in the shop presented me with the rebuilt bike and politely offered to make adjustments. He then asked me how much I had paid for it. I told him. 'You know, this is actually quite a shit bike,' he said, with the air of an indifferent tour guide. 'You paid too much for it, but anyway, these ones are actually quite shit.' I thanked him and wished him a good day. 'You too – enjoy the sun!' he replied.

Rationalism is a central building block of the Nordic psyche, and surely fuelled the clear-headedness with which the region first set about eradicating poverty by uniting state and church. It has arguably made the people of the north notably pragmatic while helping to explain their efficiency, high divorce rates and transactional attitude to sex. It could well lie behind the region's healthy disdain for the 'I can achieve anything' culture – a backlash spearheaded by the popular Danish philosopher Svend Brinkmann, who encourages individuals to acknowledge their many limitations and set goals within them. Outsiders are often wrong-footed by a Nordic conversational discourse that can seem borderline rude and disrupted by an almost pedantic literalism, itself reflecting the Danish writer John Fellow's description of symphonies by Carl Nielsen in which 'all his instruments say what they shall say, no more, no less, and all of them shall have something worth saying.' There is no word for 'please' in Danish or Swedish and, similarly, there is no way Danes or Swedes would have applauded health workers during the difficult months of 2020–21; they were simply professionals doing jobs they were deservedly well paid for, entitled to respect but not congratulation. Western Scandinavians rightly pride themselves on their superior mastering of foreign tongues, but have little fluency when it comes to small talk. Honest to a tee, they will tie themselves in knots attempting to answer rhetorical questions meant by foreigners as conversational punctuation.

A natural extension, and the closest modern Scandinavia gets to living up to its Viking stereotype, is a readiness to accept and engage with the harsh realities of life – and to train for them from an early age. The world recoiled in horror in 2014 when Copenhagen Zoo invited families to attend the autopsy of its 'retired' giraffe Marius, and to witness the subsequent feeding of his remains to the zoo's lions. The event handed Danes an opportunity to cite the enlightenment principles behind the practice, rooted in the traditions of education, rationalism and responsibility. Folk hero Bengt Holst, the zoo's then director of science, explained to CNN that the entire purpose of a zoo is to 'not make nature into Disney World'.[8] On

Culture Night in 2019 – the evening on which all manner of public and private buildings in Copenhagen are opened up to the public – I visited the University of Copenhagen's Veterinary School around the corner from my apartment, which has two architecturally distinctive autopsy theatres. I hadn't bargained on the theatres being put to use for the benefit of visitors, and was met by the sight and smell of all creatures great and small being disembowelled and spatchcocked by earnest students, smiling as they answered questions from intrigued parents and children.

This hard edge manifests itself throughout Nordic 'culture' in every sense of the word, from winter swimming and endurance sports – the latter unavoidable on Swedish, Norwegian and Finnish television throughout the year – to the sternest of Sibelius's edifices and severest of Carl Nielsen's serrated edges. In a musical context, it runs deep. Many Danish parents teach their children the song 'Højt på en gren en krage', whose four brief verses are laid over a tune that shimmies through an unsettling modal shift as it describes the downfall of a crow ('en krage'). In verse one the crow takes up its position on a branch. In verse two a hunter arrives. In verse three he shoots the bird down. Verse four ends with the poetically blunt 'nu er den stakkels krage død' ('Now is the poor crow dead'). Given the onomatopoeic qualities of the Danish word 'død' and the falling structure of the melody, the impression is of an avian corpse hitting a butcher's block.

I considered this delivering of hard truths without fuss or fear when, in 2019, the debut album from one of the most talked-about opera singers of the new century was released. The Norwegian lyric dramatic soprano Lise Davidsen was born in Stokke, a rural town 70 kilometres south of Oslo, and had some of her first professional singing experience alongside Tora Augestad as a member of the Norwegian Soloists' Choir. The album included opera arias by Richard Wagner and orchestral songs by Richard Strauss, and was nothing if not direct. 'Davidsen does little more than pour out the voice in long, even lines,' was one *Financial Times* critic's take on the soprano's performance of Richard Strauss's 'Four Last Songs'. 'I believe it's my mission to be clear,' said Davidsen when I met her in a café near her apartment in Copenhagen to discuss the recording. 'I try to approach the songs with clarity and an attitude of "this is what it is" . . . It's not my responsibility to interpret. I am just the messenger. Strauss tells us how he feels and invites the audience to respond. It's not actually me feeling all of these things. It's you, the listener.'

Her words put me in mind of Olafur Eliasson, the Icelandic-Danish artist who designed the striking exterior shells of both the Harpa in Reykjavík and the auditorium of the Alsion in Sønderborg. Eliasson's structures create a sort of cognitive field between the physical objects themselves and the person encountering them, as if the essence of their artistic worth is found in our reaction to their form. It was revealing to hear Davidsen apply an obviously post-modernist concept to such an iconic work of late Romanticism as Strauss's 'Four Last Songs'. But the truth of her statement was undeniable, as the essence of any piece of music lies in our individual reaction to it. In music, 'the work' itself doesn't tangibly exist.

Davidsen's career echoes musical history with a convenience bordering on the serendipitous. Like the iconic soprano Kirsten Flagstad before her, she is a woman from rural Norway singing heavy opera on big stages with a rich consistency of tone (it was Flagstad who gave the first performance of Strauss's 'Four Last Songs'). The distinctiveness of her delivery is most obviously connected to the depth and power of her voice across its range. But it is also connected to the expressive directness she described to me, something that seems embedded in the Norwegian psyche. Andsnes described the 'Scandinavian traits of directness and sincerity' when we discussed matters of interpretation in Grieg's music in 2018. British critics were taken aback by the very same sense of directness when they heard Grieg's wife, the lyric soprano Nina Hagerup, perform her husband's songs on a visit to the country in the 1890s. It's not a lessening of feeling, just a less egocentric orientation of it – much like that referred to by Kuusisto.

Andsnes was born in 1970 not far from Haugesund. Remarkably, for a pianist considered to be among the finest alive, he was trained entirely in nearby Bergen. Like most of Jorma Panula's conducting students, at the conservatory Andsnes was guided by factors other than the prospects of an international career. 'I always thought of myself as someone who needs time, and that therefore, a small conservatory where there was no competition was a good place to be,' he told me in 2018. Another graduate of the same institution is Christian Ihle Hadland, a pianist's pianist and a busy soloist both inside and outside Norway. 'In Norway, you have a lot of time and there is a lot of patience,' reflected Hadland when we met in London during his two-year participation in the BBC's New Generation Artist scheme. 'There is the room to grow, because there aren't 100 others knocking on the same door.'

Maybe not hundreds, but Hadland's homeland has given the world a sizeable cohort of exceptional soloists on piano, violin, viola, trumpet, voice and other disciplines. As well as perceptive independent music schools with their ears to the ground, we have our old friend oil to thank. The scholarship scheme established by the state oil firm Statoil allows young musicians of serious potential, at one point including Hadland, to take time out from trying to make a living and focus on development instead.[9] In wealthy Norway, money can buy you time. Even more of it.

A specialist agency was established in the country in 2015, with the aim of applying lessons learned in the training of Norway's successful Olympians to the classical music sector. Talent Norway works with a network of mentors to fund bespoke development packages tailored to individual musicians, allowing them to focus entirely on artistic growth without having to endure the rollercoaster of the mainland European and American competition circuit – the normal route to a career as a soloist and a rock on which many a potential career is dashed. In 2020, Talent Norway launched an initiative to identify, support and platform conducting talent from across the country in both the amateur and professional sectors, aiming to establish major careers but promising to make Norway 'a nation of conductors' either way. In Norway, it had not gone unnoticed that Finland had produced its steady stream of renowned conductors by focusing on local opportunities.

▲

In August 2019, Andsnes was back in his erstwhile base Copenhagen for an unusual performance of Grieg's Piano Concerto. It was happening exactly a century and a half after the piece had its premiere, and in the same city. Included in the orchestra were the very drums that had been used in that first performance in 1869 and which, in Grieg's score, get the first word. The rest of the orchestra was made up of instruments from the mid nineteenth century or reconstructions – the sort that might have been around in Copenhagen at the time of that performance. Andsnes himself played a Blüthner piano from around 1876.

Historically informed performance (HIP) is the biggest trend to have visited the playing of notated music since Edison's phonograph kick-started the art of recording. The bandwagon got going in earnest in the 1970s with the performance of music by obscure baroque composers such as Schütz and Schmelzer using 'period' instruments: strings made from animal gut, woodwinds with more rudimentary mechanics and brass instruments with no mechanics at all – in other words, the sorts of instruments those composers wrote for. When these old instruments and the more considered playing techniques they engendered started to affect the performance of more popular works by the likes of Bach and Handel, the HIP movement began to stray beyond the domain of sandal-wearing specialists and into the classical music mainstream.

As audiences have got used to cleaner, lighter and often faster renditions of music from the baroque and classical eras, so the idea of using appropriate playing techniques and instruments has expanded its chronological remit. These days, it often embraces music of the twentieth century. The aim is usually the restoration of a work's original colours, which pays particular dividends in the case of overfamiliar warhorses like Grieg's concerto. Under the rollercoasters of the Tivoli Gardens in Copenhagen, the concerto sounded with a new elegance and a startling ferocity at the 2019 concert, thanks to Andsnes's Blüthner, Concerto Copenhagen's nineteenth-century instruments and conductor Lars Ulrik Mortensen's characteristically uncompromising view of Grieg's score.

Predictably enough, the HIP movement has advanced more slowly in the Nordic countries than in its Dutch, Austrian and British heartlands. Still, Concerto Copenhagen celebrated its thirtieth birthday in 2021 and is even credited by Nicholas Kenyon as having made the finest recording of Bach's Mass in B minor.[10] Counterparts including the Helsinki Baroque Orchestra have risen fast. Despite its three decades in existence, at the turn of the decade 'CoCo' still felt like an ensemble in the throes of infancy – a touch more naïve than its counterparts in France, the Netherlands and the UK but less jaded for it.

That suited Mortensen, its artistic director. He was born in Copenhagen but started his career as a harpsichordist in London, just when the HIP movement was becoming a public concern in the 1980s. He has been unapologetic in his conclusion that the movement, initiated to kick against orthodoxies and challenge creative autopilot, has started to develop the very ossified rules and habits it was initiated to resist – in mainland Europe, anyway. Not so much in Scandinavia, where even Mortensen can see the benefits of his own orchestra's relative obscurity.

I spoke with Mortensen in March 2020, on the day before Denmark's musical life was locked down, for the first time, by the Covid-19 pandemic. He made no bones about his desire for CoCo to have a bigger voice in the national musical conversation. In fact, he suggested it should be jostling for power, with Denmark's civic symphony orchestras in its sights. 'I don't think the future lies in maintaining everything in the world of traditional symphony orchestras,' said the musician in his dressing room in the eaves of Copenhagen's old opera house, where he was conducting his ensemble in a production of Monteverdi's *L'Orfeo*. 'It doesn't seem a completely far-fetched idea that in a country the size of Denmark, one of the fully-funded orchestras could be allowed to be a little bit different to all the others.' His comment encapsulated the new reality facing the Nordic region's network of symphony orchestras: that while they lumber on, even the broader classical music world has changed. In the last decade, Denmark has spawned another nimble, self-governed, privately funded freelance orchestra that has no geographical or seasonal commitments and can travel anywhere at the drop of a hat – the Danish Chamber Orchestra led by Ádám Fischer.[11]

Mortensen is an intriguing figure, with a half-raptor-, half-peacock-like demeanour on and off the podium. His energetic, distractible disposition sees him seize upon morsels of conversation, gnawing deeply upon them until such time as another more interesting one should turn up. Whenever we have met, he has appeared to care as little about the various potentially hurtful critiques of his conducting style as he has about which members of polite society his own words might offend. He is just the sort of nonconformist the Nordic region has long struggled to cope with and the sort that Jantelov was designed to guard against.

Not that Mortensen has acted on anything but principle, and often selflessly so. In 2003, he consciously ostracized himself from the musical mainstream by vowing never to conduct a modern symphony orchestra again, which effectively put him out of the reach of every orchestra in Denmark bar his own. He epitomizes the lot of the Scandinavian pioneer: to attract the suspicion and even the hostility of the societies from which they emerge, until such time as their genius is certified internationally. Even then, respect is hardly guaranteed.

This social friction is seen throughout history – in the philosopher Søren Kierkegaard, the playwright Henrik Ibsen, the painter Edvard Munch, the film director Lars von Trier, the writers Selma Lagerlöf, Karen Blixen and Karl Ove Knausgaard, and so many more. When working in Norway, 'You have the constant feeling that you are a pioneer', the maverick Norwegian opera director Stefan Herheim told me in his penthouse apartment in Berlin in 2017. That, he said, was the reason he left: 'Feeling like an exotic bird all the time estranges you.'

I have heard it put more fiercely. In 2018, a Norwegian composer collared me in a Helsinki bar, railing against the 'self-denial that means you can't stray from a strict moral code' prevalent in his country. In 2009, I interviewed a Norwegian violinist on the brink of great things, who at the age of 24 had already seen the advantages of having left. 'Norway is very comfortable, clean and safe, which is not really the best background for a cultural life,' she said. 'The mentality is that you should play for fun and not feel any pressure. But sometimes you need those pressures, because without those ugly feelings you will have nothing to give of yourself. You need to know what it is to be jealous, to be desperate.'

It was Edward Gardner who enlightened me on the Norwegian concept of 'bygdedyret', as we discussed the title character in Benjamin Britten's opera *Peter Grimes*. Literally 'the village animal', the word refers to the shunned outsider – a madman, yes, but also the dreamer whose imagination stretches beyond the confines of a small society.[12] I saw the idea clarified with piercing insight in a novel production of a different opera, Wagner's *The Flying Dutchman*. In Lotte de Beer's 2019 staging at Malmö Opera, the character of Senta was portrayed not as the Norwegian village's misfit loner but as a visionary artist, prone to creating daemonic, progressive canvases in black oils – an Ibsen-like figure in more ways than one. When the Dutchman arrived, all Senta needed do to prove their symbiosis was paint with him. The couple didn't fling themselves into the sea at the opera's final curtain. They disappeared into the deep black of their own finished artwork, to the disdain and confusion of the locals (the chorus) looking on.

The Nordic countries would have produced significantly less of real artistic value were it not for pivotal individuals willing to step out of line in societies mechanized by conformity. Many of them were destined to trouble the deep-rooted disciplines of poverty and restraint on which those societies are built. And just as many came from abroad. Finland's orchestras may still be conducted almost entirely by Finns.[13] Danish, Norwegian and Swedish ones are led by conductors from Italy, France, Spain, Germany, Great Britain, the United States and New Zealand and have been for decades. Denmark has a long tradition of importing principal conductors from Italy and in 2021 could count two from that country as well as two from Japan. And none, save Mortensen, from Denmark.

Scandinavians have long been prone to fetishizing talent imported from abroad while underestimating, ignoring or wilfully misunderstanding talent raised at home. The reason for the latter springs straight from Jantelov: outstanding talent puts a strain on social conformity even without the wealth, privilege and ego that often come with it. Scandinavians enjoy little more than basking in the reflected glory of one of their own making it big abroad, often the only guarantee of societal respect. But they also like their most successful sons and daughters to have come from nothing, to appear surprised or even embarrassed by their success and to prove it hasn't changed them.

Carl Nielsen and Hans Christian Andersen scored highly on those fronts but plenty of outstanding artists have found it difficult to contort themselves into similarly ingratiating positions. The opera director Kasper Holten had a rough time from the Danish media, for various reasons, during his stint as the exceedingly young boss of the Royal Danish Opera. When he subsequently moved to London to run the Royal Opera in Covent Garden, his every move was fawned over back home. It's tempting to speculate whether Holten might have had an easier ride in the first instance had his mother not been the head of Denmark's National Bank.

Mortensen, meanwhile, has immunized himself against national treasure status by virtue of his eccentricity – that and his flair for refusing to tow the nationalist line. In 2017, the conductor marked two hundred years since the birth of the patriarch of Danish music Niels Gade with a performance of an iconic piece of national romanticism, Gade's *Elverskud*. But Mortensen replaced the work's Danish text with one in German and was pilloried for it. 'The most important thing about *Elverskud* isn't that it's Danish,' he told me later that year on the patio outside a café in Østerbro, Copenhagen's Islington. If quoted in a domestic tabloid rather than a niche British music magazine, the comment would have provoked a scandal.

At its most benevolent, Jantelov's social code is admirable. It insists we all eat from the same table, suggesting every citizen is family; that their actions, whether prompting national shame or national pride, reflect our collective successes and failures and urge us to do better – a philosophy underlined by Norway's humane, collectively responsible treatment of its own most heinous criminal Anders Breivik. It's little wonder the many Nordic musicians raised on those principles have progressed so readily in a wider world awakening to the idea that ego and individualism are no longer prerequisites to creative endeavour.

That process works both ways. The Nordic region's attitude to imported talent is a complicating factor, especially as politicians have begun to bristle at the sight of Nordic musicians working increasingly away from the homelands that trained them. The ascent of the region's music life has resulted in plenty of nationalistic calls, in Scandinavia at least, for more Danes, more Norwegians, more Swedes (and fewer foreigners) to lead cultural institutions – understandable, given the tendency from British artistic directors in the region to invite processions of compatriots to work with them in what have been interpreted as acts of unconscious colonialism. Still, it's a parochial argument that presumes cultural identity can only be nurtured and preserved by one born into it.

One day in 2019, I was on my way to Bergen when I met Christian Ihle Hadland at Copenhagen Airport, on his way home to Oslo. We had time for a coffee, and as we observed the slow ballet of manoeuvering aircraft our conversation turned to the internationalism that is beginning to consolidate itself in Norwegian music life. 'There was a tendency in Norway to want to be so international that you ended up being very provincial; to be desperate to book foreign soloists when you could have had Norwegians who were just as good,' said Hadland. 'It was supposedly open, but it was actually very cramped.'

Hadland has just about the friendliest face you could hope to be fixing you in conversation. He continued, citing the shift in emphasis from the visiting soloists to actual ensembles. 'Look at the Bergen Philharmonic. In the 1990s life was comfortable. It didn't really matter what the result was like at the end of the week as long as it was competent. When Simone Young [Australian, chief conductor 1991–2002] arrived that started to change. The orchestra went international. It knew it still existed for the people of Bergen, but the players realized that if they wanted to travel they had to be sharp all the time. This feeling that "it's good enough" disappeared. There was suddenly a strong will to make music.'

Hadland pointed to the more recent transformation in Kristiansand: the building of a new concert hall and the signing of the experienced French musician Nathalie Stutzmann as chief conductor of its expanded orchestra. 'Suddenly, the orchestra needed to be as good as the acoustic,' Hadland said. 'You go there now, and they're all sitting on the edge of their seats.' Increasingly, foreign musicians are coming to Norway because of what its infrastructure and musical culture offers them, rather than the other way around. 'I think I've done some of my best music-making in Norway,' the American cellist Alisa Weilerstein told me in 2018, a few months into a new association with the Trondheim Soloists. 'The musicians like to rehearse, to work and to explore new ideas and repertoire. There is an openness to absolutely everything. It is liberating.'

◢

The British conductor Simon Rattle visited Copenhagen in February 2013 to accept the Léonie Sonning Music Prize, an honour that comes with a cheque for €130,000 and carte blanche to plan a concert with one of Denmark's orchestras. Rattle opted to lead the Royal Danish Orchestra in performances of Nielsen's Symphony No. 4, the Double Concerto for Piano and Violin by the Danish composer Hans Abrahamsen, and Sibelius's Symphony No. 7. A few days after the concert, a DR employee sent me an off-air recording of it.

Sibelius and Nielsen may have been born in the same year, but neither knew an awful lot about the other and the two never hit it off socially. Still, Sibelius recognized progressive symphonic music when he heard it. When he finally met Nielsen in Copenhagen in 1912, he managed to suppress his own rampant ego sufficiently to pay his colleague a compliment, albeit in Swedish (it was, apparently, reciprocated). There are huge contrasts in the two composers' entire concepts of musical structure and purpose. But there are revealing parallels too, not least their mutual quest to harness particular forms of musical energy.

That project occupied both men throughout their creative lives, which stopped at more or less the same time. While Nielsen cultivated his Darwinian concept of musical energy, exploring how his musical 'life force' might be compelled to prove its capacity for survival in different ways, Sibelius gradually freed himself from the orthodoxy that a symphony had to arrive somewhere conclusive or win an argument hands-down before it ended – from the notion that the symphonic circle must, at all costs, be closed.

By the time of his final symphony – the Finnish composer's last orchestral word before *Tapiola* – Sibelius had apparently concluded that a form of centrifugal energy, gently manipulated by rhythm, could take his music wherever it needed to go; that the symphonic circle might, therefore, not close at all.[14] The Symphony No. 7 is his most magnificent realization of that idea. It was born of the squalor of alcohol addiction and the abrasion of a marital breakdown, yet sounds profound, majestic and humbling. In its short, single-movement span, the symphony appears to live a whole life, traversing dark and light as it plots a course through three statements of a trombone melody traced over the top of the orchestra like a silhouette. In some performances, the inconclusive radiance that floods the symphony in its final pages appears to have been searched for intensely. In others, you sense it was there from the start.

To my ears, Rattle's Copenhagen performance fell into the latter category, despite the variegated chart of blues, browns, yellows and golds the Liverpudlian conductor mined from the instruments of the Royal Danish Orchestra. It was a fundamentally dark, slow, settled performance and an extraordinarily moving one even from the recording. Whenever I have found myself talking to members of the Royal Danish Orchestra since, I have tried to direct the conversation towards that performance. The respondents always seem to focus on Rattle getting them to 'play out' – to combine their own operatic sense of colour with something more foregrounded and present.

In 2019, a magazine article about the provenance of the orchestra's collection of string instruments led me to the leader of its double bass section, Meherban Gillett. This conversation went a little deeper, literally. We live in the same district of Copenhagen, and in the basement of our local library, Gillett outlined his firm belief that despite the cut-and-thrust you hear in the opera house, his orchestra has always prized nobility over bombast. Critics have long talked of the orchestra's rich, mellow sound and have tended to associate it with the ensemble's six centuries of history. Another more tangible reason is those strings – a treasure trove of Stradivarius, Guadagnini, Storioni, Gragnani and Amati instruments collected over the same time period.

Gillett, however, returned time and again to the idea of democracy. 'The difference in this orchestra is that playing together is about creating a consensus in real time, without anyone really having talked about it,' he said. 'There is a firmness in the orchestra's sound that reflects its history but also its day-to-day work playing opera – when you get used to a singer changing their phrasing or timing from night to night. Rattle admitted that we probably play more "together" than his orchestra in Berlin [the Berlin Philharmonic] but he also noticed that we tend to trust each other more than we trust our actual, collective sound.'

Sibelius knew the Royal Danish Orchestra and wrote for it. Further into the twentieth century, the orchestra worked with the best – Herbert von Karajan, Otto Klemperer, Leonard Bernstein and Mariss Jansons. When Daniel Barenboim conducted the ensemble on receiving the Sonning Prize in 2009, he referred in his acceptance speech to the former King of Denmark Frederik IX, 'for whom ruling your country was not enough – he had to feel the power of being a conductor. Or maybe it was the powerlessness of being a conductor that made him want to be King.'

A good conductor knows that absolute power is self-defeating. A great one can brew a convincing performance while getting an orchestra with some sense of collective memory to sound as much as possible like itself – of its own tradition. Sibelius imagined an Austro-German orchestral sound in his symphonies, even if the central European orchestras that specialize in that heavier, more calorific sound have never given the composer's music much time. Despite its Scandinavian blood, the Royal Danish Orchestra errs in that richer direction, with a fulsome midriff and what Gillett describes as a 'gentlemanly' cut-and-thrust. Hundreds of years of employing musicians from the European mainland have probably helped cultivate it.

In Copenhagen, Rattle's Sibelius resembled the 'river of lava' that one critic heard in the same piece with the same conductor, but from the once Sibelius-sceptic Berlin Philharmonic. In Copenhagen,

Rattle had the benefit of an orchestra with direct links to the composer. Under his baton, the Royal Danish Orchestra throbbed with a tension that ratcheted as the music's weave became more multi-layered. The symphony's tensing and slackening, its collective strain and cohesion, was magnified bracingly.

The terms in which Gillett described his orchestra's playing style were intriguing. 'In other orchestras, the basic framework has a greater priority; people will talk about playing in rhythm, about playing in tune, about how to play on the conductor's beat,' he told me, drawing on experience playing in orchestras in Britain, France and elsewhere in Denmark. 'But these things are almost completely dissolved in the Royal Danish Orchestra. It is the ultimate in democracy: we retreat into a unity, a oneness – because of course, I'm not more important than you, but I am way, way stronger when I am with you, *part* of you. I don't really know another orchestra that thinks so beautifully backwards about it, but I do think the sound of this orchestra is what it is because we do.'

Eventually, Sibelius's Symphony No. 7 hauls itself towards what Rattle has described as 'the most depressed C major in all of musical literature'. There is a fatalistic feel to this ending to the greatest symphonic corpus the region ever gave the world. And there was something particularly binding about the sound of it under Rattle in Copenhagen – the sense of a community held in a tight embrace, confronted by the dazzling white light of a new experience.

3

Off Piste

"There are harmonies in the landscape and the climate, the truest harmonies that exist."

Jón Leifs

Kaukonen was described as a village but I searched in vain for a shop, a café or even a wall that could support a cash dispenser. Its central feature was a confection of rusting tractors, lined-up on a verge next to the gravel road that tracks the River Ounasjoki. I arrived here one afternoon in June 2016, reporting for duty as a volunteer at a homespun arts festival after a 100-minute drive north from the capital of Finnish Lapland, Rovaniemi. 'At Silence Festival you will experience art, beautiful nature and a very special atmosphere,' promised the website.

Silence Festival has no need of visiting journalists, which is why I had to sneak in under the guise of a volunteer. The next morning, I was tasked by the festival administrator Ninni with helping to move two industrial refrigerators from a lorry into a side-room of Kaukonen's Village Hall, which would function as the festival bar.

With two bulky Finns for assistance, I was supervised by the bar manager Heidi, who rolled cigarettes on a fence post as she directed us. After offering me coffee from her flask, she poured her own into the small hollowed-out chunk of wood that hung permanently from a loop on her cargo pants.

Later that day I was sent out into the village with a pile of laminated posters and a staple-gun. I learned the lie of the land and the deep river that cuts through it. Its banks were lined with verdant sloping meadows and stony wastelands. At the end of a track, the stump of an old wooden bridge gestured at its amputated partner on the opposite side of the water; a new, concrete bridge had long since been built a few kilometres upstream, signalling the death knell for this one. At Silence Festival's headline show some days later, the acrobat Sanja Kosonen would cross the river here on a tightrope while the musician Marzi Nyman stood on the opposite bank, in a red pin-striped suit, playing psychedelic loops on an electric guitar while villagers and festivalgoers looked on.

Kaukonen, with its huddles of three or four ramshackle wooden buildings, felt like an inhabited wilderness. There were copious parallels with the American Midwest but they took human form in the festival security officer, Snuupi. An early retiree from Finland's special forces – or so everyone said – he stalked about Kaukonen all week as if on the trail of a dangerous animal, all manner of tackle and weaponry hanging off him. He wore a rock-like expression on his face, which shifted as little as the intonation in his voice. I've not encountered another human being whose very presence was at once so reassuring and so unsettling.

For the first three days of Silence Festival, Storm Solomon lashed Kaukonen with unceasing wind and rain. That didn't stop Snuupi rowing me out to the middle of the river's widest point, where I clambered onto a small floating platform accommodating a wood-fired sauna the size of a small garden shed. I stripped and went inside, where a freelance philosopher was waiting, under orders to discuss whatever was on my mind. We talked about silence and music, and about the emotional duress of organized religion, heading outside to swim in the cold river now and then before stepping back into a heat so fierce it roasted the back of your throat at the first breath. After an hour, Snuupi reappeared in his kayak to take me back to shore.

I was bivouacked in a rickety cabin about a kilometre from the village hall, which had its own wood-fired sauna. The surrounding birch trees held the little structure in their silent embrace. After days of persistent rain, the air and ground started to dry and the skies lightened. At this latitude there was no real darkness at night, but the dank weather ensured there was also no direct sunlight for much of the festival either. In the early hours on my last night in Kaukonen, deep into the festival's closing party, a woman burst into the throbbing village hall with the announcement that the clouds were parting. A dozen or so survivors of the festivities rushed onto the veranda to see the sun pour itself out onto sloping meadows and unpainted wooden barns. Newborn, unfettered sunlight at 3 a.m. – the purest form of inland light there is.

There was no artistic normal at Silence Festival. I heard bandoneon music from Argentina played straight in a wooden church, a useful reminder that the biggest Argentinian musical export, tango, was received more wholeheartedly in Finland than anywhere else (though the Finns insist on transposing their tangos into minor keys). An emotionally strenuous choreographic piece saw two dancers wrenched apart from one another while two musicians protested in the corner to tunes by Toivo Kuula and Einojuhani Rautavaara – Sibelius's contemporary and protégé respectively. At an art gallery in a neighbouring village, there was a performance of Stravinsky's *A Soldier's Tale*. I was joined for some meals and drinks by the festival's co-artistic director Outi Tarkiainen, a Rovaniemi-born, London-trained composer whose own piece 'Kunnes kivi halkeaa' ('Until the Stone Splits') was played one lunchtime by the violinist Minna Pensola. It is a monologue for violin that obsesses over two adjacent notes. Over the course of six minutes those notes are prized apart by an overwhelming grief.

Silence Festival was less about its individual events and more about our collective journey through them as performers, staff, audience and villagers – the latter two groups amorphous. One afternoon, we were led through a forest by the dancers Sade Kamppila and Viivi Roiha, who gradually shed their clothes as they told emotionally humid stories of animals and men. When we thought the performance of their dance piece Metsä had ended – the two girls having capered away nude, hand in hand – we trudged towards home before hearing the sound of faraway singing. Off in the distance, Kamppila and Roiha were sitting on a cliff edge overlooking a quarry, waving us farewell as they tended a fledgling fire.

The festival felt most real during the variety performances at the village hall, which ranged from poetry readings to a covers band, with equally strong emphases on contemporary music and circus arts. Watching them cross-legged on the floor was like being sucked into the parallel reality of an Aki Kaurismäki film. This was an analogue domain that refused to indulge the metropolitan or the digital but had room for the occasional twenty minutes of blazing avant-garde. Every performance was received by the audience with a sort of deadpan acceptance, except by the drunks who heckled or roared with laughter.

That audience included an elderly man, motionless in a wheelchair, his delight expressed through wide eyes and twitching feet. A Finnish-Japanese teenager from Helsinki had made the journey from her parents' new home a few kilometres away, intrigued by what might be going on here having seen a listing on Facebook, bored stiff by her summer holiday. There was a group of 30-something lads, baggage handlers from the nearby Kittilä Airport, who had heard that for one week only Kaukonen would have its own licensed bar. That is where they cornered me one night, full of conspiracy theories about unmarked Russian aircraft on the airport's apron. At the same bar stood Tarkiainen's erstwhile composition professor, having made the journey north to support his former pupil.

Marzi Nyman's performances lingered long after I had re-entered the real world back in Helsinki, wondering if Silence Festival had been for real. He popped up on so many occasions during the week, always able to pull whatever musical discourse he found himself embroiled in up to another level, no matter what instruments he had or didn't have at his disposal. His own performances ranged from atonal free improvisation to David Bowie covers with the rough-cut Kaukonen Village Band.

On the festival's opening night, Nyman's own trio played at Villa Magia, the little hut that is Kaukonen's spiritual home, while Storm Solomon played a cat-and-mouse game with the electricity supply. The moments when the power cut out were the best, as Nyman and his co-conspirators simply made music as it came to them with whatever was lying around – literally unplugged. On a drier, calmer day later in the week, he stood in a huge forest clearing and belted out riffs on his guitar like a rock star warming-up in an empty stadium built of trees. Wailing through an amplifier, his stilted tunes started to resemble yoiks, the traditional, existential songs of the Sámi, Lapland's indigenous people.

◢

Yoiking is thought to be Europe's oldest continuous musical tradition – a personal, spiritual form of communication through song that conforms to few of the conventions of western music. Like the Aboriginal songlines, yoiks and yoiking defy hermetic definition, have a certain amount of existential philosophy built in and traverse numerous regional variations. But some commonalities bind them into a discernible entity, one being the tribe that spawned the practice in the first place. The Sámi have survived for centuries herding reindeer across the planes of northern Norway, Sweden and Finland, often driving them up frozen rivers like the Ounasjoki.

The practicalities of reindeer herding have produced their fair share of utilitarian yoiks. At its purest, the expression is more personal – evoking a person or animal not so much by describing them as by conjuring them up in sound. The use of 'yoiking' as a transitive verb suggests a person is 'yoiked' in the same way a flower is painted, but some Sámi believe person and animal can transform into one another during a yoik. Most yoiks have no use for lyrics, though exceptions are found in the 'leu'dd' – the yoiks of the eastern Sámi that take a more epic, narrative form plotting geopolitical or folkloric stories. The more common yoiks from the north and south, the 'luohti' and the 'vuolle', tend to consist of verses determined by the duration of a lung's exhalation. They stack up awkward intervals and loop them, with ornamentation woven on top – freestyle decorative elements like an opera singer's trilling or elaboration. The rhythmic groove is the individual yoiker's fingerprint.

Yoiking has suffered together with the Sámi. As Scandinavian and Finnish civilizations have encroached the north, the Sámi have lost land and seen their way of life diluted – serious wrongs that the respective nation states have been slow to acknowledge. Before the enemy of the Sámi was free market capitalism and climate change, it was the church. As they Christianized the far north, bishops viewed yoiking with disdain, condemning it as a practice soaked in sin (odd, given its respect for creation and its obvious spirituality). In much of Scandinavia, yoiking was illegal until the middle of the twentieth century. Since then, the practice has had to contend with the vested interests of the commercial music industry and its geopolitical offshoot, the Eurovision Song Contest. Yoiks can hardly help but feel personal and authentic; they conjure up an image of the continent's only existing indigenous tribe, its last people uncontaminated by greed and materialism. Just the ingredients to get other nations reaching misty-eyed for 'douze points'.

In their purest form, yoiks tend towards the raw, the unclean, the microtonal (using the notes-between-notes you can't access on a piano). They don't conform to the musical etiquette of introduction and ending, still less to the classical principle of exposition and development. They simply start and stop, often stopping far sooner than their elongated cousin, the rune song. The yoiks you hear polished-up and chirruped-out at Eurovision are plastic by-products of countries trying to make good on past crimes. So keen were the Sámi to make the distinction that they organized their very own Eurovision-style contest, under the title Sámi Grand Prix.[1] Here, Sámi take to a modest stage one by one, sometimes in pairs, delivering yoiks with only a microphone for assistance. Even from the distance of YouTube's edited highlights, it's easy to sense a tradition centuries in the making – all the associated idiosyncrasies and ingrained ornamentation practices included.

It can be tricky to wrestle the average yoik down into a particular 'modality' – the genomes of melodic construction that western musicologists use to map idiosyncratic musical traditions onto their own definable scales. Yet clear melodic patterns *are* often discernable in yoiks and can therefore be combined with more standard western musical forms. In 2010, the Swedish organist Gunnar Idenstam invited the yoiker Simon Marainen to join him and other musicians at a wooden church built to resemble a huge Sámi hut or 'kata' on the banks of the River Torne in Kiruna, high up in Swedish Lapland. Inside the square church, once voted the most beautiful building in Sweden, they recorded 17 songs shaped by Idenstam's experiences growing up among the Sámi and their music. The result, the album Jukkaslåtar, is a journey through the Sámi's eight seasons and from birth to death. One song, a lullaby mingled with a dirge, is 'dedicated to all those who have lost their lives in the Torne'.

Idenstam's depiction of the Sámi god of the winds, Bieggaolmai, invokes a howling gale courtesy of Marainen's agitated, murmuring yoiks, Thorbjörn Jakobsson's keening saxophone, Jonas Sjöblom's apocalyptic drum kit and the church's organ roaring under Idenstam's feet and fingers. In 'Renhjord över isen' ('Reindeer on the Frozen River'), singer Brita-Stina Sjaggo weaves a simple Swedish folk tune over saxophone and synthesizers to lure the winds of Idenstam's organ into being once again. As the instrument thunders out, Marainen's yoiks themselves become animals – squawking, pattering, stuttering and yelping. The track then collapses into its successor with a colossal organ chord, like something lifted from the pages of the French composer Charles-Marie Widor. Suddenly, we're into a capering Spring Dance.

One of Idenstam's tunes, over which Marainen threads first a gurgling growl and then the throaty yawl, is a light-footed Finnish polka, 'Finländares dans'. It is thought to have originated on a nyckelharpa. The tune was transcribed in 1799 by the Italian explorer and composer Giuseppe Acerbi, who recounted his experiences in the far north in his 1802 book *Travels through Sweden, Finland, and Lapland, to the North Cape in the Years 1798 and 1799*. So desperate was Acerbi to persuade a 'pastoral Laplander' to yoik for him that he resorted to offering money and liquor. He wrote of the results: 'The utmost I could accomplish was to extort from them some hideous cries, during the continuance of which I was sometimes obliged to stop my ears with my fingers.' To urbane Europeans, a lack of diatonic harmony was the mark of the barbarian.

If yoiking is an acquired taste, Jukkaslåtar lubricates its path into unprepared ears without veering into kitsch, insincerity or appropriation. The album conjures up the spirit of the far north, its blazing light and eerie gloom, its majesty and ferocity. But it also poses the central ethical question of whether yoiking fraternizes with notated and harmonic music at its peril. In Norway's 1980 Eurovision entry 'Sámiid ædnan', a yoik from Mattis Hætta symbolically interrupted Sverre Kjelsberg's metropolitan lounge song – a protest against the Norwegian Government's plans to build a dam and power plant on the River Alta in Finnmark that would have eradicated an entire Sámi village. A decade later, a Sámi-owned record label was established, Jårgalæddji, to propagate popular music seasoned with yoiks – or the other way round, depending on your vantage point.

In the short term, the commercialization of Sámi music, its inevitable debasement when straightjacketed into accepted harmonic and rhythmic rules, didn't do it many musical favours even if it did draw attention to the plight of its people. In the longer term, the attempted ransacking of the yoik tradition by an asset-stripping music industry has apparently only strengthened that tradition in its purest form. The lack of harmony and textural paraphernalia that so alarmed Acerbi is one of yoiking's fundamental principles, as underlined by the Grand Prix.

But perhaps even the Grand Prix operates to a false pretext, pitting yoiks and yoikers against one another as if the same battle lines could be drawn between individual poems and prayers. Among the yoik's most alluring features is its sense of ritual. I had my purest, most memorable taste of it in 2016, locked in the darkened vault of a former bank in Oslo along with twenty or so other adults, including an Associate Professor of Law at the University of Tromsø, Ánde Somby. In this instance, Somby was also the yoiker. He specializes in herding yoiks from east Finnmark, towards the Norwegian–Russian border – the region of the River Alta dispute.

Adopting an aloof persona, Somby introduced his audience, spread over the vault's floor, to the Sámi concept that human can transubstantiate into animal. 'The wolf asks only one question: what happens to a world that kills all its wolves?' he posited, before launching into a pained, melancholic wolf-cry that soon burst into a wrenching chest-voice. 'Here is my friend the mosquito,' he proffered later on, his falsetto fluttering and buzzing about in the darkness, a long way from Somby the tenured professor. There's a video on YouTube of a man yoiking over a fire in a tent, unclean and rough, which is probably the nearest you can get to the tradition in its purest form without visiting the Arctic. But creativity mutates according to time and place. In the vault in Oslo, I think I understood, courtesy of Somby, what a yoik really is behind its surface noise – and started to hear the music in it.

Jukkaslåtar is a meeting of musical traditions that really shouldn't get along, in which sense it reflects two centuries' of development in Nordic music. The region's entire musical identity rests on the concept of vernacular and formal styles meeting one another at a time when rapid social developments tended to prevent particular forms of music from being cordoned off from certain social groups. There have never been the same barriers of perception towards classical music in Finland and Scandinavia as those that exist in the UK and the USA. Music festivals across the Nordic region, even major European events like Roskilde Festival, include both popular and classical genres and frequently stop short of denoting them as such. 'Something has happened and we have learned to speak to each other,' the violinist Pekka Kuusisto told me in 2017, reflecting on the porousness of musical borders in his own country of Finland. 'There is more collaboration between people who are really good at orchestrating for bassoons, and people who are really good at making hip hop. It is a super interesting situation,' he added. Sibelius's reinvention of orchestral music along the lines of a circular, organic rune song may not have alerted audiences to the everyman soil in which his music was grown. But the titles and stories he borrowed from the *Kalevala* would have.

Sibelius's peers and successors raided the same sources for material and inspiration, among them the strong individual voices of composers Uuno Klami, Aulis Sallinen and Einojuhani Rautavaara. Klami's extraordinary *Kalevala Suite* of 1943 already suggested, in its primary-coloured violence, that the world of progressive notated music was moving in a psychologically expressionistic direction that would remove itself, eventually, from folk literary sources. Despite a blip in the 1980s, when Finns started churning out operas on national romantic themes, the world of the *Kalevala* had shimmied onto a different track.

If any musician has eclipsed Sibelius in conjuring up a musical image of Finland for foreigners, it's a gentleman from Rovaniemi christened Tomi Petteri Putaansuu. These days, he goes by the name of Mr Lordi. In 2006, Putaansuu took his band to the finals of the Eurovision Song Contest in Athens and won – the first time either Finland or a metal band had claimed victory at Europe's annual musical jamboree. For many who knew little of Finland but could point to it approximately on a map, Lordi's winning song and the manner in which it was performed became synonymous with the idea of country so near to the hinterland of Europe that it might just as well sit on the border between reality and myth. The victorious song was Hard Rock Hallelujah. At the heart of its musical structure is a hymn-like refrain built of a three-chord cadence. It is easily traced over the big tune Sibelius used to end his Symphony No. 2.

Lordi – the name is authentically pronounced by drawing the first syllable out and down, topping it off with a lightly rolled 'r' – show no signs of hanging up their monster masks. The band's stage demeanour invokes a sort of kind-hearted, self-mocking horror much like the succession of eye-rolling puns that title its albums (Arockalypse, Deadache, Scare Force One). But for metalheads inside and outside Finland, the sort who wouldn't be caught half-dead watching Eurovision, one band reigns supreme and has done since it was founded at around the same time as Lordi. First it went by the name of Black Water, before assuming the moniker Stratovarius.

Stratovarius made its name with dense songs fuelled by melody but filled with finger-twisting guitar shreds and harpsichord figurations, a style referred to by the cognoscenti as power/speed metal. More taut and virtuosic than Lordi's hard rock, much in Stratovarius is nonetheless underpinned by anthemic, richly harmonized melodies rendered that bit more majestic, aspirational and symphonic. In assaulting the senses with consonant volume and harmonic derring-do, many Stratovarius songs can be compared to the high-octane orchestral tone poems of the German composer Richard Strauss.

Where Strauss pushed the symphony orchestra to its limits, Stratovarius exerts the same structural pressure on the rock band. In keeping with Nordic tradition, many of its songs are filled with existential alternations of major and minor keys – Søren Kierkegaard's internal angst writ large, but with a wild Finnish streak.

The classical elements in the Stratovarius sound extend beyond the band's name, a portmanteau of two instrument makers from across the rock–classical divide. Neo-baroque harpsichord runs give the band's songs a seam of psychedelic brilliance while choirs and brass sections are roped in to bolster climaxes. Nature and mythology provide narratives and determine titles. The Finnish metal scene is awash with strong national romantic vibes, Stratovarius member Lauri Porra told me in 2015. 'If you think of the set of people around Sibelius who set out to imagine Finnish identity through the idea of the forests and lakes, spreading the old folklore stories of the *Kalevala*, this is something that has clearly been continued in Finnish metal,' he said. He should know – Sibelius was his great grandfather.

In 2015, Finland and Denmark celebrated 150 years since the birth of both Sibelius and Nielsen. Porra marked the anniversary by performing his great-grandfather's songs, arranged for bass guitar and trombone, on a tour of Finnish primary schools. That year, I talked to rappers, hip hop artists, folk musicians and rock musicians in Finland about their plans to mark the Sibelius anniversary. In Denmark, the Danish Broadcasting Corporation commissioned a series of pop musicians, including one of the previous year's *X Factor* finalists, to record cover versions of songs by Carl Nielsen with bespoke music videos. Sys Bjerre, one time presenter of *Boogie*, Danish television's weekly answer to MTV, offered her own take on Nielsen's song 'Tit er jeg glad'. It is one of the most beautiful and sympathetic performances of a Nielsen song ever recorded.

On the trail of these open-minded tributes, I found myself in Hämeenlinna, a sleepy town midway between Helsinki and Tampere distinguished by the fact that Sibelius grew up there. For a town made famous by music, Hämeenlinna was ominously silent. Too big to provide an idyll, too small to compete as a destination, its principal export appeared to be people. 'It's not a blossoming place in any sense,' I was forlornly informed by Rami Vierula, a local musician. 'When you're 18 or 19, you leave. You go north to Tampere or south to Helsinki.'

Sibelius did the latter. So, much later, did Rami, leaving for Kallio, Helsinki's Shoreditch, where he hoped to make it big with his Hämeenlinna-formed band Delay Trees. In June 1885, just before he took the new train south to Helsinki, Sibelius wrote a String Quartet in E minor, which seems to pre-empt his journey by rail in combining two planes of velocity, like a person walking along the gangway of a train speeding in the same direction. It is a structural device that would become a Sibelius hallmark.

In 2012, Rami and his fellow members of Delay Trees said their goodbyes to Hämeenlinna with the valedictory album *Doze*. Its song 'Pause' does something similar to Sibelius's quartet, using a speed-within-a-speed that might, technically, have come straight from the composer. Rather more obvious, and evident not just from the band's name, is the album's Sibelius-like interest in trees. Everywhere on *Doze* you hear the strips of forest that surround Hämeenlinna given musical form: fixed notes in the bass suggesting vertical growth and horizontal stability; the delay pedal merging the midriff of the band as if to form a middle-ground horizon – Finland's ubiquitous dado-rail of forest. Both devices contribute to what the musicologist Julian Johnson has referred to, with reference to evocations of nature music, as 'an avoidance of linear motion' that 'seems to suspend time'.² In *Doze*'s song 'Pause', which doesn't ever move from its home key, there is even less linear motion than in *Tapiola*.

The taxi ride from Keflavík to downtown Reykjavík is surely the most disorientating airport run in Europe. For a few successive years I happened to arrive in Iceland on the same date, 13 June, and even at the peak of summer the sky hangs heavily over the country's unique landscape. That landscape appears almost entirely bereft of greenery and trees, yet alive with growth, the ubiquitous solidified lava resembling a creeping green-brown fungus. Teetering piles of stones stand and stare like haunted figures at the road and its passing traffic. These, I have since learned, are 'steinvarda' – cairns fashioned as way markers. 'To be in a country like Iceland is to be brought face to face with unfathomable geological timescales, a powerful reminder of the fragility of our own lives,' wrote Martin Cullingford, editor of *Gramophone* magazine, when he travelled to the country to put the fast-rising Icelandic pianist Víkingur Ólafsson on his magazine's cover in 2019.

Soon the airport road is drawn towards the sea, where outer Reykjavík starts to resemble something like coastal Norway but with dwellings of corrugated iron rather than wood, staircases and verandas clamped abruptly to their sides and pastel-coloured paint jobs deployed to puncture the prevailing greyness. There is no avoiding the Icelandic capital's potent combination of the dramatic and the drab. The predominantly squat, flat-roofed city is peered at by Mount Esja on the opposite side of the bay. Now and then, an exceptional man-made structure rears up in splendour or severity: the architect Guðjón Samúelsson's spectre-like basilica Hallgrímskirkja, or the same architect's National Theatre, resembling a giant, neo-gothic electrical plug.[3] Otherwise, Iceland has an abundance of what appears to be architecture without architects.

One notable exception is also the structure that dominates the waterfront – predictably enough, a twenty-first-century concert hall in steel and glass. Harpa was designed by Henning Larsen and Olafur Eliasson, reunited following their collaboration on the Copenhagen Opera House, and opened in 2011 as a flexible, multi-auditorium home to the Iceland Symphony Orchestra and the Icelandic Opera. If you turned on an Icelandic television on 4 May that year, you will have happened upon the building's inaugural concert, which was carried live on the state broadcaster RÚV. The Russian musician and Icelandic citizen Vladimir Ashkenazy conducted the symphony orchestra and Ólafsson joined them at the piano.

Harpa very nearly fell victim to the financial crisis of 2008, which itself very nearly cast credit-inflated Iceland into economic oblivion. First the building's main sponsor collapsed, one of three banks responsible for gambling three times the national GDP on credit. Iceland allowed its banks to fail and construction work on Harpa was halted indefinitely, before the state stumped up the cash for it to resume. For more than a year, it was the only structure being built in Iceland while dozens of other construction projects were mothballed, their cranes frozen where they stood, statuesque symbols of the nation's fiscal hangover.

Nimble Iceland emerged quickly from the crash, however much the experience still scars the national psyche. The country reignited the growth that had already taken root in its fledgling tourist industry, and Reykjavík once again assumed the status of party town it had earned itself in the 2000s. But more and more of those doing the partying held non-Icelandic passports. The unrecognizable exchange rate had made it financially viable not just to fly to this lump of volcanic rock halfway between Europe and North America, but to eat, drink and shop there too.

Iceland's determination to market itself to foreigners has brought international exposure to a music scene that almost defies description. After the last concert of the Iceland Symphony Orchestra's season on 13 June 2013, I spotted orchestral musicians stumbling about the city long into its sunlit night. One of them turned up in a band I was watching, hours after accepting his applause on the stage of Harpa having played Prokofiev but still in his white tie and tails. 'Oh yes, there are some people who play in the Iceland Symphony Orchestra who also play in a couple of the metal bands,' Ólafsson told me when I sought his assurance that I hadn't imagined it.

It's a cliché that every tenth Icelander has written a book, but it's a fact that Icelanders buy more books than any other nationality. Both reinforce the impression that creativity isn't so much a part of life on this island as a way of life. In Iceland even more than Finland, music is just music. On my first full day in Reykjavík, I visited the record store 12 Tónar on Skólavörðustígur, where the proprietor Lárus Jóhannesson insisted on making me a coffee and sitting me down on his blue sofa to drink it. Cardboard boxes all over the floor sprouted Björk, Bach, Ragnheiður Gröndal, Múm, Low Roar, Sigur Rós and Haukur Tómasson CDs. In less than half an hour, the shop proved its status as a meeting place for music fans and professionals of every stripe. Six months later I bumped into Lárus at the Roundhouse in north London, and somehow recognized him through a haze of darkness and alcohol. He asked me how I'd enjoyed the record I'd bought at his shop back in the summer: a performance of music by Grieg, issued seven years previously on the shop's own label, from a young pianist I'd never heard of called Víkingur Ólafsson.

'In Iceland, everything is possible,' Ólafsson told me another six months on, when we met at Harpa on 14 June 2014 for a magazine interview. By this time, the pianist had upped sticks to Berlin to give himself a base in Europe, but was still well known at home and about to curate his own festival in Reykjavík. RÚV had also broadcast the first series of Ólafsson's television documentary *Útúrdúr*, itself prompted by an appearance on a talk show a few years earlier during which he'd migrated to the studio piano to make a point.

As a result, RÚV commissioned a series of forty-five-minute episodes on the subject of playing and listening to classical music. 'The level of discussion in the practice room about the direction of a phrase, which voice am I going to emphasise, the contrapuntal element of this or that, is so far beyond most people's care,' Ólafsson explained to me. 'Initially, the idea was to see if I could do something with the media of television to open some windows onto this for people.' Among the guests that made it onto his show was the British philosopher Roger Scruton, long since banished from TV screens in his native land. 'I was really not sure if I would get away with talking about fugue and sonata form and counterpoint, and the message of Schubert's 'Winterreise', on prime time television,' recalled Ólafsson. But get away with it he did. A second series was commissioned, and both went on to win an Edda – an Icelandic Bafta.

▲

Iceland's journey to nationhood echoes that of Norway, but on a different scale and at a different pace. Its democracy was Europe's first, after Roman times. The Icelandic parliament, the Althing, was established in 930 and is the oldest surviving institution of its kind in the world. But the island's expanses of tundra and sand and its brutal meteorology have long made it a challenging place to live. Just when the country's population should have been soaring in the eighteenth century, the catastrophic eruption of a volcano in 1783 prompted a mass exodus. In the immediate aftermath, the colonial power Denmark considered declaring the island uninhabitable and moving every single Icelander to Jutland by force. The country's entire population of trees had long since been felled for fuel.

In the nineteenth century and for much of the twentieth, Iceland was a land if not without music then without music as a progressive intellectual and cultural pursuit. When a noted recitalist visited the country in 1914, he was forced to play his Beethoven sonatas on an upright piano, the only instrument available. A symphony orchestra wasn't heard on the island until 1926, when, on 31 May, the Hamburg Philharmonic Orchestra docked in Reykjavík, staying for seventeen days and giving fourteen concerts at venues ranging from the city theatre to a tuberculosis sanatorium.

The visit was described by the critic Árni Thorsteinson as 'The greatest event in the history of the arts in this country,' a statement that speaks volumes.[4] While the rest of Europe was falling for cinema, a lucky bunch of Icelanders had been enthralled by the entirely new experience that was an acoustic symphony orchestra. It was a political and artistic coup and had been pulled off, with a certain degree of luck, by the man who led the performances from the conductor's podium – an Icelandic musician named Jón Þorleifsson. Hoping to jump-start his career, Þorleifsson had moved to Germany a decade earlier and changed his name to Jón Leifs. Growing up in tandem with the new century, Leifs set his mind to becoming Iceland's first nationally representative composer. He succeeded, even if he'd never become a national figure like Sibelius or Nielsen (Leifs attracted more anger and ridicule from his countrymen than respect or adoration). Once again, the process was motivated by a dislike for the colonial power and the search for a national musical identity among vernacular sources.

Leifs and his music were as different as Iceland itself. The composer was determined to draw a raw, uncompromising and separatist picture of his nation in charcoals rather than watercolours or oils, and without Sibelius's inclination to reimagine existing European practices. A fervent and at times deluded nationalist, Leifs initiated an impulsive and direct musical response to the physical terrain and meteorology into which he was born. He sowed seeds that are being reaped with ever more imagination and success in this new century, in which his vision of a distinctive Icelandic aesthetic appears to have held out. As a Finnish composer remarked to me in 2018, it's practically impossible to identify a contemporary composer's nationality through their music, unless that composer happens to be Icelandic.

As an Icelander looking to define his country in sound, Leifs was enviably light on musical baggage while benefitting from his country's ancient literary tradition and unique topography. To those he added dubious ideas about masculine heroism and a 'Nordic renaissance' that he believed would spread out into the wider world. Combined, those elements made for potent, thrilling and fresh-faced music. Leifs's work had greater pertinence for the fact that a good portion of it was written not in Iceland, where his combination of the vernacular and the modernist proved adept at emptying concert halls, but in a musically fertile Germany that was busy fetishizing all things Nordic. Like Kurt Atterberg, this drew Leifs into something resembling collusion with Hitler, though Leifs was stopped just short of getting into bed with the Nazis courtesy of his own ferocious nationalism and rampant ego. Still, it must have looked to Leifs like he'd chosen the right side when the Führer took control of Denmark in 1942. By default, the authority of Iceland's unwelcome sovereign, King Christian X, was revoked. Iceland became the only country effectively liberated by Hitler.

Musicology interrogates the extent to which climate, landscape and national temperament (or stereotypes thereof) shape the work of composers, but Jón Leifs presents us with an open and shut case, as argued in Árni Heimir Ingólfsson's penetrating recent biography of the composer.[5] It was Leifs's stated aim 'to let the cool, strong gale of the Icelandic weather rush into the world's music'. He carted a phonograph around his inhospitable homeland, recording folk songs and other oral traditions. He let what he heard inform his music's irregular rhythmic and melodic shape, inspired by the laconic structure of ancient Icelandic poetry to create his own notably un-upholstered music. He consciously broke off the shackles of the European harmonic style that characterized the handful of notated scores created in Iceland before his own. Leifs preferred to stack chords on top of one another and fix notes in parallel formations, both off limits in polite European musical company.

As much as Leifs derided anything Danish, the only schooled composer who had a significant technical influence on his style, beyond his beloved Beethoven, was surely Carl Nielsen. In 1919, Leifs was in Copenhagen for a performance of Nielsen's Symphony No. 4, *The Inextinguishable*. He would have noticed the Danish composer's building of harmonies based on triads and tritones,[6] and would surely have been fired up by Nielsen's pitting of two of the orchestra's drummers against one other in the symphony's infamous apex of violence. Similar devices are found all over Leifs's music, suggesting he picked up on those ideas and ran with them. Either way, it's likely the general rough and tumble of Nielsen's symphony stoked Leifs to take his own ideas to their extremes.

Towards the end of his career, now back in Iceland, Leifs wrote four great orchestral tone poems reflecting his country's most distinctive natural phenomena: 'Geysir', 'Hekla', 'Dettifoss' and 'Hafís', respectively a geyser, a volcano, a waterfall and drift ice – the latter Iceland's most treacherous natural hazard. The score for 'Hekla' is literally huge: Leifs was forced to glue pieces of manuscript paper together to write it. The music sounds just as colossal, befitting the musical conjuring-up of one of Iceland's biggest volcanoes, in which task the composer calls for choir, organ and orchestra with an augmented percussion section including rocks large and small, metal chains, two sirens, a gunshot and an ondes Martenot – an electronic French instrument beloved of sci-fi film scores.

'Hekla' launches with what the composer termed 'quiet ice and the glacier's nobility' before slipping into a full-on eruption, nothing if not rational in its prioritizing of danger over awe. Percussionists provide the spouting and spurting before a benediction is bestowed upon the event by a chorus singing words by the poet Jónas Hallgrímsson: 'violent are the howls of death / in the deep depth; from there red / flames lead the boiling lava / over the [humble] land'. As cited by Ingólfsson, Leifs chose to omit the word 'humble' for obvious reasons.

As well as an invigorating listen, 'Hekla' is broadly representative of Leifs's entire modus operandi. The first thing we hear is the interval of a fifth spelled out by trombone and tuba – the very interval Leifs had noticed all over Iceland's own folk songs, the tvísöngur, before channelling it into his own works to the disdain of traditionalists who believed it crude. He makes good use of similarly barbaric 'parallel harmonies', two pitches tracking each other at a fixed interval. Soon we hear the juddering modulations characteristic of the composer, together with major and minor triads (the most fundamental three-part chord) piled up on top of one another without apology. Smooth, traditional, rhetorical cadences are avoided. Instead, the music changes its key from bar to bar, like the footsteps of a lumbering giant.

Leifs was a savvy enough composer to have alighted upon a method that could be adapted depending on expressive need or context. In his Elegy Op. 53, a memorial to the composer's mother, he uses the same abrupt modulations but to soothing effect. In his many songs, the human voice often provides a conciliatory counterpoint to the piano's steady churning through stacked chords, as dense and inexorable as flowing lava. The song 'Torrek', a grief-stricken response to the drowning of the composer's daughter that uses a lament from one of the sagas, speaks of a different sort of pain but with the same means; the piano part consists simply of five minor 'triad' chords in the right hand laid over a steady open fifth in the left.

The grand project of Leifs's creative life was a set of three mammoth oratorios based on the *Edda*, medieval poems and prose texts telling of the Norse gods, Odin and all. It was a conscious effort to wrestle ownership of the stories back from their hijacking by Richard Wagner in the four operas of *Der Ring des Nibelungen*, works dismissed by Leifs as a 'terrible misunderstanding of the Nordic character' (it hadn't crossed Leifs's mind that Wagner might have been aiming for something more universal). The *Edda* oratorios, which occupied him throughout his life, demonstrate just what Leifs meant by that character.[7] The stories are recounted with fearsome, relentless determination by singers requiring lungs of steel. They ask for all manner of instruments including lurs, the ancient Nordic wind instruments familiar these days from their appearance on packets of Lurpak butter. The musical structure is held in place by yet more of those lumbering harmonic footsteps, deeply driven sonic piles that reference the hexagonal basalt columns formed all over Iceland by the cooling of lava.[8]

Critics heard in Leifs's music precisely what he wanted them to. Unfortunately, that couldn't make them like it. 'Horribly monotonous, cold and quite frankly unpleasant,' ranted a review in a Gothenburg newspaper of Leifs's Iceland Overture, using words that could come straight from a contemporary Tripadvisor account of a hike through the Icelandic wilderness.⁹ Leifs himself was no more pleasant, a man whose company was by all accounts best avoided. At one point in his life, he apparently conceded that he might be schizophrenic. At another, he suggested coldness and emotional detachment were personality traits that could be positively extolled as Nordic. One local critic who defended the composer in 1932 got it right, castigating his colleagues with the keen observation that 'to judge Leifs's songs by the aesthetic standards of classical music is as absurd as to judge the Icelandic wilderness by the standards of French formal gardens'.¹⁰

When 'Hekla' was performed at the Nordic Music Days in Helsinki in 1964, it was mocked. The composer's methods felt at once undercooked and old hat, while Romantic notions of evoking a native landscape seemed passé in a Finland that had fought those ideological battles many decades earlier (as an independent nation, Iceland was barely out of its teens). At home, Leifs's music sounded disorientating and off-puttingly modernist. He may have been of his place, but Leifs was arguably fifty years ahead of his time. That put Iceland a hundred years behind it.

Leifs's music has never sounded more prescient than it does now. With its uncompromising noise and its strident scissoring through successions of keys, it foreshadowed Finnish metal music from Lordi and Stratovarius and much more notated music from Scandinavia, Iceland and throughout the far north. Leifs's belief in the Icelandic landscape as a resource has since been seized upon by a new generation of composers and across genres. Iceland owes its very existence to a heaving, wrenching tectonic movement between Europe and North America and the country's twenty-first-century compositional identity seems born of a similar aesthetic tug-of-war, with American minimalism and rock of the 1960s on one side and the stern edifices that had characterized much twentieth-century Scandinavian and Finnish music on the other. That very dynamic courses through the work of one of Iceland's biggest musical success stories, the post-rock band Sigur Rós.

If Iceland's glaciers, waterfalls and volcanoes remind us how fleeting our time on this planet is, recent history proves how nimble the country's political cycles have become. Back in 1930, from the chamber of the re-established Althing, the future president Ásgeir Ásgeirsson reminded his people that their literary tradition had 'saved the nation from ruin at times when ... bad harvest and misery had nearly cut her life's thread in two'. In the process of soul-searching that took place after the financial crash, when Iceland's Nordic neighbours slunk off to side with its critics, the need to assert Icelandic identity arose once more. Many of Iceland's composers, most of the best-known ones women, have found strikingly original ways of handling the modern symphony orchestra as they have sought to capture a new vision of their homeland in sound. In the third decade of the twenty-first century, no country on earth has reinvented the language of the symphony orchestra on such distinctive and locally relevant terms as Iceland has. Since 1950, thanks in no small part to Leifs, Iceland has had a symphony orchestra of its own.

▲

Before notating her works conventionally, Anna Thorvaldsdottir literally draws them, producing pristine pencil illustrations that seem as evocative as the works they're meant to help her write. One of these drawings, reproduced in the artwork for the album *Rhízōma*, features a consistent yet bumpy horizon of two almost-horizontal lines tracking each other in tight counterpoint, not unlike Leifs's parallel fifths. Beneath that, multiple roots gather towards a single, thick trunk before breaking into four branches, fraying outwards at their end points – perhaps a forbidding volcano, perhaps a weedy turnip.

In 2015, the New York Philharmonic named Thorvaldsdottir its inaugural Kravis Young Composer, a major endorsement from the oldest orchestral institution in the USA. In the years since, the composer has produced a string of orchestral canvases that echo Leifs's 'natural' tone poems of the 1960s. The orchestra is Thorvaldsdottir's medium, and she handles it exceptionally, aware of a large ensemble's capacity, as was Sibelius, to produce music that appears beyond human control. The drawings she creates help her 'map where a piece is going'. But they bear a striking resemblance to the landscape of Thorvaldsdottir's Iceland: the craggy moonscape with its repeating patterns, the protruding volcanoes and the sense that something timeless and inconceivable lies underneath it all.

Her first major work, *Dreaming* (2010), treats the symphony orchestra as an organism apparently capable of autonomous growth and metamorphosis; it is a piece in which the music, like the Icelandic sky, appears to change colour suddenly despite – or perhaps because of – its slow basic speed. Thorvaldsdottir's next work, *Aeriality*, has become a signature piece, performed around the world and recorded commercially twice since it was completed in 2011 (once on the prestigious German label Deutsche Grammophon). It opens with a snap and a creak, the juddering of tectonic plates, before quickly coming to rest on a deep pedal note. A giant tapestry is then woven from the orchestra's vaporous assembly of 70-plus instruments, thick and dark low down but swirling and luminous higher up, invested with a heaving, restrained power. New pedal notes emerge, taking the place of their predecessors almost by stealth, tricking the ear into surrendering spatial and pitch orientation like a musical counterpart to glacial movement – the rate of change sufficiently slow to feel imperceptible. At the peak of the piece, a cluster of quarter-tones – those 'notes between the notes' again – shatters at the top of the orchestra like an eruption.

Thorvaldsdottir's works convey, in the composer's words, 'my own distinct experience of nature'. They don't often sound like Leifs, but they frequently look like his on paper. Leifs himself used quarter-tones to give his music a sense of creeping progress. *Aerality* sits on rails of parallel open-fifths, like so much from the pen of Thorvaldsdottir's predecessor. Its creaking and snapping picks up on the hammering eighth notes with which Leifs depicted the cracking of ice sheets in 'Hafís'. Like Leifs before her, Thorvaldsdottir knows the power of an eruptive climax and can find exceptional colours from an acoustic orchestra. Leifs talked about nature providing composers with 'the truest harmonies that exist'. Thorvaldsdottir moves that idea into the domain of orchestral colour. 'Nature teaches you that brown is never just brown,' she once said in a post-concert talk in Copenhagen, referring to the manner in which her music moves in directions determined as much by colour and texture as by rhythm and harmony. Parallels with *Tapiola* are everywhere.

As *Aeriality* begins with an adjusting tectonic creak, so does *Lendh*, an orchestral score by the Canadian-born, Iceland-resident composer Veronique Vaka. What follows is another organic orchestral landscape, this one shifting from deep darkness to piercing luminosity and back by imperceptible degrees, floating like an ever-transforming cloud, a huge canvas subjected to micro pressures that gradually exert an influence on the whole. *Lendh* feels less anchored by pedal notes, more tethered at its midriff. There is still less sense of a human hand at work in this piece, as if colours and textures are controlled entirely by meteorological phenomena. Gestures spread through the orchestra like a virus.

Vaka has studied idiosyncratic Icelandic singing styles and used them in her works, with particularly interesting effects. Much like Leifs before her (though with a degree more sophisticated science), she has also made it her mission to translate what she experiences of Icelandic topography, and the country's geological processes, into musical form – 'the inaudible made audible' as she puts it. *Lendh* is based on analyses of steam and rock features around Krýsuvík, a geothermal hotspot 35 kilometres south of Reykjavík, subsequently 'converted' into musical notation by the composer. Her Viola Concerto *Vanescere* (2021) maps the slow melting of the Sólheimajökull glacier onto a temporal grid, compressing the 12-month contraction she recorded into the course of the concerto's twelve-minute duration. We hear the glacier's changing shape in movements by degrees: the shifting of one note in a chord or the slight contracting of a texture. Detailed, chronological photography – images of the same spot at different times, superimposed above one another – guide not just timescales but also the composer's choice of colour through instrumentation. Vaka's is landscape music as much by scientific design as emotional inspiration.

Across genres, Icelandic music appears to be unified by its lack of speed. The rest of the continent's failure to master the Viking Thunder Clap at soccer's European Championships of 2016 suggested that Icelanders are locked into a different psycho-physiological tempo to the rest of us, an idea born out in swathes of music from the country. We think of the Icelandic sky changing its outward appearance with uncommon rapidity. In musical terms, the changes are as slow and imperceptible as those that twist *Lendh* and *Aeriality* into new states and colours. Perhaps it's wrong to describe these pieces as 'slow', as, in both cases, their music changes our perception of speed.

In 2018, the Iceland Symphony Orchestra began to chronicle an outstanding new generation of Icelandic orchestral composers with a series of recordings. Across all three albums, titled *Emergence*, *Recurrence* and *Occurrence*, are works by the composers María Huld Markan Sigfúsdóttir, Hlynur Aðils Vilmarsson, Anna Thorvaldsdottir, Páll Ragnar Pálsson, Haukur Tómasson, Þuríður Jónsdóttir, Magnús Blöndal Jóhannsson, Veronique Vaka and Daníel Bjarnason (also the conductor on all three).[11] The vast majority of the scores included are slow by anyone's definition. In many, it's difficult to ascertain where the scored beat lies.

In 2019, I spoke to Bjarnason about the trend over my own kitchen table. He insisted there was plenty of Icelandic music that is manifestly *not* slow, including some of his own, and other pieces included on the Iceland Symphony Orchestra's recording series. But he also acknowledged the trend: 'I could say, I don't want to do any more slow, droney music, but at the same time I think this is some of the best music that has been written in Iceland.' He then went a little further: 'we did a concert at the Dark Music Days in Reykjavík this year, and all the tempi were below 60 [beats per minute]. I think Anna's [Thorvaldsdottir] piece was the fastest, like 80 or something. That tells you a lot.' This being Iceland, the trend is not confined to notated 'classical' music. It is a fundamental characteristic of Hildur Guðnadóttir's throbbing score for the TV series *Chernobyl*, of whole swathes of Sigur Rós and even of the electronic dance music made by the group Vök and the DJ Janus Rasmussen.[12]

◢

After the financial crash, the international press relished the chance to set Iceland's riches to rags story in a broader Nordic context. Iceland, they wrote, had let the side down. Journalists feasted on the idea that the country had become everything a Nordic nation was supposed not to be: fiscally irresponsible, short-termist, decadent. It was the wild teenager that had ignored the lessons of its frugal Scandinavian parents. A now-famous *Vanity Fair* article, 'Wall Street on the Tundra', went further. It suggested Iceland's attempt to reinvent itself as a financial superpower before the financial crash was a manifestation of red-blooded, hotheaded Viking values that had lain dormant for centuries. Even worse, suggested its author Michael Lewis, Iceland was corrupt.

The Nordic countries pride themselves on their disdain for corruption and their proven curtailing of it, one reason for high levels of societal and communal trust. So how could the world's oldest democracy, Iceland, become so badly embroiled in multiple corruption scandals? Principally because corruption in a country the size of Iceland is a natural hazard rather like weeds in a garden. Iceland's entire population is equal to that of Gothenburg, which makes for a smaller, more proximate state. Many MPs have second jobs in the hospitality or creative industries and if you're an Icelander, the chances are you'll know a handful of them. Before a spell in Paris, Jón Leifs was taught French by Vigdís Finnbogadóttir, later her country's President and the longest-serving female head of state anywhere in the world.

Iceland is spread over 100,000 inhospitable square kilometres, which draws a huge imbalance of power and resources to Reykjavík. The city has Iceland's only international airport and is the seat of its organized cultural life to an overwhelming degree. European capitals are expected to mount film festivals, host conferences, house embassies and media companies and offer high-level training in disciplines ranging from drumming to surgery. In Iceland, it all happens in a city with fewer inhabitants than the UK city of Gloucester. Physical proximity to politicians, artists, novelists, musicians and filmmakers has tended to suggest to the many young Icelanders who pass through the capital that they can be any of those things themselves – simple 'role model' theory. Meanwhile, all are bound, challenged and focused by the topography and climate that have formed such a distinctive part of the nation's creative and political history.

Things happen quickly in Iceland. The sorry mess of the late 2000s was a story of deals done after chance encounters with politicians in bars, restaurants, onboard aircraft and even at church. It was the same limited distance between conversation and action that saw the country emerge so rapidly from the hole into which it had dug itself. 'The good thing with Iceland, and it's an Icelandic speciality, is that I can do whatever I want at any given time,' Ólafsson told me. 'I love Iceland for how small and intimate it is. But at the same time, it's almost too small and intimate.'

Plenty of Icelandic poachers and gamekeepers found themselves in bed together in the years before the 2008 financial crash. But the same sort of proximity has had a fertilizing effect on the country's music scene, which has become one of the most distinctive on earth.

Even more than its Scandinavian and Finnish counterparts, Iceland got to know classical and popular music in tandem. It has increasingly little appetite for wasting time differentiating between the two.

Icelandic genre-blindness is a by-product of a single music scene concentrated on a small capital where the sharing of resources is not optional. The Icelandic University of the Arts is the only institution in the country offering degree-level courses in music, of whatever genre. Many of those studying classical music there will, by necessity, be involved in popular music genres and vice versa. 'Most people [in Iceland] are just interested in music in the same way that Björk is interested in music,' a student there, Torgrummur Torsteinsson, told me in 2019. Music has long been a part of general education in Iceland. In 1945, a huge shipment of pianos purchased cheap from London was distributed to all corners of the country courtesy of the publisher responsible for bringing the works of the Icelandic novelist Halldór Laxness to the world.

The tale of those pianos is often recounted by Björk Guðmundsdóttir, the Nordic region's most iconic living musician. She was born in Reykjavík in 1965 and was sent to the city's children's music school six years later, where she studied piano and flute. In her teens she joined the Hamrahlid Choir, which sang baroque, folk and avant-garde music under conductor Þorgerður Ingólfsdóttir. 'I think every single Icelandic musician you have heard of was brought up and musically baptized by this miraculous woman,' Björk tweeted in 2020, 53 years into Ingólfsdóttir's leadership of the ensemble.

Accordingly, it was Björk's singing voice that came to the attention of her schoolteachers. They sent a recording of her performing to RÚV, which operated a single radio station at the time meaning everyone with the apparatus was listening when the station broadcast the demo.[13] Björk was signed to the record label Fálkinn and released an album straightforwardly titled *Björk* at the age of 11. It was a collection of well-known songs from elsewhere translated into Icelandic and delivered with a voice that immediately pricked up the ears. Even then, despite its childlike expression, it was a voice apparently freighted with experience and lined with mystery.

Björk's musical interests sprawl across four centuries of the avant-garde to the popular music of her own time and the full sonic landscape of her home country. In 1996 she gave a performance of Schoenberg's *Pierrot lunaire* at the Salzburg Festival. More recently, she took time to review Ingólfsson's biography of Jón Leifs. Her fondness for Johann Sebastian Bach, Karlheinz Stockhausen and Arvo Pärt – she interviewed the latter two composers for Dazed & Confused and the BBC respectively – stem from her considered musical education and its pathway into Reykjavík's small but intense musical milieu, for whom a visit from any interesting musician in the 1980s would have been unmissable in both senses of the word.

Though Iceland and its language were always on her mind, Björk had to leave her homeland and return to it again before those elements started to infiltrate her music structurally. In the interview with Stockhausen, she talked of her mother's insistence that she walk around their Reykjavík commune barefoot, how it grinded against her instinctive desire to be around cars and skyscrapers. Having moved to London and immersed herself in trip-hop, world music, funk, opera and more, a visit home for Christmas in the mid 1990s apparently triggered in Björk a longing for her country and a deeper musical connection with it. After a series of break-ups, altercations and tragedies, Björk started to express her own personal pain in music that gave equal expression to the dark essence of Iceland itself.

Homogenic, the 1997 album that emerged from that process, picks up where Leifs left off but with a determination to speak in more multi-dimensional and emotionally complex terms. The song 'Jóga' opens with those touchstone parallel fifths in strings, the interval stepping upwards twice before resolving onto a third. Björk sings of 'emotional landscapes' while the beat manifests itself as tiny volcanic microbursts, exploding underneath as the vista of the song opens up. That beat never really gets into its groove, distorted by displaced emphases and a single shortened bar in the chorus, disorientating techniques that rarely find an entry point in commercial pop music and would literally wrong foot anyone trying to dance to the track. The album's opening song, 'Hunter', pulls similar rhythmic tricks while also fuzzing the beat into a horizontal landscape. In *Homogenic*, late 1990s electronica is as attuned to Iceland's distinctive terrain as the nineteenth-century symphony orchestra would be, in Thorvaldsdottir's hands, a decade and a half later.

Björk described the track 'Jóga' as a response to Iceland's national anthem, or at least the genre of Romantic songs from which it came.[14] Her album had advanced the language of Icelandic music using the standard forms Leifs made such a point of avoiding, and achieved far more besides. The song 'Virus' is built on a looping ground bass, the sort that underpins the cyclic downfall of the heroine's famous 'Lament' from Purcell's opera *Dido and Aeneas*. Leifs spent years trying to rid himself of the formalities he had been obliged to take on board as a European student composer. Björk spoke to Stockhausen of struggling to do the opposite, of 'learning to love regular rhythms', as if her default position were something altogether more broad, more shattered.[15] 'I thought I could organize freedom,' she sings in 'Hunter', 'how Scandinavian of me.' Icelanders had never played by *those* rules. Leifs made sure of it.

Björk squared that particular circle, partly, by rendering so many of *Homogenic*'s beats as ambiguous, sizzling little volcanoes – just one, obvious way in which her music bears witness to Iceland's landscape (the process runs far deeper). The album also shows signs of the orchestral music that would follow from the generation that came after her – of drones bending out of shape, of synthetic electronics advancing the music by colouristic means. Drop the needle anywhere in Thorvaldsdottir's piece 'Fields' for small ensemble and electronics, and you might think you're listening to a Björk track. All that's missing is that rotund singing voice, tinted by an Icelandic accent that curls idiosyncratically around English vowels. The sentences they form in *Homogenic* grapple with levels of philosophical and emotional strain that would certainly have kept Søren Kierkegaard busy.

By 2014, the time of *Homogenic*'s most tangible successor *Vulnicura*, Björk was struggling with the ramifications of a significant relationship gone bad. Here, the emotional strain is even more pronounced. The track 'Stonemilker' uses another looping 'ground' bass before 'Notget' shortens the loop dramatically, the music chanting away at a falling melodic fragment in the manner of a rune song.[16] When the loop shortens again, to just three notes, the contextual electronics and percussion grow more intense. There's plenty to occupy the brain on *Vulnicura*: the five-in-a-bar metrics of 'Atom Dance' and the double-speed of 'Quicksand' that layers jittery drum-and-bass underneath a slow ballad. But centuries of musical traditions feel most tangibly linked when Björk distills her textures right down to basics. 'Notget' echoes vernacular music from across the north, a plea for safety in the form of an incantation that becomes a growl, easily heard as a traditional Icelandic tvísöngur tune – a folk song – stripped and turned on its head.

As a volcanic island marooned between two great continental civilizations, Iceland conditions visitors to feel sucked up from one world and spat out in another. It's an oddly disorientating experience, for non-islanders, to visit a capital city where there's only one practical way in and out. No country on our fast globalizing planet lends weight to Montesquieu's theory that climate determines the character of a nation quite like Iceland does. That can be seen across cinema, literature and the visual arts as much as it can be heard in music. Hermetically sealed under a churning sky, musicians of every genre in Iceland often have more in common with each other than with those working in the very same medium elsewhere.

▲

A few days before arriving in Reykjavík in May 1926, Leifs and the Hamburg Philharmonic Orchestra sailed into Tórshavn on the Faroe

Islands, where they presented a concert in a dockside warehouse attended by a generous proportion of the town's 15,000 inhabitants. If the experience of hearing a live symphony orchestra had proved overwhelming in Iceland, on the Faroes it must have seemed miraculous. 'The music glided like a huge, well-oiled machine,' wrote the Faroese novelist William Heinesen in a fictionalized account of the performance in *The Lost Musicians*, the country's touchstone literary classic. 'It was like a furious colossus moving on lightly tripping feet.'

Tórshavn, the world's smallest capital, makes Reykjavík look like Manhattan. From a few hundred metres above the town centre on the side of a hill, you can survey the metropolis in its entirety: the enclosed harbour lined with archetypical coloured warehouses, and then the town itself – a mixture of drab industrial buildings, sleek functional homes and cutesy turf-roofed cottages that give way to verdant, chaotic moorland on one side and a vast expanse of glinting ocean on the other. Heinesen's novel paints a moving picture of an emerging music scene at the turn of the twentieth century, of a country with more than its fair share of talent and a belief not only in music as a force for good but as a means of binding a small community together. The idea ran deeper than fiction. Today, as in Heinesen's time, music on the Faroe Islands is first and foremost a community pursuit.

Lutheran hymns of Danish–Norwegian extraction have shaped Faroese music as much as 'skjaldur' – rhythmic nursery rhymes that deal with the standard Nordic bedtime fare of havoc and death. But the Faroese ballads, or 'kvæði', dominate, forming the basis of the country's distinctive oral tradition. Their stories are drawn from the sagas of Iceland and from Norway's formative myths.

The Faroese will tell you that the ballads are danced, but to everyone else they appear to be sung to choreography: syllabic, tuneful loops chanted by a similarly tight circle of human beings, each individual's right arm entrapping their neighbour's left, hands clasped beneath. Feet plod determinedly two steps in one direction and one in the other, slowly but surely ratcheting the circle around. On a wooden floor, the steady thump of feet on every other beat is as hypnotic as the apparently infinite unison singing. 'You reach a sort of trance that makes you understand why the repetition is necessary,' the Danish conductor Thomas Dausgaard told me of his participation in chain dancing at a Faroese wedding, as we discussed similar musical devices in the music of Sibelius. 'You can't get into the trance without a level of repetition way beyond what you're used to hearing – that sets its own time, its own dimensions.' The dance, Dausgaard said, 'went on for hours; you don't change it when the story becomes more dramatic, but you may stamp your feet a little harder.'

Chain dancing was once common all over Europe. The sort that has survived on the Faroe Islands has a steadfastness that stands in stark contrast, according to ethnomusicologists, to its long extinct and more celebratory counterparts from Spain and elsewhere further south. There is a primitive feeling to the dance and its music, but, as Dausgaard's comment suggests, the chants generate a minimalistic sophistication of their own. You quickly detect a call-and-response pattern at work. The individual doing the calling, the 'skipper', is not necessarily the participant blessed with the best voice but the one deemed to be most inside the atmosphere of the story being told – tales of remarkable feats, sorry domestic tragedies, heroics at sea and the triumph of good over evil.

For all its homespun integrity, the Faroese music scene has tasted international success in recent years and grown wise to the fashion for far-flung Nordic artists with a sense of mystery in their eyes. Right now the country's most successful international export after knitwear is Eivør Pálsdóttir, a singer who started her career chanting the ballads. Pálsdóttir was born on Eysturoy, the second largest of the country's 18 chunks of oceanic rock. As a child she devoured Kate Bush and Leonard Cohen, but would sit with her octogenarian grandfather as he chanted the ballads with his friends. Her first album, unequivocally titled *Eivør Pálsdóttir*, rerendered many of these ballads and their associated tunes in the garb of simple but sturdy pop, jazz and blues. Pálsdóttir had been to Reykjavík to study at the Icelandic University of the Arts, but, after returning home and shedding her surname Björk-style, she found herself slipping and sliding increasingly between genres. In 2010, she sang the role of Marilyn Monroe in an opera about the film star by the British composer Gavin Bryars. It was not her first appearance on the opera stage.

Eivør's frame of musical reference expands with every collaborative album she records. As with Björk, one constant is her soulful voice, highly distinctive despite its chameleonic abilities. After a string of albums collaborating with jazz bands, orchestras, string quartets and professional choirs, Eivør released the album *Lava* in 2010, a collection of gothic power ballads etched like chamber music. The lyrics border on the trite and the sci-fi undertones feel synthetic. But the delivery fixates as much as the arrangements fascinate, seizing the attention with strong gestures knowingly juxtaposed. So strong is the musical glare Eivør emits throughout *Lava* that it distracts you from wondering whether the whole enterprise is tongue in cheek. However well the singer marshals the album's sprawling musical accoutrement, she knows she doesn't really need it, which proves its magic bullet. It is the work of a folk musician at heart, one who still appears on stage chanting ballads and songs from all corners of her throat while pounding on a Sámi drum.

The strength of national feeling on the Faroe Islands is rooted as much in pragmatism as pride. Solidarity is fuelled by the small population's distribution over 17 different landmasses – all but one of the islands is inhabited – and by the ever-present issue of Danish sovereignty, a thorn in the side of Greenland, too. The Faroese parliament answers to the Danish crown, its currency is effectively an imprint of the Danish krone and anyone seeking higher education in a whole raft of subjects must leave the country, with the tacit expectation that it will be to Denmark or maybe Iceland (again, as in Greenland). On

29 July every year, Faroe Islanders celebrate nationhood on the feast of St Olav. They do so partly by filling the country's streets and harboursides with examples of their living folk tradition, chain-dancing the ballads. Politics and geography explain why that tradition has survived – even if it remains endangered – while so many equivalents have disappeared. The practice has inevitably seeped into the country's wider music scene.

Like a great deal in the Faroe Islands, that music scene resembles Iceland's in microcosm. It thrives on community traditions and personal need. But those things connect to the tip of a professional musical iceberg that is no less interesting. A good way for the uninitiated to immerse themselves in the nation's music scene is to show up at the annual Faroese Music Awards, which squeezes the majority of the country's well-known musicians into the Nordic House in Tórshavn for a ceremony carried live on local television. It is presented in Faroese – a blend of Germanic west-Scandinavian with Old Norse Icelandic.

When I attended in 2017, Eivør was awarded Best Female Singer but, in a mark of her success, she was too busy touring to accept the award in person. Another major artist otherwise engaged, despite being newly local, was Teitur Lassen. After years living in the United Kingdom, the United States, Sweden and Denmark, Lassen had moved back home some months before. It was a homecoming foreshadowed in the song 'Your Great Book', in which Lassen sings in his own droll way that 'you have to leave the country to rise again from misery'.

Teitur, who has also jettisoned his surname in favour of international cut-through, came to widespread attention with a collection of middle-of-the-road love songs titled *Poetry and Aeroplanes*. But he soon veered off course, abandoning his US conglomerate record label as he readied himself to probe and disembowel the whole idea of 'the song' with revealing results. His ditties stayed lucid on the surface – eight of them have been coopted into Denmark's national hymnal – but took on a new emotional depth and plenteous musical and philosophical complications. His album *The Singer* stripped everything back, its title track dissecting the profession in unnerving terms but delivered, like a good proportion of everything that comes out of Teitur's mouth, with an audible smile if not a physical one. 'I sing about my loneliness and in return you thank me,' goes 'The Singer'. Teitur's music might not sound so Faroese, but its combination of rural piety with Scandinavian openness taps into something absolutely of the place. So does its tendency to range dark clouds over simple pleasures.

In 2011, after collaborating with a series of artists including Seal, Nolwenn Leroy and Corinne Bailey Rae, Teitur wrote a song cycle, *Weekdays*, for the DR Symphony Orchestra and Girls' Choir. Another cycle, for voice, pre-recorded voice and string quartet, 'Romeo Answers', followed in 2015. In 2017, the singer sat down with the American composer Nico Muhly and the Holland Baroque Ensemble to create *Confessions*, described by one critic as 'an elaborate Baroque fantasy' but one that found ever more resonant ways of rendering the gently ironic tearfully profound.[17] Working increasingly in notated, acoustic music for large and varied forces, Teitur knew who to call for help.

Sunleif Rasmussen is the most high-profile composer on the islands, and was once used in a campaign by the Faroese tourist board. It featured an image of the composer reaching upwards and outwards from the edge of a dramatic Faroese cliff, as if conducting the birds and the clouds above. I first heard Rasmussen's music in 2013, at the Barbican Centre in London, when the BBC Symphony Orchestra opened a Saturday night concert with the composer's Prelude for Brass – a work whose brevity and simplicity concealed its depth.[18] What sounded on the surface like a succession of rather obvious pointillist patterns was actually the charting of a gradual, fascinating transformation.

Rasmussen's music can resemble one of those wall posters ubiquitous in student bedrooms of the 1990s; relax your eye muscles suffi-

1. A 30-year-old Björk Guðmundsdóttir performs at Lowlands Festival in Biddinghuizen, the Netherlands, August 1996.

2. Emilia Amper plays her nyckelharpa. The traditional Swedish folk instrument combines the extra resonating strings of a Norwegian Hardanger fiddle with elongated mechanical frets.

3. Western Norway at its most distinctive: a dramatic curve in the Geirangerfjord, north of Bergen.

4. Turf-roofed cottages, a lagoon and a waterfall at Saksun – a village on Streymoy, the largest and most populous of the eighteen Faroe Islands.

5. Icelandic composer Anna Thorvaldsdottir stands among the stone cairns that are scattered throughout her country's unmistakeable terrain.

6. Sade Kamppila and Viivi Roiha perform their dance piece Metsä - The Forest Project in a wood outside Kaukonen, Finland, at the 2016 Silence Festival.

7. If Sibelius designed buildings . . . Architectural model in wood (1959) for the auditorium of Alvar Aalto's opera house in Essen, Germany.

8. Inside Marko Kivistö's Musiikkitalo concert hall complex in Helsinki, opened in 2011. Banks of seat rows in the principal auditorium are arranged at acute angles, referencing the Finnish industrial practice of floating felled timber down rivers.

9. Norway's first purpose-built opera house, opened in 2008 to a design by local architects Snøhetta. The building resembles an iceberg rising from the Oslofjord in white marble.

10. Façade of Musikkens Hus ('The House of Music') in Aalborg, Denmark – a playful response to severe Scandinavian design traditions by Austrian architects Coop Himmelb(l)au.

11. Monster rock band Lordi celebrates victory at the 2006 Eurovision Song Contest in Athens – the first time a metal band, or one from Finland, had claimed victory at the event.

12. Finnish conductor Sakari Oramo conducts the BBC Symphony Orchestra at the Last Night of the 2017 BBC Proms. A year later, every one of the BBC's six full-time ensembles would have a chief or principal guest conductor from the Nordic countries – or would have announced the imminent arrival of one.

13. The South Jutland Symphony Orchestra at its concert hall in Sønderborg, Alsion. The Nordic region's unparalleled network of regional orchestras and concert halls was developed in the mid-1900s as a direct result of social democratic cultural policy.

14. Where the greatest crime is to have no money: Graham Vick's 2016 staging of Kurt Weill's *Rise and Fall of the City of Mahagonny* at the Royal Danish Opera. The set used replicas of the Copenhagen Opera House's distinctive maple balconies and glass chandeliers.

15. Models at the 2017 Paris Fashion Week showcase Marimekko textiles. Curtains to the rear are adorned with a version of Maija Isola's pattern Unikko.

16. Sámi reindeer herders in Pajala, Sweden, mark the ears of their flock's young calves. The Sámi, guardians of Europe's oldest continuing musical tradition, are already suffering the catastrophic effects of climate change.

ciently and an image would float out from the apparently flat, regimented scheme of dots or shapes. The composer explained the process to me with recourse to one of his frequent sailing trips around the Faroese islands of Sandoy, Skúvoy and Stóra Dímun: 'When you are on the water, things change slowly. You may know how a particular island looks, but when you sail around it, you experience entirely different perspectives on the same place and you hardly notice it happening. That's what I try to express in my music.'

Outlining his quest to capture the essence of his country using notated and mostly acoustic music, Rasmussen compared himself to Jón Leifs. You could easily stretch the comparison to Grieg, Sibelius and Nielsen. As a composer of symphonies and chamber works that have been performed around Europe, Rasmussen is a towering figure on the Faroes, even if there are plenty more composers and musicians of other genres for him to associate with. His music speaks unequivocally of its place, reflecting the utilitarian nature of music on the islands without patronizing its people and at the same time breathing something of the country's harsh, wet and blustery air. From simple ingredients, he explores varied perspectives on familiar themes and objects.

The composer's Symphony No. 2, *The Earth Anew*, is another reclamation of the Nordic creation myth from Wagner in the manner of Leifs's *Edda*. In its final movement, the sun turns black, the land sinks into the sea and a rebirth takes root, echoing the apotheosis of Wagner's *Der Ring des Nibelungen*. It is a huge score for orchestra and singers that writhes and wriggles, cackles and cascades, sounding as though it has been hauled up from beneath the surface of the earth. Like Sibelius's Symphony No. 5, Rasmussen's symphony is not so much a description of the creative process as an embodiment of it, giving the impression of a language being formed and refined even as it's being spoken. Its music is punched out and present, every rhythmic impulse felt in the bones yet sufficiently crafted to bring perspective in the moment and a residue long after it. More urbane composers have striven for a lifetime to achieve the same directness.

At the award ceremony in Tórshavn, Rasmussen's symphony picked up the Faroese Music Award for Best Composition. That his work resonates domestically in a way Leifs's never did is surely down to its proximity to themes everybody here knows. The composer learned the Faroese hymnal as a child and was drip-fed the ballads by his grandmother. Isorhythms – consistent, anchoring rhythmic patterns like those that form a chain dance – fix much of his music onto clear metrical tracks even as its energy levels surge and wane. For a while, Rasmussen kept actual Faroese hymns and skjaldur out of his own scores, not wanting 'to become another Bartók', referring to the Hungarian composer who hung his music off indigenous folksongs. More recently, Rasmussen has allowed those elements to come to the surface of his works, however well disguised.

The day before the ceremony, Rasmussen approached me between formal engagements and suggested we head out on a drive. Having read my review of his symphony in *Gramophone*, he wanted to show me where the music actually came from. We took the road north out of Tórshavn, along the ridge of the island of Streymoy that climbs ever higher over the fjords that cut into and between the islands. On a map, the Faroe Islands resemble marks left by inky fingers dragged momentarily down a sheet of paper in a south-easterly direction.

The Faroes are more verdant than Iceland, but no less dramatic. Water is almost constantly visible, usually over the edge of a teetering cliff or ebbing onto a slender black sand beach. Black sheep roam the grey-green moors, ambling down roads and even into the city. Colonies of puffins gather on cliff edges and on rock formations, staring placidly out to sea. Waterfalls pour liquid patiently back into the Atlantic, resembling upended columns of thin candle smoke. At the dead of night, the spring moonlight was breathtaking, illuminating what felt like the entire surface of the sea in a rippling silver.

When its beauty isn't bewitching you, the overbearing impression of the Faroe Islands is of a place that really doesn't want you around.

Just being there feels like an incursion onto terrain that could, at any moment, react angrily to your presence. The further we drove, the more extreme the weather became. The winds whipped up while mist and rain draped a heavy grey blanket over the hills. When the gloom momentarily dispersed, the scale of these shards of rock was revealed in its breathtaking severity – the west of Norway but bigger, blunter, less earthly. At Mjørkadalur, a settlement on a tight curve at the end of a long finger of fjord (the name means 'valley of fog'), the country's prison is cut into the side of the hill, looking straight down the valley. The views from its cells, the locals say, are the Faroese penal system's most efficient and effective means of rehabilitation.

Rasmussen appeared fixated on the landscape throughout our drive, as though it was demanding his attention. I asked what these monumental views meant to him. His opaque response is best summarized as 'everything', but was post-scripted with a few muttered words of disdain for the city. When I see the composer around the streets of Frederiksberg in Copenhagen, where I live and he has an apartment, he seems somehow a fish out of water. 'The one common thing is the birds,' he once told me outside our local 7-Eleven. 'I try to exclude the cars and focus on the birds.'

◢

Far from all Faroese music is dark, brooding, ritualistic or organic. At the Faroese Music Awards, the gong for Best Song was given to a band called Danny and the Veetos for their song 'Alright', a feel-good number that might have been written in Birmingham. Some acts strived for metropolitan sheen. Best Newcomer Konni Kass achieved it, singing louche, sophisticated songs with self-blown saxophone ritornellos. Still, oral traditions and their subjects proved remarkably persistent throughout the ceremony, rumbling even under the surface of electronica and rock. As younger Faroese musicians have been drawn into separatist political positions by globalization or the overbearing influence of everything Danish, many have turned, like Rasmussen, to local source material. Like their equivalents in Finland, the Faroese ballads and nursery skjaldur have fed into a fertile metal music scene described variously as Viking metal, doom metal and death doom metal. Much of its music is as related to Rasmussen's symphony as it is to Eivør's use of haunting choirs of children and adults.

The doom metal band Hamferð takes its name from the phenomenon of long-drowned sailors appearing to their loved ones as apparitions. The band uses music from the Faroese hymnal and stories from the kvæði, one of the primary sources for the ballads, as does its folk-metal counterpart Týr, named after the Norse god.[19] Hamferð's stated artistic aim is to root its music in the territory it comes from. The extraordinary lungs of the band's singer Jón Aldará combine with the music's dark, monolithic qualities and slow, slithering gait to conjure up the meteorological atmosphere of the islands as a counterpart to the Faroese tunes and language used.

In his fifth solo album, *Story Music,* Teitur made his own diversion homeward. After a series of songs in defiance of the international pop industry ('Rock and Roll Band') and global connectivity ('Antonio and his Mobile Phones'), the song 'Hard Work' reinforces a very northern Atlantic view of the societal usefulness of music. After that, the song 'Monday' ropes all manner of Teitur's Faroese countrymen in for assistance, including radio announcers and choirs. Somewhere in the background is the sound of a chain dance. In total, 78 Faroese citizens are heard on the album, ranging in age from 7 to 83.

Isolation, more than landscape, keeps the chain dances turning and returns the Faroese perpetually to music, now as much as in Heinesen's day. Social proximity has lumped Faroese musicians of different aesthetic outlooks into the same creative Petri dish, where many of them have discovered they share the same musical DNA after all. Even more than in Iceland, this is a music scene that can feel inbred, for better or worse. That much was apparent when watching the Faroese Music Awards, as a good number of nominated artists popped up in each other's bands (it was impossible not to wonder how many of them would be back next year, too). I thought I recognized the show's well-coiffed host, but couldn't place him until another journalist did: he was the stranger who'd helped find us a taxi on the harbourside the night before. We'd been drinking in the little room above the Hawaiian-themed bar Sirkus, at a performance that took in the long-breathed incantations of string duo Hettarher and the raging of post-punk band 200. A day or two later, when an official was referring to the country's culture minister in conversation, he told me I'd already met her that night in Sirkus. She'd been behind the bar.

◢

An adult Eivør Pálsdóttir first appeared on stage as part of the Faroese ensemble Yggdrasil, a group that seeks to expand the outlook of Faroese music by welcoming musicians of all nationalities and traditions into its ranks.[20] Yggdrasil plays everything from world and rock music to experimental opera, and in caves and on mountaintops as well as in concert venues and bars. But it allows itself to be rooted by the hymns and ballads of Faroese tradition. It was founded by Kristian Blak, a Dane who upped sticks from Jutland in 1974 to move to Tórshavn, where he still lives on the proud little peninsula of white wooden buildings that also includes the Løgting – the Faroese parliament.

Blak's own composer credits include a string of works that adapt, refract, remix and recontextualize the sounds of Faroese nature including wind, waves and birdsong. He has made a speciality of cave concerts, in which audiences float into dark sea caves, remaining on their open boats for elongated performances that ride the mesmeric natural acoustics. In 1977, Blak changed the footing of Faroese music by establishing Tutl, a record label, publishing house, shop, museum, management company and aggregated ticket agency for Faroese concerts of all musical genres. Eivør and Teitur both started out releasing albums on Tutl's imprint, which was also the first to publish Rasmussen's music on record.

For all its transformative activities, Tutl is first and foremost a physical presence in Tórshavn. Its shop on the capital's main drag Niels Finsensgøta gives the town something London no longer has: a specialist, independent, cross-genre record store with a regular concert series (every Wednesday in the summer months). On my three visits across the same number of days, the shop was patronized by a steady procession of islanders and visitors, talkative and quiet, old and young, fresh-faced and weather-beaten. Friday nights throughout the year are generally 'release party' nights, and the one I attended was memorably convivial. Standing by the till – short, bearded, as steady and expressionless as a sea captain – was Kristian Blak.

While not prone to verbosity, Blak did possess an unreadable wit that betrayed his Danish roots. He described the shop itself as a cultural embassy. 'There was a time when the Faroe Islands were marketed as a destination using fish and mountains,' he told me. 'Now the country is marketed using fish, mountains and culture. We get high-class tourists coming here who are interested in the cultural life of the place. They're not here for the sun.' Most Faroese musicians will tell you that, without Blak, there would be significantly less culture here for them to visit.

Musical training on the Faroes has been formalized since Heinesen's day. A network of 13 specialist music schools across the country now feeds the flagship Faroese Music School, which in 2019 moved into new premises incorporating a chic concert hall. Courses are offered in 30 instrumental disciplines as well as music theory and ensemble playing – a long way from the music without instruments that forms the country's sonic DNA.

On the Music School's faculty is Bernharður Wilkinson, the very model of a formally trained musician. He started his education as a choirboy at Westminster Abbey in London, before joining the Iceland Symphony Orchestra as a flautist, by way of the Royal Northern

College of Music in Manchester. His father, a sometime organ scholar at Cambridge University, had been posted to the Faroe Islands with the occupying British during the Second World War, where he married a local. Wilkinson eventually felt the allure of his maternal homeland, and made the move south-east to Tórshavn from the only place such a move is navigationally possible. With a degree of pride in his voice, he told me how many young musicians the Faroe Islands regularly despatch to conservatoires in Denmark, Sweden, the UK and the US. Subsidies from the Faroese Government mean children pay 2,000 Danish kroner a year (around US$300) for ninety minutes of musical coaching a week including theory, oral and instrumental tuition.

Keeping Wilkinson busy these days is the development of his adopted homeland's own professional symphony orchestra, which gathers for around seven projects a year including New Year concerts broadcast live on Kringvarp Føroya, the Faroese Broadcasting Corporation. The orchestra is staffed by teachers from the music school network joined by professional Faroese players drawn from the ranks of symphony orchestras in Glasgow, Copenhagen and elsewhere. That such an ensemble can even exist on the islands has aroused the curiosity of international news networks including ABC and France 24. At 50,000, the population of the islands is twelve times smaller than that of Wyoming. Naturally, the islands also boast their own dedicated contemporary music ensemble, Aldubáran (the Faroese word for 'little wave').

The Faroese Symphony Orchestra has premiered music by Rasmussen, Blak and others, as well as supporting Faroese musicians from other genres. Slowly but surely, it is introducing its populace to live performances of the classical repertoire. 'Last season we had the Faroese premiere of Tchaikovsky's Piano Concerto No. 1 and Mozart's Symphony No. 35,' Wilkinson told me when we spoke in 2018. 'Next season we will introduce Beethoven's Ninth Symphony to the islands. And we have an Icelandic soloist called Víkingur Ólafsson coming down to play Grieg's Piano Concerto.'

When not working on the orchestra's sound, Wilkinson has the responsibility of arguing the case for its funding. 'It depends who is in power, but when you press them [the politicians], they tend to admit that it's an essential part of the cultural life here,' he told me. At least the conversations are easily had. 'You meet the politicians in the street, you sit next to them on the plane – that makes it much easier to plead your case.' So far, the pleading has been successful. Why wouldn't it be? Playing, singing, dancing and listening are more pervasive, intrinsic activities on this cluster of oceanic mountains than they are in Vienna or Bayreuth.

And yet, notated music has a relatively short history here. It can feel historically disorientating to think of Sunleif Rasmussen laying the foundations for such a tradition in the post-acoustic age, while his homeland grapples with its own identity and autonomy. It was all smiles at the music awards, but the country still struggles with issues ranging from Danish dominance and youth emigration to accusations of brutality towards the very sea life its export economy relies on. The country's annual ceremonial whale cull has prompted reams of negative press and even international boycotts. Perhaps it's as simplistic to recoil from the techniques by which whales are hunted and killed by the Faroese as it is to romanticize the country's landscape – or patronize it by measuring its extraordinary musical creativity against its size.

More recently, Faroese music has willingly joined the global cavalcade. When Eivør's albums are reviewed by international publications like the *Guardian*, the economic benefits wind their way back to Blak's not-for-profit label, thus creating opportunities for the next generation. Music and the music business are two different things, but Blak's running of his country's most pivotal musical enterprise as a community concern ensures the former is never likely to overbear the latter on this strange and songful archipelago, however much locals look to capitalize on the rise of Brand Nordic. The central, communal message of Heinesen's *The Lost Musicians* still holds sway. For the time being, at least.

OFF PISTE

▲

Through a combination of accident and osmosis, a colonial hangover from Denmark once wormed its way into the musical traditions of the Faroe Islands. Thomas Kingo was a Danish hymn writer and theologian whose 1699 hymnal was used widely in Denmark and Norway for a century or more, until liturgical fashions moved on. On the Faroe Islands, where fashions of all sorts are notably lethargic, Kingo's tunes were found to be in common use well into the second half of the twentieth century.

In the intervening years, something strange had happened to those tunes. Left to marinate in the individuality of human habit and generational change, Kingo's melodies sprouted wild and fascinating ornamentations. What were referred to even in modern times as 'Kingosálmar' ('Kingo Hymns') combined the remnants of the original tunes with freestyle additions and melismas that frequently incorporated quartertones – those notes-between-the-notes so beloved of the twenty-first-century avant-garde. When the Danish musicologist and conductor Marianne Clausen discovered these practices during her various research trips to the Faroes, she got her choirs back in Copenhagen to actively imitate the sounds Faroese congregations were making.

One March I took the Lillehammer express train north out of Oslo, changing at Hamar station onto a small, two-carriage train for the winding journey up to Røros, a former mining town in the region of western Norway that hugs the Swedish border just before the country narrows from the bulbous into the spindly. The journey, through a geologically dramatic landscape almost entirely whitened by snow, was the stuff of fantasy. The vistas were vast, appearing all the more so from the warm side of a train window. All was sweeping and majestic up to Lillehammer, the big train kicking white spray down the sheer hillsides as it went. On the rattler to Røros, things got more precarious. The pair of carriages heaved themselves up and up towards the town, spread over a hillside 180 metres above sea level. Getting there seemed to depend as much on divine providence as on horsepower.

On the journey I was listening to the Norwegian Soloists' Choir's recently released album *White Night*. Like Marianne Clausen before her, conductor Grete Pedersen had asked the members of her choir to break most of the established rules of choral singing. Ensemble unity and blend, precise tuning and the cultivation of a clean tone from the throat or the chest were abandoned – or consciously forgotten. *White Night* consists of traditional hymns and folk songs stripped of what Pedersen describes in the liner notes as their 'sophisticated wrapping'. Yet in the context of performance practice, the part of musicology that deals with how music has and can be performed, what you hear is enormously sophisticated. It is Björk's 'learning to love' musical regularity slammed into reverse; a painstaking process of 'unlearning' various disciplines that for most classical musicians have become instinctive.

White Night takes us back to how things were in parts of rural Scandinavia centuries ago, and to something like the tradition that held sway on the Faroe Islands in the not-so-distant past. Gjermund Larsen's Hardanger fiddle weaves its way through many of the album's songs and hymns. Its characteristically non-standard tuning influences the way the choir sings, gently luring it away from the rigidity of major/minor scales – away from what Pedersen refers to as the 'black and white of the keyboard' towards 'a more personal approach'.

'Nådigste Jesus – Jesus Styr du Mine Tankar' ('Merciful Jesus Guide My Thoughts') uses a tune handed down by the folk singer Ragnar Vigdal. It opens with an incantation, sung from an open throat and littered with keening ornaments by the folk singer Berit Opheim Versto. Before long, a sort of improvised polyphony emerges from the assembled voices. Each singer moves at his or her own speed, a cantor leading much like the skipper in a Faroese chain dance. The voices swarm, eventually flipping unanimously onto an extraordinarily placed chord, elaborated by one soprano with soaring aerial decoration. In the individual freedom of each voice, the theology of Luther's universal priesthood finds musical form. The faithful offer their devotions as one, but at their own pace and in their own style.

Røros, population 2,200, is plainly arranged on a gentle slope with a tree-speckled hill at the top and a plateau at the bottom. In winter, skiers weave among the trees above while the white smoke of industry resembles gaseous snow below, rising from the whiteness all around. A copper mine was established here in 1644. The town sprang up in the years that followed and has barely changed since, its outlying streets scattered with turf-roofed wooden cottages, Faroese-style. In 1980, Røros attracted UNESCO World Heritage status. In 2016, Simon Rattle and his Berlin Philharmonic Orchestra opted to perform their annual European Concert in the town's impressive octagonal church, with the Norwegian violinist Vilde Frang for company.

An ascendant main artery lined with squat villas and shops cuts Røros in half down the middle. After disembarking from the train I took a taxi up the hill to a hotel with a woman I later learned was Lise Fjelstad, one of Norway's most distinguished actors and the daughter of Øivin Fjelstad, sometime chief conductor of the Oslo Philharmonic. Having come here to write about an orchestra, I was even more surprised to find Grete Pedersen and the Norwegian Soloists' Choir in town. After their concert, I chased the conductor down and arranged to talk to her.

We met the next day at Peder Hiort Mathus, a restaurant inside a stern grey building at the bottom of the hill surrounded by a white picket fence. We talked through the interpretative journey of *White Night* full-circle: classical music polishing-up folk music in the nineteenth and twentieth centuries; twenty-first-century classical musicians learning the impure techniques of the folk singers to better understand how that music was conceived and restore some sense of respect. Pedersen appeared to me a serious, stern individual, her default facial expression a rugged frown. As we spoke, a woman passed ferrying a tray of drinks and caught wind of our conversation. 'Grete is the real pioneer in this field – she went to these places before anyone else,' the woman said. This, Pedersen explained, was Anita Breivik, director of the choirs at Trondheim Cathedral. 'I paid her to say that,' Pedersen laughed, her frown loosening momentarily.

Pedersen experienced considerable resistance when she started to change the way classical musicians performed folk-inspired music. Parallels with the historically informed performance movement are obvious. As there, Pedersen talks of opening ears to methods previously deemed unthinkable. 'There is a way of singing folk music, just like there is a way of singing Verdi and a way of playing jazz,' she said, while emphasizing a shift in the idea of ownership: 'before, you couldn't sing folk music if you were not born in a place like this. I didn't grow up with it at all. That doesn't mean I can't familiarize myself with the style.'

The sound of Pedersen's choir in *White Night* is perhaps the closest a classical ensemble has ever come to sounding uniquely Scandinavian, with a little help from the Norwegian language. Others have taken her ideas forward. The ensemble Pedersen founded, the Oslo Chamber Choir, released an album in 2020 titled *Veneliti* on which it presents a series of ballads, chants and laments – some deftly recomposed by Ørjan Matre – with a similar approach. On *White Night*, the entire Norwegian Soloists' Choir put down its printed music to learn the hymn 'Und mig, Gud' ('Forgive Me, God') aurally from the folk singer Unni Løvlid, to whom it had been passed down via Ragnar Vigdal (1913–1991), who encouraged the brooding, semi-ornamented approach taken. For anyone trained as a singer in one of the churches or choral societies of England (or, indeed, one of Scandinavia's clean-lined metropolitan chamber choirs), it feels extraordinary to hear choral singing visited by the raw, earthy spirit of the yoik, the rune song and the chain dance.

The practice is not confined to singing. Ensembles including The Trondheim Soloists have taken a step back from conservatoire perfection in certain Norwegian and Scandinavian repertoires. They have consulted folk fiddlers and even folk dancers for stylistic input, consciously cultivating a less cultivated sound, ensuring it's not just the notes in eighteenth-century Nordic music that refer to folk traditions but the playing of them too. 'The people behind the establishment of The Trondheim Soloists were extremely connected to the "Old Norwegian" tradition,' I was told by the ensemble's then artistic director Øyvind Gimse in 2009, when I visited the city to investigate the roots of the orchestra's distinctive sound. 'These were guys who loved running around naked in the mountains, eating sheep shit and all that – they were really crazy!'

The roots of Vigdal's tune for 'Und mig, Gud', as well as its text, go back centuries. The subject matter isn't exactly celebratory. But in truth, a streak of melancholy runs through almost everything on *White Night* including the rousing wedding song that rounds it off with teary eyes, 'Bruremarsj fra Valsøyfjord' ('Wedding March from Valsøyfjord'). Pedersen writes of this pervasive melancholy in the booklet notes: 'There is a vulnerability and fragility, regardless of the circumstances.' Discussing the frisson that charges the performances on *White Night*, Pedersen closed the circle: 'We have done this a little bit with Grieg too – with his *Four Psalms*. Do you know these works? We brought a little bit of the folk style to our recording of those.'

4

Nordic Noir and Snow White

"Anxiety is the dizziness of freedom."

Søren Kierkegaard

Sibelius laboured long and hard over his Symphony No. 5, wondering how the pieces of the mental jigsaw strewn about his head might fit together. It was the mid 1910s. Europe was slipping towards war, which spelled disaster for Finland's hopes of independence (or so the nationalists thought). As he sweated through bouts of depression and heavy drinking to finish the score, Sibelius was thrown a lifeline. On 21 April 1915, he stepped out onto his veranda to see sixteen migrating swans soaring upwards from the lake close to his house, Lake Tuusula. 'One of my greatest experiences,' he wrote in his diary. 'The Fifth Symphony's finale theme ... legato in the trumpets!'

In fact, the theme is first heard on trumpets shortly after the midpoint of the symphony's first movement, born of travailing strings. The trumpets soar upwards from the orchestra, elaborating on the interval of an ascending perfect fourth (think the first two notes of

'Away in a Manger'), widening it by one step to form a major fifth (the first leap in 'Twinkle, Twinkle Little Star'). A little after a minute into the symphony's final movement, double basses can be heard spelling out that same interval of a fifth. Moving to the horns, the fifth starts to form the basis of a looping pattern, its bottom note dropping twice before stepping back up. The movement traces the graceful rise and fall of a wing while the repeating top note echoes the monotone hoot of Finland's national bird. Here are the Lake Tuusula swans.

On aerodynamic horns, the oscillating wing-flap theme gains pace and grandeur. Suddenly, the music shifts key: double basses drop down like the falling away of a runway. Magically, gloriously, the swans take flight. Soon they can be heard in the distance once more, circling as if for a final salute. Back on trumpets, they push on upwards, now fighting tangled rhythmic and harmonic obstacles formed by the rest of the orchestra. Eventually, against overwhelming structural odds and with huge emotional force, the swans break free. It is surely the single most exhilarating and moving passage of music Sibelius wrote – the agony of life transformed, through nature, into something higher.

Even in a mediocre performance of that passage, the sense of release can be overwhelming. For a few decades, one place you could be sure to hear it played rather well was in the unassuming Finnish city of Lahti. After a series of recordings made in its Alvar Aalto church conducted by Osmo Vänskä, the city's municipal orchestra won a reputation as the music world's most ear-tweaking interpreter of Sibelius's symphonies. Hearing those symphonies played by the Lahti Symphony Orchestra at its pristine lakeside concert hall has been one of the great privileges of my professional life. But no amount of nature transcending drudgery can take away from the fact that Lahti, in the autumn, is depressing as hell.

Like Hämeenlinna's, Lahti's biggest export after classical music appeared to be human beings. On a Saturday morning I hiked up the hill towards the altitudinous transmission mast and ski jump that loom over the town, hardly encountering another soul on the way. I was looking for the Lahti Television and Radio Museum, which I found in a stern neo-classical building by the side of a running track among the trees. After paying the entrance fee to the solitary teenager manning the front desk, I was left to negotiate the interactive exhibits alone, monitored half-heartedly by the teenager and her boyfriend (who arrived later) as I did so. What started out mildly humiliating soon became a test of resolve and, ultimately, an exercise in self-knowledge. As my days in Lahti slipped by, each resembling the next in its lack of action but with a chunk of striving Sibelius in the evening, I started to do something Nordic folk have tended to do for centuries: think too much.

Søren Kierkegaard believed the greatest despair was that of not knowing oneself. But he quickly found the process of making one's own acquaintance to be no picnic either, using the word 'angst' to describe the natural anxiety that comes with realizing what being alive is likely to encompass. Before becoming philosophy's staunchest advocate of human suffering, Kierkegaard surely sensed the residual comfort of everyday melancholy – the sort that comes with solitude, bad weather and good art. In Lahti, I settled into the depressive air as if it were the blue-green water of a warm bath. At the end of each day there were Sibelius's symphonies to indulge my mood, each one half-freeing itself from sorrow, hard labour or mental strain with eyes-clasped-shut exultation. These works stop short of the sort of symphonic victory proclaimed by Beethoven and Mahler. Even in the sunniest examples, Sibelius seems to be searching for little more than release from the intensity of his own thoughts.

Attempting to define the particular brand of introspective melancholy that is said to underpin the Nordic psyche makes for quite some psychological fishing trip. The author Robert Ferguson attempted it in his excellent 2016 book *Scandinavians: In Search of the Soul of the North*. Any revelations he offers are couched between the lines, but one of the more explicit theories he probes is that Scandinavian melancholy is a literary construct, an external view of societal behaviour stretching back to the seventeenth century that became self-fulfilling.

One of Ferguson's interviewees even suggests, with his tongue in his cheek, that an English immigrant to Denmark helped invent the character of Hamlet after he'd returned home and regaled his old friend William Shakespeare with tales of his travels. That immigrant was John Dowland, the lute player and composer who joined the Royal Danish Orchestra in 1598. For Dowland, the sight of morose courtesans fighting existential problems in the dark corners of cold palaces would have been all too familiar. Their predicament certainly seeped into the music he wrote in Denmark.

Ferguson's point is that outsiders tend to project their own sense of melancholy onto the North just as they automatically associate more colourful characteristics with cultures further south. We *want* our Nordic art to be dark and miserable because it fits a stereotype and makes us feel better about ourselves. The Nordic film festival I routinely covered in London in the 2010s gleefully presented a quagmire of cinematic alcoholism, betrayal, loneliness and family breakdown. At the same time, subtitle-savvy types all over the UK were held in thrall by the Danish television series *The Killing*, an epic crime thriller depicting a Copenhagen saturated by rain, shrouded in darkness and filled with troubled souls. Settling in the same city in the spring of 2015, I found a place bathed in apparently eternal sunlight and populated by energetic, contented folk. On television, the very same actors from *The Killing* were gurning and goofing for laughs in romantic comedies.

The international success of the Nordic noir genre is tangled up in our fascination with the so-called 'Scandinavian Utopia'. *The Killing*, *The Bridge*, *Deadwind* and others provide a tantalizing counter-narrative: that the wholesome, Volvo-driving Scandinavian isn't so wholesome and may well have a body stashed in the boot.

But that's little more than a happy coincidence. Nordic noir was never intended to entertain Europeans; the genre emerged from within, a symptom of the same stringent democracies it seeks to interrogate.

The series of Marxist novels led by the character Martin Beck, that are said to have kick-started Nordic noir as a genre, were designed to expose abuses of power and vested interests in Sweden's social democratic system, echoing Kierkegaard's use of fiction to critique what he saw as the hypocrisy of the church. Apart from being distinctly well woven by their authors Maj Sjöwall and Per Wahlöö, the Beck stories gained traction because they reinforced the democratic fundamental that nobody is above the law. The underlying messages were private as well as political. Like their many successors, the Beck novels' ugliest truths concerned the deep personal flaws of those trying to uphold some sense of morality. In Nordic noir, the good guys rarely get the moral high ground to themselves. That way, we all feel a little better.

Kierkegaard's belief in the inevitability of human suffering suggests Nordic melancholy isn't so much externally projected as bluntly rational, an unavoidable side-effect of engaging with the realities of life from philosophy to meteorology. That there is a disproportionately significant dark streak running through Nordic art of almost every form is undeniable. The question is whether it's fundamentally aesthetic or expressive – effect or message, means or end?

There's an answer, to some degree, in the way Sibelius manages to render even the most heavily straining music so utterly beautiful. Ingmar Bergman's cinematic psychodramas packaged up the darkness of the Nordic soul for an international screen audience, but that darkness was on the inside; most of Bergman's films were shot in summer sunshine outdoors, the only way his cameras could get sufficient light and the only time Swedish actors employed by state theatres were free to film. In the late 1990s, the Danish film directors Lars von Trier and Thomas Vinterberg gained recognition for their literal production techniques referred to as Dogma 95. But those techniques were only dreamed up to embroil cinemagoers more deeply in the maelstroms of personality disorder, sexual abuse and torpedoing angst that are the films' subjects. Three of von Trier's subsequent films have already been converted into operas, a testament to their huge dramatic tension, ripe with musical potential. The director's own staging of Wagner's *Der Ring des Nibelungen* would have been seen at the Bayreuth Festival in the 2000s, had his concept not been pulled at the last minute. It was literally deemed too dark.[1]

Plenty had been there before. For over two centuries, Hans Christian Andersen's fairytales have acquainted Danish children with the inevitability of unfairness, inequality, lost innocence and sexual frustration. The *Kalevala* has been telling of violent tragedy in Finland for far longer. In Norway and Sweden, the playwrights Ibsen and Strindberg often echoed the Icelandic sagas, in which human pain is projected back into the mind of the reciter – where, in a telling anticipation of postmodernism, the audience must fill in the blanks when told of a character whose 'eyebrows hang low'. Strindberg's newfangled Intima Teater (Intimate Theater) insisted audiences and performers be immersed in the emotional horror of a play for cleansing and bettering effect.[2]

One of Strindberg's favourite tricks was to make extensive use of that trusty dramatic device, silence. He injected it judiciously into his scripts much as Sibelius did in his music. 'In silence, you can't hide anything,' says a character in Strindberg's *The Ghost Sonata*, the story of a strange, rotting abode whose inhabitants bask in their own misfortune but have little desire to talk about it. Sibelius knew Strindberg's comment was even truer in music than in conversation, but that didn't stop him deploying silence strategically in both contexts. When asked clumsily about the meaning of a symphony, the composer was prone not to answer at all, letting the silence speak for itself.

After the last of Sibelius's symphonies had resounded in Lahti, I found myself at a drinks reception standing next to the man who had just conducted it, Okko Kamu. 'Does this orchestra bring something special to Sibelius, would you say?' I asked him crudely in a moment of panic. 'Yes,' he replied after a pause, before returning his gaze to his wine glass. Never ask a Finn a polar question.

◢

In 2019, the so-called 'Lost Wallet Test' placed Helsinki at the top of sixteen world cities, ranked according to how likely its citizens were to turn in a wallet full of cash rather than pocket it for themselves. The test prompted a flurry of pseudo-psychological articles on Finnish honesty, one even carried by BBC News.

A blunt survey it may have been, but Finland's poll-position in the honesty stakes reveals a great deal about the country's communicative habits. Conversation doesn't always flow in Finland as it does elsewhere in the world, nor in Sweden. But this tendency towards inter-conversational silence could be interpreted as an honest manifestation of the fact that, for most people and for most minutes of the day, there is actually very little to be said. Small talk, not silence, is fundamentally dishonest – a hunt for unnecessary information that contravenes the strong Finnish–Swedish tradition of propriety.

A better way to think of conversational silence in Finland and Sweden, and across the Nordic region to a lesser degree, is to consider it the natural state of communicative comfort – the centre of gravity. In the sauna, silence rules until the emergence of something deemed worthy of breaking it, which in turn encourages a greater imperative to listen, a skill not in short supply in Finland. Riding the silence that can permeate even a business lunch in the country can take some getting used to. Doing so can be a liberating exercise for non-Finns raised on the principle that silence is socially unacceptable. In terms of physical and mental discipline, it is almost comparable to mastering a breathing exercise or a martial art.

Silence is prevalent in the most sparsely populated countries in continental Europe. But the silence here, in climates prone to acoustically dampening snow and in landscapes strewn with tall forests, is all its own. 'I have long been interested in this,' the German composer Sid Hille told me in 2015, reflecting on three decades living in Finland. 'I first went to Lapland in the winter of 1995. I was in the middle of the forest, where the snow was reflecting what little light there was, and there was a complete and utter silence. I cannot imagine that it doesn't influence a person.'

A native journalist once noted that the average Finn's ideal home is one from which no neighbours can be seen. Across the whole of the Scandinavian peninsula from Bergen to Inari, the desire to put as much space as possible between oneself and one's fellow man persists, even through an acknowledgment of the often painful loneliness it engenders. The saxophonist Jan Garbarek has compared the Norwegian herding calls known as 'kulning' to 'the cry of a lonely person with no one to speak to'. And yet, outside the Nordic city even more than inside it, speaking to a stranger can feel as intrusive as touching them. All must have the right to silence and solitude. But all must learn to confront it.

Before the technical and emotional breakthrough of the Fifth Symphony, Sibelius was in the wilderness. In 1908, he had been forced onto the operating table several times, where surgeons successfully removed a tumour from his throat. As a result, he was ordered to forgo his two most steadfast companions, alcohol and tobacco. Both had been doing a good job of distracting him from colossal debts.

In the wake of all this, Sibelius set forth for Koli, one of the few significant peaks in Finland whose treeless summit of white quartzite looks out over an archetypical patchwork of lakes and forests. The visit took place in early autumn, just as the light of summer was transitioning into something cooler and sharper. With fog and snow, it most likely made for quite an atmosphere, a permeating whiteness underpinned by a luminous glow. The composer's diary entries from the time of the trip are full of dark concerns and depressive rants. But Sibelius didn't head to Koli to counteract his bleak mood. He went there to make sense of it.

The experience produced the composer's Symphony No. 4, famously compared to a pencil sketch in contrast to the variegated oils and watercolours of its European counterparts. It is an elusive masterpiece that struggles to sustain symphonic momentum and breaks down, time and again, into a silence that lays Sibelius's emotions bare. What music we do hear is ranged as if out of reach, echoing and glinting here and there, moving at unquantifiable speeds – wholly intangible. Like menial tasks in the depths of a Nordic winter, many of the symphony's gestures seem to take twice as long as they should. Uniquely in the history of the symphony up to that point, this one doesn't frolic in final triumph or settle into hallowed sleep. It simply disappears. Like a character in one of Ibsen's plays, it gets lost in the enveloping whiteness. Suddenly, the symphony is no longer there.

Silence had been used dramatically in music before. Handel and Beethoven deployed it strategically to make their audience hold its breath: a silence charged by rhythmic emphases carried through suddenly empty bars, like test-dummies in a crashing car. Tchaikovsky embedded silences deep in his symphonies as glances into the abyss. But in Sibelius's Fourth, the emptiness is more pervasive – as if only the silence can tell it like it is. Strindberg knew about that and was writing it into the *Ghost Sonata* at precisely the time Sibelius was breathing it into his radically conceived symphony. Painters were attempting the visual equivalent. The Swede Richard Bergh captured it in oils in his 1893 canvas *Silence*, a foreboding glimpse of an empty graveyard in front of a uniform rank of trees. 'In the North,' said Bergh, 'art is not a product of happiness, it is a product of longing.'

Some years before Sibelius's trip to Koli, his brother-in-law, the painter Eero Järnefelt, had travelled to the same spot. While there, Järnefelt wrote of landscape painting's hold on the emotions: 'joy, angst, hatred'. Other Nordic painters of the period had celebrated solitude and loneliness in their work: the individual in the awe-inspiring landscape, the painter as explorer on the threshold of danger. One of them turned the process on its head. Edvard Munch once proclaimed that 'The angels of fear, sorrow and death have stood by my side since the day I was born.' In his paintings, he swivelled 180 degrees from the orthodoxy of National Romanticism's confident outward gaze, turning subject into object in an obvious parallel to Sibelius's suddenly introverted symphonies. In the foreground of his forbidding landscapes, Munch painted the souls lost in them. In an increasingly urban Norway, he noticed that his countrymen no longer needed to head for the wildernesses to feel alone. The loneliness of the city was infinitely more painful.

▲

On my last night in Lahti, the bright lights of the metropolis beckoned – all three of them. On the large decked terrace of a sports bar, an American colleague and I got talking to a man of a similar age, Jussi, who despite declaring no knowledge of classical music whatsoever was keen to tell us precisely how the Lahti Symphony Orchestra had achieved greatness under its former chief conductor Osmo Vänskä. His thinning hair waxed upwards, Jussi sported a goatee beard and stereo earrings. I began to suspect he had a good ear when he demonstrated an assortment of British regional accents with astonishing accuracy, claiming to have learned them while gaming online.

His tongue lubricated by alcohol, Jussi did a good impression of a motormouth. He and his two female friends appeared to know everyone else in the establishment but were apparently happy enough talking to us. 'I don't like the city,' said the otherwise worldly Jussi early on in our conversation. 'Helsinki is big and impersonal; I would admit, it actually scares me.' After a fifth beer, by which time his two friends had moved on to an apartment party and my American colleague had called it a night, Jussi slowed the tempo of his chatter and began to describe his wooden hut some 20 kilometres away by the side of Lake Kutajärvi. He talked of the smell of the trees, the need for silence and solitude and of the physical and mental demands his little hut placed on him. 'It is where I go to feel my brain working as it was designed to,' he said.

'And what do you do there?'

'Hmm . . . nothing much.'

The readiness with which Finns (and to a comparable degree, Norwegians) will up sticks to escape the city has to be seen to be believed. It very nearly straddles the entire year but comes into its own from April to November. On Friday afternoons, flotillas of boats head off from coastal towns in search of uninhabited archipelago islands on which their owners can camp out for the night, first come first served. Many are furnished with jetties and barbecue equipment for the purpose. Some Finns will head for their own island or lakeside huts and summerhouses. Very little will stop them making the journey there. The prospect of enduring cold weather, rain, mosquitos and impatient children supposedly trumps that of staying put in warm houses and apartments contaminated by the hum of the city. 'We have not been an urban culture for very long,' responded the conductor Esa-Pekka Salonen in 2017 to my question on the subject, justifying the urge.

When Jussi went to fetch yet another round of drinks, I used the isolating hubbub of the bar to try to imagine the silence of his lakeside hideaway. Even within reach of Lahti, the quietness would have been heavy indeed, the sort that Andrew Brown describes, in *Fishing in Utopia*, as inducing 'a concussion that persists for three or four days'. I sensed it at my hut in Kaukonen during Silence Festival, alongside the particularly Finnish feeling that when your little patch of the planet is at its quietest, you have the clearest impression of not quite being alone in it. Jussi's experience seemed uncannily redolent of the Finnish novel I was reading at the time, Arto Paasilinna's *The*

Year of the Hare. It describes a journalist accidentally injuring a hare on the road while driving to an assignment. He takes the animal into his care, but instead of ferrying it back to the city, heads with it into the wilderness for a new, more organic and more fantastical life.

Finns and Norwegians may be its most uncompromising exponents, but the niggling need for silence and isolation is a pan-Nordic phenomenon. The idea of being taken into nature, more than simply reflecting or describing it, resounds through whole swathes of music from the Nordic and Baltic countries and is not confined by genre or epoch. In 2020, the Faroese DJ Janus Rasmussen was nominated for the Nordic Council Music Prize for his album of electronic dance music *Vín*, an organically mixed, cumulatively complex tapestry that Rasmussen claimed was shaped by weeks in a hut in Iceland and the nature that surrounded it. The more you listen to *Vín*, the more the paraphernalia of technology with which it was created floats away – just as the urban contraption that is the symphony orchestra dissipates when it curls around itself to reflect the same curious landscapes in Anna Thorvaldsdottir's tone poems.

▲

The Nordic region's fierce resistance to the habits of the metropolis explains, in part, why its cities are so determinedly clean, quiet, efficient, frequently devoid of human life and increasingly filled with nature-inspired architecture. Shortly after I moved to the Copenhagen district of Frederiksberg in 2018, its council declared that every occupied residential room within its boundaries must have a view of a tree. That same year, another Frederiksberg resident became the second Dane in as many years to win the unofficial Nobel Prize for composition, the University of Louisville's Grawemeyer Award. It was given to Bent Sørensen for his concerto for three instruments and orchestra, *L'isola della città* ('The Island in the City').[3]

I first encountered Sørensen's music in Trondheim, at the unveiling of his 2010 accordion concerto, *It Is Pain Flowing Down Slowly on a*

White Wall. Sørensen's works consistently look to unfasten themselves from the pressures of existence, to slip their moorings and drift away. His music floats and percolates of its own accord, haunted by remembrances of things past, dragged down by the weight of its own sorrow. 'From the moment we are born, there is one way – a slow slippage into decline,' the composer commented in the mid 1990s when his violin concerto *Sterbende Gärten* was first performed. He likes to remind journalists that the comment is decades old. But it could feasibly preface almost every work he has written since. And yet, despite its extreme emotional fragility, Sørensen's music is that of pure aesthetic indulgence, crammed with as much beauty as is tastefully possible. 'I suppose I am afraid of my music disappearing,' he told me in 2017. 'I often get a terrible sorrow after it is played.'

It's easy to relate to those words when listening to Sørensen's music. Much of it has a habit of finding solace just when it's too late. In his Trumpet Concerto, the trumpet discovers its full voice after the piece has effectively finished. In his concerto for piano and orchestra *La Mattina*, the piano tries to sing out the Bach chorale 'Ich ruf' zu dir, Herr Jesu Christ' but can only find the confidence to do so, for eight seconds, just as the curtain falls.

Silence is the aesthetic basis for most of Sørensen's works, the 'white wall' that becomes increasingly dominant as his narratives dissolve or, occasionally, resolve. Sometimes a Sørensen score will instruct an entire symphony orchestra to lay down its instruments and hum quietly together. Sometimes it will ask an entire orchestra to walk off stage, musician by musician, until only the first violinist and conductor remain. The first piece the composer wrote for Jean Nouvel's new vineyard-style concert hall in Copenhagen, *Sounds Like You*, is a sound-play on the theme of an individual joining a tightly packed, all-seeing concert audience and feeling a crushing, horrifying loneliness sat among it.

I first met Sørensen in an apartment just off Copenhagen's main square, Kongens Nytorv, on a hot day in 2016. Some years later I learned that this apartment, once occupied by Leif Ove Andsnes, was 'the island in the city' to which the composer's award-winning triple concerto refers. High up on a narrow Parisian-style street, it was an oasis of calm from whose solitary balcony Sørensen and his wife Katrine Gislinge could observe pedestrians below, weaving around one another like the voices of the Beethoven fugue that drifts in and out of earshot in 'The Island in the City'.

The concept of a throbbing metropolis surrounding a quiet space – almost inaudible, almost invisible – is reflected in the concerto's configuration. A large orchestra lies dormant, making hardly any noise but clearly signalling its ability to overwhelm the trio of soloists like a tsunami, though of course it never does. Foreground activity is mostly confined to the violin, cello and piano soloists. That trio finally gets to play a consonant chord, a simple G minor triad, just as the concerto evaporates.

As he prepared to accept the Grawemeyer Award, I asked Sørensen what he planned to do with the US$100,000 prize money. He would, he told me, purchase an actual island in the city: a soundproofed workshop where he could compose while Gislinge, a pianist, could practice at home or vice versa. He had long since moved back into town after an experimental period in the countryside. 'When I moved to the country people presumed it would be very inspiring. But that's ridiculous because the inspiration is inside,' the composer told me in a bustling Copenhagen café. 'The inner soul of the music is the same. You get a light from something.'

Over the course of a series of conversations with Sørensen, I tried to get to the source of that light – not easy in the company of a composer whose demeanour feels entirely at one with his music, but whose words protest to the contrary. 'I never really felt like a churchyard Romantic, a gothic composer,' he said during the conversation in the café, referring to some much-reproduced descriptions of his work. 'I wasn't depressed, that was just my style. Some pieces have a sadness because they're . . .' he trailed off and his eyes sank, '. . . sometimes in music it's hard to reconcile sadness, sorrow and so on with beauty. Because the way you describe sadness *is* with beauty.' We discussed the words 'decay' and 'disintegration', often used to describe his music. 'We've just spent four weeks in Italy. What would Italy be without decay? Decay is so beautiful, so human.'

Outsiders can be wrong-footed by the Scandinavian people's pervasive acceptance of melancholy. 'While it might be said that the Englishman takes his pleasure sadly, the Scandinavian takes his sadness pleasurably,' wrote the American historian Daniel Kilham Dodge in his 1911 article 'Scandinavian Character and Scandinavian Music'. Little, arguably, has changed. In a part of the world where getting, spending, succeeding and manipulating are yet to entirely eclipse some sense of a deeper meaning to life, folk tend to accept a broader range of moods beyond those which semaphore 'success'. Besides, social democracy's institutionalization of human kindness removes the need to worry about material extremes anyway. You won't fall into poverty given strong societal safety nets and there's not much point amassing extreme wealth, as you'll give the majority of it back in tax. Like the financially comfortable Kirkegaard before them, all modern Scandinavians are left to worry about are the fundamental questions of existence.

Meanwhile, the more pronounced changes in weather and light from season to season appear to suggest to Nordic folk that a full cycle of moods is entirely rational; that those moods can be compartmentalized and even indulged. 'We are very good at accepting darkness,' the Danish music journalist turned orchestra manager Trine Boje Mortensen said during an open discussion on the subject of Nordic music in 2018. 'Musically, aesthetically, we find it totally acceptable to be in one mood for a whole piece – you don't have to change.'

Dwight Eisenhower failed to see the benefits when he went on the rampage against Nordic social democracy. The sometime President of the United States linked the politics of the region to soaring suicide rates in 1960s Sweden and Denmark, suggesting the taking of one's own life could only be expected in countries where the individual's right to freedom and initiative had long since been waived. In the second decade of the twenty-first century, suicide in the Nordic region appears to be back under control, though it remains easy to comprehend how it might have soared in the years immediately before. As Kierkegaard posited, the fear of falling off a cliff is nothing compared to the fear that you might jump, a state of mind only antagonized by the Lutheran and linguistic condemnation of the act not just as the sin of self-killing but that of self-murder ('selvmord').

Centuries ago, Lutheran music rooted itself in the principles of penance, suffering and considered spirituality. Even in the grandest Lutheran churches at the height of the Baroque, musical exuberance was occasional and contained – heard only in stern rhythmic gameplay or slim ribbons of brass fluttered over the summit of a score by rudimentary instruments with a narrow choice of notes. Before Bach, the Swedish-Danish composer Dietrich Buxtehude had prepared the ground with cantatas pious, frugal and resolutely whole-grain. Common to many were the hymn tunes or 'chorales' that formed Lutheranism's musical DNA, as savoury and reassuring as the deep brown wood that furnishes so many Nordic churches. Naturally, chorales were bound by the strictest of musical rules.

Just as the Nordic region has proved all too ready to supplant theological Lutheranism with its economic and social equivalents, the chorale has taken on its own set of secular but largely positive values. It has come to represent the non-denominational sound of solidarity and fortitude, one loaded with an acknowledgment that something bigger exists to bind us together, however divergent our definition of it. Luther may well have initiated this desanctifying of the once sacred when he pointed to nature as the most obvious manifestation of God's work, without imagining God might one day be airbrushed out of the picture. The most significant elements of Lutheranism's legacy these days are secular. The chorale continues to underpin the language of European music from Eurovision to the BBC Proms. In the Nordic countries, it has its own distinct significance.

Much of Abba's output thrives on the harmonic sorrow and satisfaction of the Lutheran chorale, foregrounded most obviously in the opening call-and-response of 'Lay All Your Love On Me'. The striving, hymn-like tunes that emerge towards the end of almost every one of Sibelius's symphonies use the same vertical, harmonic, chorale-derived form. Nielsen wrote his own hymns, tailoring them for a new Danish hymnal before embedding them into concert works. The composer's Wind Quintet uses his own stoic tune for the hymn 'Min Jesus, lad mit hjerte få' in its last movement, subjecting the tune and its beautifully austere and characteristically Danish harmonization to a set of variations.[4] Nielsen effectively coopted the thrust of his own most famous, pithy, popular and overtly socialist song 'Jens Vejmand' ('Jens the Road-Mender') for the final movement of his *Sinfonia Espansiva*. But it's notable how many, including the British composer Julian Anderson, have also heard allusions to that song in Nielsen's most brittle and incendiary symphony, No. 5.[5]

Bent Sørensen hides Lutheran chorales in his works, drawing back the disguise now and then to offer momentary glimpses of them – the fleeting feeling that yes, all shall be well. His erstwhile pupil Christian Winther Christensen, in music even quieter and more calligraphic, does much the same but with a tendency to make you laugh more than cry, despite his music's unspeakable fragility and tenderness. In Iceland, Daníel Bjarnason has made a speciality of burying bits and pieces of chorales deep in his music, marshalling the orchestra, like a giant octopus archaeologist, in the rediscovery and reconstruction of them. The effect is of music that feels somehow anchored, pulled with a centrifugal certainty back to something ordered and totemic. Bjarnason's 2019 piece for the centenary of the Los Angeles Philharmonic, *From Space I Saw Earth*, has bits of a chorale move at three autonomous speeds across three divisions of the orchestra that dock into one another at pivotal junctions. When the pieces click into position, the earth's rotation seems to fall back onto its rightful axis.

It wouldn't work were the chorale not so embedded in the aural consciousness of all sorts of Europeans, courtesy of their respective national anthems. Most of these anthems, learned by children and presented ceremonially at major sporting events, are chorale tunes harmonized by the book. In the Nordic region they are unanimously so, but the sentiments of their lyrics reveal a good deal about national psyche all the same. 'Eternity's flower, with its homage of tears, reverently passes away,' sing the Icelanders. 'Although things looked dark, after all the fights our fathers fought and tears our mothers wept, we won our rights,' sing the Norwegians. 'We have no rising hill, no mountain grand and no northern beach, yet still we love this land,' offer the Finns with characteristic pragmatism. The once-imperial Swedes and Danes focus on environmental beauty, the latter seeing no reason to highlight the fact that, like the Finns, they have no mountains either.

There is something of the melancholic vulnerability cited as endemic, by Norwegian musicians in particular, in these anthems. There is even more so in the Danish–Norwegian youth movement song 'Til Ungdommen' ('To The Youth'). The song's long text, draped over a stern minor-key tune by Otto Mortensen, talks of resolve in times of hardship and determination when all seems lost. It is this piece of music, not a triumphant proclamation of national superiority or even individual positivity, to which Norwegians are drawn in times of crisis. When the country's former Prime Minister Jens Stoltenberg appeared on the BBC's Desert Island Discs in 2020, he chose 'Til Ungdommen' as the one record he would cherish over all others.

◢

While their Nordic counterparts battle with the burden of existence, Norway's composers are saddled with the predicament of existing specifically as Norwegians. In 2014 the unfailingly hip Ultima Festival of Contemporary Music in Oslo chose 'The Nation' as its theme. 'Being a composer in Norway has also meant taking a position on the meaning of "Norwegian",' wrote the festival's artistic director, Lars Petter Hagen, in his introduction to the festivities. He continued: 'a universal issue that touches the core of making music, and of being an artist today, is an attempt to understand who we are. It is far from being a distinctly Norwegian project.'

Perhaps not. But there is no nation on earth whose composers remain so preoccupied with the idea of national identity while at the same time distilling such progressive music from it. That could only happen in non-EU Norway, where more than a century after Norwegian independence the biggest topic of national conversation remains Norwegian independence. One composer, Ørjan Matre, has made something of a speciality out of reimagining iconic chunks of Norwegian musical history. His rewrite of a handful of Grieg's 'Lyric Pieces' short-circuits the thorny issue of nostalgia by homing in on elements of Grieg's own musicianship that have been airbrushed out of the picture for convenience: his music's layers of meaning, its strange colouring, the composer's very precise way of toying with speed in his own piano performances.

In a different corner of the same arena, Lars Petter Hagen's own music appears to be engrossed in the spectacle of an entire epoch slipping from memory, not so much railing against that process as exploiting its melancholic residue for deeper reflection. If there was any doubt that Hagen's 2013 album with the Oslo Philharmonic was determined to address Norwegian nationalism past as well as present, it was there on the cover: an image of a typical Norwegian wooden hut in picture-gallery red with white trim, perched in the snow. On closer inspection it turns out to be a kebab shop. The music encased within plays with distance, memory and the whole idea of Norway in sound – Grieg's favourite subjects. A piece called 'Norwegian Archives' presents old hymn tunes, nature images, funeral marches and even cattle noises as follies. A concerto for Hardanger fiddle pits the instrument's distinctively zingy tuning system against a clean modern symphony orchestra and bleeping electronics. The distance is palpable but the music is cutting.

The new nationalism of the European far right sustains itself on images of countries that never really existed, and with particular relish in predominantly white, traditional Scandinavia and Finland. Hagen's music affectionately teases and undermines that position by examining Norway's burdens of history (short) and tradition (often constructed) while also telling you how important those things are to him, to all Norwegians and indeed to anyone who has a soft spot for the country. His music's in-built sense of loss is that experienced by every generation of Norwegians after Grieg's, something amplified by the drama of the country's landscapes, even for foreigners. While Matre U-turns back into Grieg's world for reappraisal, Hagen picks up where the composer left off, leading his listeners into a forest of fantasies. In the vocal work *Lament*, Hagen maroons us in the dead space between a choir's painfully spread harmonies and a murmuring undertow fusing percussion and electronics – the loneliness of Grieg's *Four Psalms* rerendered for the twenty-first century.

There are more Grieg-like distancing tricks in Hagen's *Norwegian Archives*. Whole passages sound as though they might have been produced by age-old instruments left dangling in trees, played only by the wind. 'Melancholy is a reflective attitude to life, an active response to something,' said the composer in conversation with his colleague Eivind Buene in 2015, acknowledging, like Sørensen, the power of that emotion as a positive creative force: 'it is not about sadness and depression, but about the realization of finality; you know you are going to die, and accepting the fact is the only way to relate to life.'

Norwegians have been faced with pressing and disorientating quandaries since they gained independence. Their country had to confront the prospect of a rapidly globalizing world just as it was consolidating its own sense of itself. Norway became so rich so quickly that it had to import an entire working class, before coming to terms with the fact that its riches were wrought from a finite natural resource that is now tainted. The tragedy of 22 July 2011, when the terrorist Anders Breivik killed seventy-seven Norwegians with a bomb in Oslo and a gun rampage on the island of Utøya while dressed as a police officer, has led Norwegians to re-evaluate their gloriously naïve but perfectly workable sense of trust in each other. Hagen's music poses parallel questions in non-nationalistic terms. On one level the focus of his love, the thing he cares most about, is purely musical: a shapely tune, a beautiful harmony, a distinct timbre. But he knows the only way to counteract man's hopeless urge to preserve is actually to reinvent.

Hagen's music has plenteous implications outside Norway, not least for the wider cultural project that is western classical music. His piece *The Artist's Despair Before the Grandeur of Ancient Ruins* appears to put the current incarnation of that music's so-called 'tradition' in the dock. It ends as a percussionist bashes out the famous kettledrum strokes from the opening of Richard Strauss's *Also Sprach Zarathustra*, against what the critic Tim Rutherford-Johnson has memorably described as the 'tinnitus' of high strings and a farting contrabassoon. It's a resonant moment for anyone who has felt themselves caught in the classical music tradition's slipstream. But it is freighted with extra meaning in Norway, a country whose classical music infrastructure is maturing just about now, well over a century after most of Europe's.

Relistening to that passage, which seems to clasp its hands over its own ears, took me back to a conversation in 2019 with the superstar Norwegian soprano Lise Davidsen. 'I may have been developing very fast since we last met,' she said in a Copenhagen café, referring to her voice as well as her career, speaking just a few months before her debut at the Bayreuth Festival. 'It might look like it's all been going one way. But sometimes I feel as though I want to creep back to my cottage and not exist.' In Norway, it has all happened so very quickly.

Two years before Bent Sørensen won the Grawemeyer Award, the prize went to another Danish composer for whom writing music could be interpreted as an escape from the brutalities of life. In the 1970s and into the 1980s, Hans Abrahamsen's scores slotted neatly enough into the style associated with the European avant-garde, mostly disappearing unnoticed because of it. From an austere basis, his music became gradually more overwrought until, in his own words, 'I couldn't find the right tools ... the right words to speak.' Abrahamsen had tried to maintain an essence of simplicity in his music but it wasn't working. So he gave up, and spent a decade rearranging music by Bach, Schumann, Nielsen and Debussy.

Doing so allowed Abrahamsen to make sense of the roadblock he'd got to before. 'When I started [writing] again, my music became, on one level, much more complicated but on another level much more simple,' he told me. The key to his resumption was a series of seven instrumental canons by Johann Sebastian Bach, works in which two or more instruments are braided together using the same tune but voiced at staggered intervals. 'I became totally absorbed ... and arranged them with the intention of the music being repeated many, many times as a kind of minimal music,' wrote Abrahamsen in his own essay on the work he finished in 2008 as a reaction: *Schnee* ('Snow').

Like a picture book, *Schnee* consists of ten canons in pairs, in which the two canons of each pair form the mirror image of one other. As the hour-long work proceeds, the pairs get shorter – from eight minutes to one minute – a crystalizing of the subliminal arithmetic that allows the piece to unravel into silence. As in a snowflake, complex mathematics serve aesthetic beauty. And as in Bach's *Goldberg Variations*, you don't need to know the science behind the sounds to appreciate the arching form they create. Abrahamsen instructs the pianos, strings and woodwinds of *Schnee* to play with a pure, clean tone stripped of warming vibrato – one of the methods by which he leads us to feel the essence of snow and some emotional sense of it. The limited tone colours create a sound the composer has described as 'white polyphony', but it is a sound steadily discoloured by the detuning of certain instruments. Some snow doesn't stay white for long.

Schnee was Abrahamsen's tabula rasa. It rebooted his creativity and the majority of the music he has written since bears an umbilical connection to the piece. 'When I was very young it was my goal to write music that was completely unexpressive: just a white page, a simple piece on the piano,' the composer told me in 2019 in the kitchen of his bungalow outside Lyngby, north of Copenhagen. In *Schnee*, he had worked out how to do it.

The first major work that followed was that which won the 2016 Grawemeyer Award. In *Let Me Tell You*, Shakespeare's words for *Hamlet*'s Ophelia are rearranged by the writer Paul Griffiths to open a new window onto the character's soul, sung by a soprano impersonating Ophelia accompanied by a large orchestra. It opens with the twisting melody of *Schnee*'s Canon 1b – a preliminary purification. From there, *Let Me Tell You* opens up, a showpiece that isn't a showpiece; a product of extraordinary subtlety and relentless focus in which an elasticated soprano and anti-gravitational orchestra move through space and time as if telepathically linked.

Underpinning much of the score to *Let Me Tell You*, its precise geometric footprint included, are the miniature overlapping canons of *Schnee*. Finally, echoing Sibelius's Symphony No. 4, Ophelia disappears into the enveloping whiteness of snow. 'I will go on,' she sings, to the sound of sheets of paper being rubbed on the skin of a bass drum (another device lifted from *Schnee*). For Abrahamsen, snow is a technical guide. But it is also, to some extent, an escape back into childhood, to the Denmark of decades ago when serious winter snowfalls were inevitable. Stymied by all the colour and confusion of the modern world, Abrahamsen's feeling for snow was his refuge.

As he worked on *Let Me Tell You* in 2013, the composer was asked by the Royal Danish Theatre to consider writing a full-length work for its opera company. The two parties came to an arrangement within minutes: the theatre would commission Abrahamsen's first opera, the telling of a Hans Christian Andersen fairytale in which the girl Gerda journeys through multiple trials to rescue her friend Kai from the clutches of the Snow Queen and thaw his heart. Discussing the opera a few weeks before it opened in 2019, Abrahamsen compared himself to the character of Kai, who is drawn to the crystalline perfection of the Snow Queen's domain as much as he senses his need to escape from it. 'He is an artist, like Thomas Mann, not taking part in real life,' the composer said of Kai. 'That is why I have been so taken with the story: I recognize so many things about myself.' An unassuming, hesitant but demure man, Abrahamsen is as outwardly accommodating as he is internally strong-willed.

Weeks before the first performance of *The Snow Queen*, the assembled music critics of the *Guardian* newspaper in London voted *Let Me Tell You* the finest piece of classical music written so far this century. But the opera that followed wrong-footed many when it was seen later that year in Copenhagen and Munich. Cold and sparse, the music lays its mathematical foundations bare in an unapologetic, icicle-clear depiction of the Snow Queen's realm of precision and calculation. Kai's music increases in fluidity and range as the character comes to terms with love, maturity and the task at hand. Abrahamsen's finely calibrated systems operate imperceptibly underneath all the while.

When Kai manages to form the Snow Queen's ice letters into the word 'Eternity', the music blossoms momentarily. As Kai and Gerda grow old in the final scene and summer finally arrives, radiance floods the score even as it sticks resolutely to the Snow Queen's regimental tick-tocking. 'You can make perfect structures, and *Schnee* is the perfect construction from which *The Snow Queen* comes,' Abrahamsen told me. 'But in the end, it's about finding your inner child.'

Eleven years after nature flew to the rescue of Sibelius's Symphony No. 5, his orchestral tone poem *Tapiola* must have sounded altogether more equivocal, its view of man's relationship to the natural world more ominous. The title refers to the mythical god of Finland's forests. But even if the work is more figurative than literal – the forest of the mind referred to by the writer Alex Ross, the animal inside all of us for the Finnish conductor Hannu Lintu – its power and instability border on the terrifying. 'No one but a Norseman could have written this work,' concluded the German-born American who commissioned it, Walter Damrosch.

Tapiola speaks of the precarious balance of a mind teetering on the edge of order, of a life lived at the mercy of nature's procedures. Events, the piece suggests, are well beyond human control. Sure, things turn out rosy when that final B major chord arrives to protect us from malign forces like the fur coat of Finnish forest proverb. But it could so easily have gone the other way. The technical miracle of *Tapiola* is that the music seems to roll out of itself according to its own laws. For us listeners, it's as though Sibelius were as relieved by the benevolent turn of events as we are.

There was little meaningful music left in the composer after *Tapiola*. A cursory listen to the surviving fragments assumed to be from his destroyed Symphony No. 8, recorded in 2014 by John Storgårds and the BBC Philharmonic, and again in 2021 by Klaus Mäkelä and the Oslo Philharmonic, suggests Sibelius was attempting to pick up some of the sparse, frayed linguistic threads of that piece (and perhaps his experimental music for Shakespeare's *The Tempest*) but was struggling to knit them coherently together – aware, perhaps, that *Tapiola* had assumed the role of a creative farewell by default. The composer's distillation of his voice to the point of actual silence might be seen as music imitating nature, like the self-annihilating canons of Abrahamsen's *Schnee*. Then again, it could just as easily have been the sounds of jazz, tango, newsreel, traffic and the iconoclastic European avant-garde that persuaded Sibelius he had nothing much left to say. Whatever the reasoning, plenty were paying close attention. As the Nordic region's most distinguished musical figure in the middle of the twentieth century, Sibelius's three-decade silence couldn't help but linger.

In 1978, Abrahamsen enacted a musical retreat with a piece of stringent minimalist music titled *Walden*. The title was borrowed from that of Henry David Thoreau's book charting the writer's retreat into a simple life in the woods. Abrahamsen's piece, scored for a classical wind quintet, imposes the composer's usual rigorous procedures on a miniscule amount of material. The result is music that imagines the predictable unpredictability of what you might see, seated in a forest, looking in one direction for a short stretch of time. It represents a classically Nordic act of withdrawal from the industrial world – just the sort portrayed in Paasilinna's *The Year of the Hare*.

For years, Abrahamsen and Sørensen served together on the composition faculty of the Royal Danish Academy of Music in Copenhagen. Their pared-back aesthetic inevitably filtered down into the student body and the general compositional scene, more a result of admiration and proximity than any desire to influence. Allan Gravgaard Madsen, however, studied with neither composer. He was a pupil of Simon Steen-Andersen at the Royal Academy of Music in Aarhus.

Madsen's concerto for violin and piano, *Nachtmusik*, was one of the major Danish premieres of 2019. Its first movement consists of just one pitch. The two movements that follow decrease in duration by a third and then by half, a choreographed process of reverse-distillation which confines most activity and material to the brief and comparatively frenetic final movement. 'I wanted to be loyal to the idea of nothing much happening,' the composer told me after the premiere. Referring to the opening movement, in which the two soloists discuss a single E for fifteen minutes, he said: 'Your senses adjust; you hear both the macro-cosmos and the micro-cosmos.'

As individual as his realization of it might be, Madsen's score conforms to a certain twenty-first-century trend, echoing the New Simplicity movement that took root in Denmark as long ago as the 1960s. You don't have to attend the Nordic Music Days, the annual festival of newly composed music from across the region, to notice the quietness of Abrahamsen, Sørensen and others mutating into a stringent half-silence courtesy of the next generation. Sørensen, who is easy to spot at concerts featuring music by his peers, described it to me as a rite of passage. 'It's the way they find their music,' he said. 'Avoid any kind of melody, avoid any kind of tonality, start to avoid pitches and just make noise, and then have even the noise disappear so you have silence. It is a yogic process: over a very long period of time, cleaning the slate so you have the white paper you need to work on. I have always understood it as a method by which people find their style.'

More and more, like Abrahamsen before them, Danish composers in particular appear to be of the persuasion that the clean slate – the white paper – isn't so much the means as the end: it *is* the style. The Royal Danish Academy of Music's Associate Professor of music history, Søren Schauser, described to me a particularly Danish recoiling from the perceived ugliness of the avant-garde that has seen Abrahamsen assume the status of an emblematic figure – a musical craftsman, like his physical forebear Arne Jacobsen, able to create something intensely modern yet reassuringly beauteous; clean, white, lucid, palatable Danish design given musical form.

At the end of 2019, I ran that idea past Matias Vestergård, a prodigious and poly-stylistic composer who was yet to graduate from the Royal Danish Academy of Music but had already written an opera for the Academy and a ballet for the Royal Danish Theatre. 'It may be that Danish music exists in the flux between "I have to write a piece about snow which is super slow and super quiet" and "I have to write pieces that are like ..."' he said, before making a series of noises imitating flatulence. 'One thing we really hate in Denmark is taking ourselves seriously,' he continued. 'But then, we also kind of dream of being able to take ourselves seriously.'

▲

In London in 2012, I went to a concert in King's Cross which included a landmark piece of Danish modernism, *Plateux pour Deux*. It was written in 1970, by a composer named Pelle Gudmundsen-Holmgreen, for a cello and a set of old-style car horns – the sort operated by large rubber bulbs that blow air through the horn, emitting an abrupt single pitch when squeezed. I wrote about the performance for the *Guardian* newspaper:[6]

> As the cellist bowed her eloquent riffs and the percussionist honked on his squeeze bulbs, two members of the audience began to titter. The titter became a laugh. And the laugh became a guffaw. The more those audience members tried to contain their mirth, the more prominent and hilarious their noises became. Suddenly everyone in the room had no choice but to think hard on what the music they were hearing was trying to do and to consider whether or not the performance could continue with its integrity (or even its fabric) intact. If you've ever been to a self-regarding concert of avant-garde music, you might appreciate just how refreshing that sudden, new atmosphere was.

With his flatulent noises, Vestergård was referring unmistakably to Gudmundsen-Holmgreen, a composer who managed to unite almost every faction of progressive Danish music in mutual admiration. Gudmundsen-Holmgreen took the idea of radical musical simplicity in a wholly original, personal direction. He wrote bracing and refreshing music that applied the instincts of a street-busker to the principles of the avant-garde, in which intense beauty is frequently a by-product. Rarely do his pieces take themselves seriously but plenty become poignant, deeply affecting and highly serious almost by accident. His methods can appear to be pilfered from children or animals. Musical building blocks are stacked indiscriminately on top of one other; solo instruments are forced out onto tightropes; instrumental groups are bound together in unlikely coalitions that writhe and fidget like ferrets in a sack.

All are in evidence on a well-circulated YouTube video of the composer dancing to his own music. That music is *Triptykon*, a score from 1985 that pulls one of Gudmundsen-Holmgreen's classic tricks, whereby the third movement consists of the first two movements played at the same time. To its accompaniment, the composer shuffles and jolts across the floor of his composing room as if on marionette strings. The music you hear is typically impolite, alive with an animalistic heartbeat and an uneven gait, joyously self-destructive. It rejoices in a form of blind liberation that the composer took from his creative hero, the Irish writer Samuel Beckett. 'The catastrophe of meaninglessness has something deeply liberating about it,' said the composer in 1992, outlining the precise effect Beckett's works were having on his own.

I met Gudmundsen-Holmgreen for the first and only time in 2014. It remains the only encounter of its kind I have never felt able to delete from the recording device I use for interviews, which may be connected to the fact that we promised to meet again but were prevented from doing so by the composer's death two years later. Even at the age of 81, he had an energy and spirit that seemed somehow immortal, hopping on his bike at the end of our interview and confidently joining the throngs of cycle traffic on Queen Louise's Bridge.

Before that, we sat in the window of a café overlooking Blågårds Plads and the stone reliefs by Kai Nielsen that line it – a place where Copenhagen is at its most colourful, socially if not architecturally. As we talked about anything but the subject areas listed neatly in my notebook, the conversation turned to a Gudmundsen-Holmgreen work that had just been recorded by the London Sinfonietta, *Run*. I read out a part of the album's liner notes – a detailed, eloquent musicological analysis of what happens in the score by Paul Griffiths. Gudmundsen-Holmgreen responded with his own analysis: 'It's a man running. Maybe he's a man in a condition, who *has* to run. He is being whipped to run. I think actually he's a fat man. Yes: it's a fat man running.'

The composer subsequently confessed his underlying concern that the London Sinfonietta was 'afraid of being in bad company' having agreed to collaborate with him and begun rehearsals for an upcoming concert. What did he mean, specifically? 'The bad manners [in my music] were not easy for them and I did have a suspicion that they would find my music too naïve, too clumsy.' The composer's take on musical simplicity is extreme enough to suggest both those things, even if the music itself invariably communicates something deeper. He once wrote a song cycle setting texts from the business pages of a newspaper. There, as in *Plateaux pour Deux*, the absurd plays second fiddle to an almost physical examination of base relationships – how disparate musical ingredients might find a way to get along. Listen long and hard enough and both pieces reach out in an embrace.

Part of the reason for setting those droll newspaper reports was Gudmundsen-Holmgreen's belief that poetic text has a rhythm and beauty of its own, and thus has no need for obscuring or elaborating music. As a result, he consciously avoided setting poetry or 'meaningful' texts. When he did, he treated their constituent parts like the notes of the scale; examining them from an obtuse angle, chopping sentences and words up to better explore their base sonic qualities, as if the last 500 years of entwined musical and linguistic development never happened.

In the piece titled *Company*, voices struggle to spit out even the smallest verbal building blocks of John Dowland's song 'Flow My Tears', as if choked on the vowels and tripped by the consonants.

When the voices finally manage to sing out the song after ten minutes, it's obscured by accumulated instrumental growth and sent into exile by the wrong key – major instead of minor. The only concession to the material's implied melancholy is a sudden, fleeting focus on one emotionally heavy harmonic suspension. But that disappears almost as soon as it arrives. There is nothing like nostalgia for making you feel alien from both your past and your present, Gudmundsen-Holmgreen could be saying. 'Exiled for ever, let me mourn where night's black bird her sad infamy sings,' goes the poem Dowland set, one he may have written himself. Gudmundsen-Holmgreen makes sure you never hear it.

In 2005, Denmark celebrated 200 years since the birth of Hans Christian Andersen, and not even Gudmundsen-Holmgreen could avoid setting the great storyteller's words to music. For the occasion, he used separate Andersen poems as part of a two-movement work for voice and string quartet, *Moving Still*. The first movement, 'Moving', uses Andersen's poem 'In a Thousand Years' – a prescient premonition of the modern tourist industry, spoken over the top of the score. Andersen's own awkward personage finds synergy in Gudmundsen-Holmgreen's characteristic noises off, cussing and spitting, shuffling and scratching. The second movement, 'Still', changes the mood again. It has a pure, untrained and purposefully non-Danish voice sing the Danish words of Andersen's poem 'I Danmark er jeg født' ('In Denmark I was born'):

> I Danmark er jeg født, der har jeg hjemme
> Der har jeg rod, derfra min verden går
> Du danske sprog, du er min moders stemme
> Så sødt velsignet du mit hjerte når
> Du danske, friske strand, hvor oldtids kæmpegrave
> Står mellem Æblegård og Humlehave
> Dig elsker jeg, elsker jeg, dig elsker jeg
> Danmark, mit fædreland

> In Denmark I was born, 'tis there my home is,
> From there my roots and world extend.
> You Danish tongue, as soft as Mother's voice is,
> With you my heartbeats O so sweetly blend.
> You windswept Danish beach,
> Where ancient chieftains barrow
> Beach close to apple orchard, hop and mallow,
> 'Tis you I love – Denmark, my native land!

The melody, introduced and delicately harmonized by the quartet, acknowledges its antecedent by the Danish composer Poul Schierbeck but is Gudmundsen-Holmgreen's own – proof that he could knock out a tune as lovely as the best of them. It soon starts to occupy a distinctive space. The singer uses a sampler to loop his own voice, creating a vortex of echoes that feed the poem's nostalgic visions back against themselves. Next, the quartet's underlying harmony shifts in style, from Lutheran chorale to Slavic prayer, to boogie-woogie, to the Hassidic and eventually to the Arabic. It only takes a few flattened notes and ragged rhythms here and there, with a touch of elegant ornamentation from the singer, and the ethno-musicologically untrained ear believes it is hearing a quintessentially Arabic song.

The symbolism of Andersen's poem sung to an apparently Arabic melody is obvious almost to the point of being crass. Only compositional cunning means it never becomes so, instead sidling through its various genetic incarnations with a stealthy beauty and a raised eyebrow. 'We live at a time when Danishness has become a theme that arouses malaise and claustrophobia,' wrote Gudmundsen-Holmgreen in the liner notes for the Kronos Quartet's 2008 recording of the work. 'I wanted to draw attention rather rudely to the fact that Danishness is not an immutable entity, but is coloured by innumerable influences from the outside.' In the case of the Englishman Paul Hillier who sang Andersen's poem, the composer suggested his non-Danish accent 'sheds a wry light on the perception of Danishness as something you can only acquire when you are 100% a native Dane' (Hillier has lived in Denmark since 2003 and has a Danish knighthood for services to music). The Arabic qualities, even more, propose that Danishness is not quite black and white.

It was that porous idea of nationality that riled the 'new' nationalists when Gudmundsen-Holmgreen's Andersen tribute was first heard: the idea that humans who weren't born in Denmark could become Danish, yes, but more importantly that something as sacred as a Hans Christian Andersen poem could be so easily siphoned off into another cultural context and even sit quite beautifully there. Just as much as racial prejudice, Gudmundsen-Holmgreen's piece appeared to critique his homeland's often blunt level of debate around the issue, one area in which the enlightened land that is Denmark frequently appears at its most knowingly and obstinately unsophisticated.

'Generally, I think we in Denmark are a little vulgar [in comparison to Sweden],' Gudmundsen-Holmgreen told me when we met. 'We even like to make a virtue out of it.' The bilateral confusion over free speech that separates the two countries illustrates the point. Each week sees dozens of jokes published in Denmark at the expense of Swedish 'political correctness', which is bullishly and crudely viewed by plenty of Danes as an affront to Scandinavian liberalism despite being seen by many others as a blunt tool wielded for the greater humanitarian good. Factions of Danish society like nothing more than to stress-test their own country's fierce protection of free speech by doling out gratuitous offence while letting off prejudicial steam at the same time. If you can't laugh at it, it only proves you're 'not one of us'.

The *Jutland Post*'s printing of cartoons depicting the Prophet Mohammed is one of the more urbane examples. There was no public interest motive for publishing the cartoons; it was done simply to prove a point. Hardly anyone in Denmark would disagree with the principle, but plenty who recognize free speech as a privilege that comes with responsibilities disagreed with the choice to convert that principle into action – action that was always likely to provoke violence. The country's later Minister for Integration, Inger Støjberg, was not among them. A decade after the event, while in office, she hoisted up the newspaper cartoons as her Facebook cover photo. What some saw as politically passive-aggressive, others recognized as emblematic of Denmark's crude struggle to reconcile its enlightenment values with the realities of a respectful, globalized world.

The second movement of Gudmundsen-Holmgreen's *Moving Still* feels like Inger Støjberg's stunt pulled the other way, and with a sharing smile instead of a selfish snarl. It is a deeply touching work for anyone who has felt the challenges of settling in this country: the constant pressure to prove oneself au fait with the social codes; the obligation to wind your neck in lest it protrude beyond the confines of Jantelov; the years you spend earning the right to eye contact around the candlelit table – enduring warm hygge's cold shoulder.

The Nordic region can boast many liberal 'firsts' and was quick to reform in numerous arenas, from the abolition of the death penalty and the introduction of same-sex marriage to the assumption that women can and must lead. In 2014, I attended a performance at the Finnish National Opera conducted by a woman, directed by a woman, commissioned by a female artistic director who reported to a female board chair who oversaw a senior management team that included just one man. 'The most beautiful thing is if you don't have to think about gender anymore,' the artistic director in question, Lilli Paasikivi, told me shortly afterwards. 'We have a history of women in leadership positions, it's just perfectly natural here.' A few years later, Finland would elect a coalition government led entirely by women. But in the field of classical and other forms of non-commercial music, Denmark and Norway have a lamentable record on gender equality when compared to Finland, Sweden and Iceland. With only one obvious exception, all the Danish classical musicians with major international careers are men.

The problem, in still homogenous Nordic countries, is that entrenched ideas of unrelenting social progress have arguably led to complacency and even stubbornness. Brand Scandinavia has spent so long projecting the idea of perfect societies to the rest of the world that its own populations have started to believe there's no more progressing left to be done. Jantelov, by its nature, denounces positive discrimination as a cardinal sin while in western Scandinavia the sanctity of free speech suggests a bit of racist or sexist ribbing over dinner is fair game. Melvin Kakooza's finely observed situation comedy *Sunday*, which fictionally echoes the writer's own journey from Uganda to the Jutland town of Fredericia, can't help but mock the African nation as much as it does small-town Denmark – a neat summary of the egalitarian principle that everyone must take a joke. Whether that joke hurts some more than others is, apparently, beside the point.

Absurdity came in useful for Gudmundsen-Holmgreen, as for Beckett, in making some sense of the torture of his own creative responsibilities. Like Carl Nielsen's, Gudmundsen-Holmgreen's music ingratiates itself downwards, not upwards. 'Sometimes I prefer Nielsen to Brahms, which I know is a ridiculous thing to say,' Gudmundsen-Holmgreen said on Blågårds Plads. 'It's like a very deep brown, mahogany desk in the Ministry of Justice. Brahms is on the right side of the desk – so convincing, so right, so beautiful in his heaviness. Carl Nielsen is on the wrong side: a little out of tune, the naughty boy, not the cleverest in the class but definitely the most inventive. You couldn't confuse him with anyone else.' That makes two of them.

◢

In December 1925, Nielsen's last symphony was first performed, part of nationwide celebrations in Denmark to mark the composer's sixtieth birthday. 'One looks in vain for original, spontaneous inspiration,' wrote a critic on the newspaper *Nationaltidende* of the composer's Symphony No. 6 – a curious conclusion, given those things are precisely what the score appears to contain in abundance.

These days, commentators are more likely to cite the Sixth as Nielsen's unsung masterpiece, perhaps even his truest, most personal symphonic creation. If you have no history with Nielsen or even with 'the symphony' as a musical tradition, the Sixth might just be the most accessible of them all. It's only a curveball if you know what went before; it only ties you up in intellectual knots if you've grown up with symphonic architecture in your head.

For everyone else, the Symphony No. 6 can exist happily as an instrumental show with all the ingredients of a *commedia dell'arte*: jokes, riddles, feigning elegies, lurching contradictions in mood, instruments cast as parodies of themselves. Some contemporary musicologists believed Nielsen's symphony was prophesizing the collapse of meaningful music, particularly in the parody of new aesthetic trends that appears in its second movement, a cheeky 'Humoresque'. More recently, the musicologist Daniel Grimley has argued the opposite: that Nielsen's Sixth is less about demise than about renewal, 'a desire to bring music more vividly into the realm of the lived experience'.[7] If the Sixth was going to resemble a comic strip, clarity and directness would be key. Only the cognoscenti would fail to see the wood for the trees.

Like Gudmundsen-Holmgreen after him, Nielsen had straightforward words to describe his aims in the symphony. 'I have written a contentious movement for small percussion instruments, which bicker and quarrel and get bogged down in their own likings and fancies,' he remarked of the 'Humoresque'. 'I regard the various instruments as persons who lie sleeping whom I have to awaken into life,' he said of the symphony as a whole, which would explain why the instruments of his slimmed-down orchestra adopt such distinct personas.

Nielsen went a step further when describing the score's final movement, and began to reveal the detail behind all those instrumental personas. The music takes the form of a set of variations on a doleful tune, its underlying sadness suggesting the tears of the clowns that have entertained us up to now. As the variations veer from crazed elation to despair, an episode arrives described by the composer as 'death knocking at the gate' (this, deduced Nielsen's friend Thorvald Nielsen, was Variation 11: 'The big drum the knocking; the xylophone bony Death; the deep tuba the black void'). Nielsen corroborated and indeed elaborated: 'But I want to defy death – and then follows the flourish.' The flourish he referred to is a fanfare that could have come straight out of *Tom and Jerry*.

Nielsen was surely blowing a raspberry at his own mortality, just as he sensed it most acutely. At the time, the composer had suffered a number of heart attacks related to his chronic angina. A few days before his heart stopped forever, Nielsen had been backstage at his former workplace, the Royal Theatre in Copenhagen, as its opera company prepared to revive his own opera *Maskarade*. Always up for a caper when the opportunity presented itself, the composer joined a group of stagehands trying to untangle a piece of scenery, proving he was game by climbing up a rope. It was too much for Nielsen's 66-year-old heart. He collapsed and was taken to Copenhagen's Rigshospitalet, where he died a few days later.

There's a famous series of nine photographs of the adolescent Nielsen, taken on a family vacation in the 1880s and quickly thrown up by a Google image search. As Grimley has suggested, these portraits of the composer pulling nine insolent faces are as relevant to the Symphony No. 6's theatre of mimicry as they are to understanding of the composer's worldview more generally. There is anxiety in the Sixth Symphony; the spectres of Nielsen's faltering marriage and his concern for the 'spiritual syphilis' that he concluded, like Gudmundsen-Holmgreen would, lay behind Denmark's increasing nationalism. But the real theme was surely death. And the nearer death got, the more ready the composer seemed to throw up his hands and rejoice in the game of life. You have to laugh, or else you'd cry.

In the assorted disguises and masks of Nielsen's Symphony No. 6, there was a conscious echo of *Maskarade*, an opera that hinges on the themes of decadence, youthful abandon, pervasive equality and the importance of good times in a city where even the town hall bells chime in a minor key. In Denmark, *Maskarade* is presented almost as a national pantomime. It reminds us that the puncturing of authority is necessary for societal progress but also that partying and gameplay – and alcohol – are decent enough tools for survival in the meantime.

▲

Before its many champagne corks are popped, *Maskarade* begins with a hangover – a very Danish placing of the negative consequential cart before the horse. Alcohol is a constant theme in the opera that follows. As Nielsen was recalling it in the score for his Symphony No. 6, Sibelius was at work on what would become *his* last symphony, No. 7. Whisky, not champagne, fuelled Sibelius's nighttime labour on this symphonic last word, which would sound as profound as Nielsen's would impertinent. After numerous themes, schemes and drafts were discarded, Sibelius wiped the slate clean in 1924 and started over. By March he had finished the manuscript, the greatest he would ever write.

Alcohol was prohibited in Finland at the time. Sibelius was taking delivery of contraband hooch courtesy of contacts made through his physician brother, who at the very same time lectured on the dangers of alcoholism at the Imperial Alexander University, perhaps prompted by his father's death from the disease. The composer's justification was that it steadied his shaking hands – allowing him, literally, to commit the notes to the page. As he struggled to find intellectual release from his last and most heavily straining symphonic argument, Sibelius freed himself physically through drink.

Did the composer's boon companion ethyl alcohol play a deeper role in the development of his most fluid symphony? 'Alcohol to intoxicate nerves and mind,' he wrote in his diary in January 1924. His long suffering wife Aino had recently witnessed her husband stop the Gothenburg Symphony Orchestra mid-performance, so drunk he momentarily believed he was conducting not a concert but a rehearsal (that time, it *had* been champagne). The intangible, organic, free-flow rapture of the Symphony No. 7 speaks of the sweet spot of inebriation when usually inaccessible connections and ideas become readily available to the mind; when thematic fluidity, in life as well as art, presents itself with rare clarity. The real reason Sibelius never accepted a major teaching post was that he believed himself unable to rationalize or explain his methods. The best of them seem to have come from the hinterlands of his consciousness.

The morning after a night of slow progress through the symphony and the bottle, Sibelius would be discovered by his wife slumped over his desk. You can still see the desk, in the house the composer had built for himself in the woods and subsequently named after Aino. It now stands as a museum. A removable screen divides the living room in two, a physical reminder of how unequally the burdens of family life were distributed in the Sibelius abode. Aino hadn't the space, substances or creative distractions with which to immunize herself from the pain of infant mortality and the labour of raising a family. Her husband would simply draw closed the screen of his male privilege and pour himself a drink (precious about extraneous noise, he even forbade the installation of running water). In the adjacent room stands the desk. Next to it is the bed on which the composer died.

There was a mournful atmosphere at Ainola on the bleak Sunday in October when I visited. After a while, I managed to extract myself from the group being herded regimentally through the house and sneak outside. The villa and its small complex of associated buildings sit on the edge of a small, ordered patch of the Järvenpää woods, surrounded by unusually tall pine trees. Nearby is Sibelius's grave, covered by a rectangular copper slab on which the composer's name is spelled out in bold, sans-serif capitals. Aino's name, lower case and italicized, sits at the bottom right corner.

As I stood over it, trying to think deeply about Sibelius's life and the meaning of this place, an angry wasp had the same idea and I had to stagger away out of its orbit. I walked a few feet down an incline and looked towards Lake Tuusula, but could hardly make out its surface in the gloom. I found my way to the clearing where Sibelius's old sauna sits. This place felt more real and resonant than anything in the museum, and while inside I managed to shut the world out for a few minutes. Via my phone, I listened to the Hymn of Praise from Sibelius's incidental music to the play *Swanwhite*. It is a beautifully melancholic piece lined with a sense of Finnish resolve and built of repeating, wordless, chorale-like statements of gratitude on which glistening harp and sleigh-bells bestow their benediction. Kettledrums rumble away reassuringly underneath.

In Helsinki that night, I met with a friend in trendy Kallio for a beer. Later we joined a larger group of her friends at a hybrid bar-café serving pizzas. One of them incorporated us in a round of drinks he was buying just as we arrived. Presenting me with a freshly poured pint of gaseous lager as he caressed his own, he invited me, as the foreign guest, to join him in a contest to see which of us could finish our drinks first. The loser would be obliged to buy the next round. Whether through his generosity or my desperation to impress, I beat him by a whisker. That exercise turned out to be a mere hors d'oeuvre, making for a painful flight home the next day.

Contrary to popular belief, Finns are not the biggest drinkers in the world or even in Europe. Most polls put them well below Germany, France, the UK and even Iran, though safely above their Nordic counterparts. What marks Finns out, according to Matti Peltonen of the University of Helsinki's Faculty of Social Sciences, is their pre-eminence when it comes to consuming large quantities of alcohol in short spaces of time.[8] Finns, apparently, are Europe's biggest binge drinkers.

This distinction is replicated to lesser degrees across the Nordic countries. The concept of 'a drink after work' is an alien one in Scandinavia yet, on weekends, towns and cities fill up with locals of all ages who have chosen to cram their weekly alcohol consumption into the space of one evening. According to the 2020 Global Drug

Survey, Danes admitted getting drunk more times in the space of a year than any other nationality except Australians.[9] Norwegians even have a word for weekend binge drinking: 'helgefylla'.

Social drinking in the Nordic countries is rooted in the idea of ritual and ceremony. Binge drinking has adapted with versatility to modern equivalents – confirmations (an alcoholic rite of passage more than a religious one), high-school graduation, weddings, summer feasting and the culture associated with metal music among them. Christmas is elevated with particular relish. On a pre-arranged day in November, Danish breweries release their Christmas Brew ('Julebryg') to a carnival atmosphere of giveaways and street dancing. One television show in December has two presenters and a brewing expert drink a bottle each of 25 varieties of beer until they can barely stand; the footage is then edited into 25 installments broadcast each day up to Christmas. That no country celebrates drinking quite like Denmark was marked beautifully in Thomas Vinterberg's Oscar-winning 2021 film *Another Round* (released in Scandinavia as *Druk*). 'In this country everyone drinks like maniacs,' proclaims the Swedish character Anika in despair, at the apex of her Danish husband Martin's project to supercharge creativity by maintaining consistent blood-alcohol levels throughout the working day – a method that would appear to have worked for Sibelius.

All over the Nordic region, beer constitutes mere refreshment between harder schnapps or aquavit – strong, clear spirits with proud geographical associations, each prominently racked at airports so that tourists might transport them home as cultural souvenirs. In Iceland, beer was illegal until 1989, considered dangerously quaffable – too soft and too Danish – which only raised the status of the local liquor, Brennivín. The subject of drink and drinking was the single most returned-to conversation topic during my time at two state-affiliated language schools in Copenhagen, with the same press cuttings and survey results projected onto whiteboards for student discussion.

Alcohol does its own decent job of tracing the fault lines along which the related cultures of the Nordic nations diverge. Denmark is the liberal Gomorrah, where the word for 'tip' is literally 'drinking money', where school children are all but encouraged to fill themselves with beer in their mid teens (they can buy it legally at 16) and draw their own rational action-consequence conclusions from the process. At the other end of the spectrum, Sweden upholds the old temperate values: outside bars and restaurants, serious alcohol (wine upwards) is available to purchase at restricted times from government-owned stores that have only recently shed the atmosphere of needle exchanges. Finland operates similar but less stringent rules, whose effect in tempering the country's generally extreme attitude to consumption in all forms is negligible. Norway follows Denmark's model with increasingly less restraint. Iceland and the Faroe Islands are only just past viewing alcohol as medicine or something used to mask the foul taste of rotten fish.

Binge drinking, unsurprisingly, straddles these regional variations. It is both an expression of self-control and a release from it, a discipline nurtured through centuries of seafaring. In Finland, binge drinking is only exacerbated by the collective neurosis of existing sandwiched between two more powerful and more populous former colonial masters. With typically black humour, Finns have taken to mocking their own unique urge to binge drink, even publishing an airport book on the subject of drinking alone designed to sit ironically alongside pastel-coloured guides to Danish hygge and Swedish 'lagom'. Even so, social binge drinking in Finland is still going strong – a consumer–capitalist manifestation of 'sisu', the national recourse to stamina, fortitude and resolve. At a Finnish metal concert you drink to be sucked into the black hole of oblivion. At a Finnish bar, you drink to prove your mettle as the last individual left standing.

In its less extreme manifestations, social drinking has eased many Finns, like Jussi, into the less-than-natural task of conversation. Solo sessions have had the same lubricating effect on the still more daunting prospect of making art, a phenomenon studied in relation to Finnish literature by Anja Koski-Jaunnes.[10] Alcohol is everywhere in that art: in the rivers of booze that run through Aki Kaurismäki films and Arto Paasilinna novels, in the many odes to alcohol written and sung by Irwin Goodman and even in Finland's established artistic view of itself, which has tended to focus on the flawed, alcoholic (and invariably male) creative genius figure. Finnish cinema grew sufficiently obsessed with the subject to cast the actor Martti Suosalo as Sibelius in a biopic of the composer in 2003, having had him play Goodman two years earlier. In Denmark, Tom Kristensen's novel *Havoc* plots a respectable Copenhagen journalist's descent into alcoholic stupor with as much celebratory verve as pathetic tragedy. 'Intoxication is just a poem without a form,' the protagonist Ole Jastrau signs off before one of many descents into liquid oblivion.

On canvas, a much-discussed painting from 1894 by Sibelius's contemporary Akseli Gallen-Kallela illustrates the deep roots of the issue. *Symposium* shows the musicians Oskar Merikanto, Robert Kajanus and Sibelius slumped around a table littered with empty glasses and bottles while Gallen-Kallela himself looks on. Talk has given way to stupor, but liquor has induced the fantasies of the creative mind. The painting seems to acknowledge the idea that alcohol was an aspect of the twentieth-century human's spiritual life just as much as it was, in Finland, 'the problem' – the title Gallen-Kallela gave to a sketch for the work. In Sibelius's case, it's hard to ascertain whether alcohol was, in creative terms, the problem or indeed the solution. It surely acted as a portal into the deeper levels of the composer's consciousness, the sort that may well have influenced the form of his strikingly fluid late music. The Symphony No. 7 oscillates between elation and aching strain – its gait, velocity, harmony and melody all deliciously swilled and smudged.

◢

Composing is a lonely profession, and Finland has more active, registered composers per capita than any other multi-city country. They work across a huge spectrum of styles and hold differently coloured passports. Many of them benefit from the sort of state stipend pioneered to bail out the financially unseaworthy Sibelius and still offered to artists today. In the summer of 2015, I interviewed 13 of these composers in Helsinki over the course of a week for a documentary film. It was a gender-equal selection ranging in age from 24 to 63.

'The most difficult thing is the loneliness,' said Seppo Pohjola, speaking for many of his colleagues while suggesting, in not so many words, that music had proved a safe haven in times of difficulty. That may be common to composers anywhere in the world, engaged in an introverted search for expression. Research by the musical psychologist Suvi Saarikallio has shown that Finns are particularly prone to citing music as a means of accepting personal vulnerability and facing personal difficulties.[11] The composers I spoke to in Finland had a distinct way of articulating loneliness and melancholy, but also of seeing it in broad and nuanced terms. 'Happiness is really not a concept I am happy *with*,' said the composer Aki Yli-Salomäki. 'I would rather say I was never happy, unless I am happy to the extent that I am not suffering.'

Yli-Salomäki was an interesting case study. He described the loneliness of the city in much the same way Jussi had in Lahti. He admitted that he struggled to cope with the Finnish winter and was 'probably born in the wrong country'. His solution was to head to Australia for a portion of the year. I asked him what he did there. 'I go to a really nice beach where there is nobody – I am there by myself – and I go swimming. That is one guaranteed way to achieve solitude: to go a little bit away from home.'

Some of the Helsinki interviewees spoke of the mental challenge of working as a composer in a country whose most significant cultural figure had the same profession. Some seemed perpetually challenged, as if untethered and alone in a hostile world. Others talked of the privilege of the job, of striving for something abstract and beautiful every working day and participating in a society that set great store by that endeavour. Plenty went the whole hog, claiming they couldn't survive doing anything else. The filmmaker I worked with on the interviews, Raimo Unnila, shot our subjects walking with their dogs, pushing their prams in snow-covered woods and meadows or retreating into corners of Helsinki bookshops.

The following summer, I spoke to the American violinist and composer Sara Pajunen, whose itinerant existence has included stretches living in Asia and Helsinki. She was raised in Minnesota by her Finnish-speaking father, the son of immigrants. We talked about the dramatic cycle of seasons in Finland and of surviving meteorological extremes. 'In general, if you're very affected by the natural world, you go to darker places when it's darker, and you potentially have to do something to take care of yourself in those places. That's possibly why people create a lot,' she said. 'I think a lot of powerful work comes out of that cycle; it mimics the manic depressive cycle, its ups and downs. I can't imagine living in a place near the equator where there's a consistent amount of light. There's nothing to respond to.' The pianist Víkingur Ólafsson talked to me in 2017 of the 'state of mind' induced by latitude. 'There is something in the inherent extremes of weather and light conditions, certainly in Iceland,' he said, 'everything in the north is extreme.'

While positioning himself as the very picture of a stoic Finn, Sibelius dreamed of sunlight and warmth. In a bitterly cold Helsinki February in 1904, he wrote a short piece, *Music for a Scene*, inspired by Heinrich Heine's idea of 'a fir tree dreaming of a palm tree' from the poem *Fichtenbaum*. It was a musical surrogate for the actual travel Sibelius indulged in when he needed light and colour in his life. He liked, in particular, to head to Italy. He would often leave his family behind.

However much Sibelius loved Italy, its warmer climates couldn't alter the course of his music. The symphony Sibelius wrote in Rapallo, his Second, was originally planned as a swashbuckling depiction of Don Juan cast in D major. The brightly coloured key remained, but any idea of a narrative chassis guided by the exploits of the philanderer quickly fell by the wayside. Surviving sketches suggest the symphony's material themes were actually associated with tragedy. The death of the Sibelius's daughter Kirsti lay behind the second movement's main tune, chanted out dolefully by a pair of bassoons playing in octaves. The final movement's subdued, lamenting music was jotted down in the wake of another death, that of Aino Sibelius's (and Eero Järnefelt's) sister Elli. Kirsti had died of typhus. Elli had killed herself.

Suicide, like alcohol, is a domain in which Finland strays statistically from its Nordic neighbours, and in the wrong direction. Finland's suicide rates still hover at the top of Europe's top-ten despite the apparent collective happiness of Finns reported in global surveys. Eisenhower's theory of socialism fuelling personal crises was roundly questioned at the time, but the idea has proved persistent. Herbert Hendin's much-reprinted book *Suicide and Scandinavia* includes some dated nonsense on gender but voices tenable concerns around mental stability in societies built on homogeneity and order. It picks up on the same pervasive loneliness as that articulated in the films of Bergman, the paintings of Munch and the music of Sibelius – as well as in the topography of the Nordic countries themselves.

Tapiola might just be the ultimate expression of that loneliness, despite its ominous suggestion that none of us are ever truly alone. Again, Sibelius wrote the work partly in Italy, travelling to Rome and Capri with the working manuscript in his luggage. But the Mediterranean sunshine could barely conceal the dark thoughts of the work's creator. As separate sections of the orchestra whir in micro-polyphonic conversation with themselves, *Tapiola* conjures up images of a brain in turmoil. Stalking the piece are the dark places and empty spaces that lie at its structural heart: the distress of bad thoughts layering up in confrontation; the emptiness of silence; the hopelessness of a harmonic language soon to have run its course.

In print and on screen, Nordic noir has taken to peeling back narrative layers more and more, forcing hard rationalism into play albeit with varying levels of aesthetic and literary success. Opera houses have followed suit, shifting the focus of the genre's tragic lifeblood away from murderous love and towards contemporary forms of psychological trauma. Many of the Nordic region's major operatic premieres of the last decade or so have taken psychological strain as their principal theme. Emotional abuse, acidic resentment and rampant selfishness grind up against one another in the Finnish composer Sebastian Fagerlund's take on Ingmar Bergmann's *Autumn Sonata*, a work of cold grandeur in which the orchestra's consistent agony speaks for everyone on stage. Daníel Bjarnason's *Brødre*, based on the Danish director Susanne Bier's film of the same name, plots one man's disintegration through post-traumatic stress disorder after active service in Afghanistan; slow, heaving music weighs the whole story down from the start. Signe Lykke's operatic take on Jakob Ejersbo's cult novel *Nordkraft* – a sort of Danish *Trainspotting* – examines the psychological pain that seeps out from between the lines of the author's three parallel stories. Also from Denmark, Louise Alenius's *Silent Zone* is a self-authored, immersive reflection on inter-familial sexual abuse that literally forces its audience into a house of horrors, having them confront the silence in between the music in a format that sees Strindberg meet Sibelius. Sometimes, the most dramatic, horrifying emotional landscapes are those found among flat-packed Swedish furniture.

The trend speaks of the introspective angst and hard engagement often associated with the Nordic mindset, but could just as easily be seen as a domestic kickback from Brand Scandinavia's insistence that everything north of the Baltic Sea is squeaky-clean. Shortcomings can be increasingly difficult to spot in rich, smart, efficient, wholesome countries that have set examples to the rest of the world in everything from green energy to penal reform. In 2016, the late British opera director Graham Vick came to Copenhagen, bringing to life a fantasy town 'where the only capital offence is to have no money'. Vick's production of Kurt Weill's satirical singspiel *Rise and Fall of the City of Mahagonny* pulled the fashionable directorial trick of pointing the finger back at the audience. In this case, there was a little more squirming in the stalls than usual.

Vick's set for the Royal Danish Opera's production was a replica of the interior of its own opera house, complete with Henning Larsen's distinctive maple balconies and Olafur Eliasson's chandeliers. When Fatty the Bookkeeper, Leocadia Begbick and Trinity Moses spotted 'gold' at the beginning of the show, a light illuminated the Mærsk-funded auditorium's gold-leaf ceiling. When Vick's cast of refugee extras took their places next to a chorus made to look like us operagoers, the singers froze in panic, as if carnivorous animals had sidled up next to them. We saw footage of Copenhagen's new Metro lines being built, of the city's gleaming new harbour districts and even its immaculate main shopping street bereft of beggars – a place where you could legitimately assume having no capital to be a crime.

Endless rules, regulations, observations and facts ticked across a screen that formed part of the set, as well as real-time stock values. Among them was a genuine question from a recent Danish citizenship test, taken mostly by poor immigrants arriving in the country with nothing: 'Which Danish restaurant was awarded three Michelin stars in 2016?' The most eye-widening statistic of all informed us that there are more cases of domestic and sexual violence against women recorded in Denmark than anywhere else in Europe. 'Ah yes, but that's because we report it more,' a singer reportedly protested to Vick. A rare instance of a Scandinavian managing to find the bright side.

5

Scandinavian by Design

"Nature was the source for endlessly contrasting patterns and variations on Aalto's key themes: the sinuous contrasting with the orthogonal; the radiating plan . . . the natural and the man-made."

John Stewart

As Europe looked into the abyss in the 1930s, officials in the Swedish city of Malmö got together to chew over what might be done to disperse the dark clouds ranged on the horizon. What Malmö really needed, they concluded, was a fully equipped modern theatre.

An architectural competition was organized and its winner named as Sigurd Lewerentz, a largely untested figure whose only notable building thus far had been an elegant cemetery pavilion in Stockholm. Lewerentz was asked to build Malmö's new theatre, leading a design team that would, in a typically Swedish act of consensus, include his runners-up Erik Lallerstedt and David Helldén. There were elements of all three proposals that the jury deemed too good to ignore.

On the evening of 23 September 1944, Malmö City Theatre was inaugurated. Its state-of-the-art revolving stage hosted a performance of Shakespeare's *A Midsummer Night's Dream* featuring the incidental music for voices and orchestra written a century earlier by Felix Mendelssohn, augmented for the occasion by local composer John Fernström. The performance reflected the multidisciplinary purpose of the new building as a home for drama, dance, opera and operetta.

Since spoken theatre was moved to a dedicated playhouse in 1992, Lewerentz's building has gone by the name of Malmö Opera. Otherwise, it is almost entirely unchanged: a large, squat structure in white marble and glass whose restrained municipal grandeur gently ennobles the art of theatre while underlining its accessibility – social democratic culture policy given physical form. Inside, foyers are scattered with bespoke furniture, artworks and chandeliers by the Swedish glassworks Orrefors, their austere beauty punctuated by a sweeping double staircase in wood and wrought iron. The auditorium itself is a perfect enclosed amphitheatre, giving every seat an uninterrupted view.

From the revolving stage to the ranks of open coat stands, Malmö Opera is a model of functionalism. Each of its constituent parts works efficiently and reveals its purpose to the naked eye, while the broader structural scheme intuitively tells the visitor where to go and how to get there. Inbuilt hierarchies are traded for universal aspiration. Attention to detail is impeccable, despite the lack of fuss. Among the house's bespoke textiles is a drop curtain designed by Vicke Linstrand festooned with images of dancers, musicians, lyres, figures from classical antiquity and dramatic masks – the very same images that are hand-woven into the upholstery of each of the auditorium's 1,616 seats.

This was all part of a wider design trend that blossomed in postwar Scandinavia and Finland and would provide the region with its first collective moment in the international spotlight since the Viking invasions. Its roots ran as deep as its intentions were broad. What the world insisted on labelling 'Scandinavian design' prioritized functionalism and a progressive, modernist form of beauty underpinned by a regard for natural forms and materials. Architects like Uno Åhrén from Sweden argued the moral case for design that curbed the appetite and cleansed the soul. A new sort of citizen would emerge from it, they believed, tempered by wholesomeness and restraint.

If there was a puritan undertone to the dogmas of the early Nordic functionalists, it soon faded in the face of pragmatism and the urge to feather nests. The movement sparked by the likes of Åhrén got less severe but no less disciplined. Its steadfast principles encouraged critical aesthetic appreciation while injecting a sense of quiet wonder into mundane domesticity. As the most iconic products of Nordic functionalism became expensive, they retained their egalitarian symbolism. Folk apparently accepted the idea that you need only buy one Arne Jacobsen lamp, confident that it would last for decades and never go out of fashion. Whatever the price tag, the lack of bling ensured no social applecarts were upset. The vast majority of the movement's staple items are still in production.

As governments sought to furnish expanding cities with hospitals, libraries, office blocks, museums, cultural institutions and even airports, they looked to the roots of the functionalist movement. The theatres and concert halls that sprang up in Finland, Sweden and Denmark emphasized universality and accessibility with clear, ascetic forms and natural materials. These were not red-carpeted palaces enshrining social status, but municipal buildings whose provisions were offered as human rights.

Many of the emerging design features were hewn from Nordic social history and nature. While Europe and the United States started to mass-produce in disposable plastic, Finns and Scandinavians looked to durable wood, leather and clay, the memory of poverty lingering still. Traditional crafts including cabinetmaking and boatbuilding were fused with the rural tradition for self-built furniture to create simple, modest but elegant domestic objects that prioritized lucidity of line and form as well as practicality.

One man who cleaved to those principals was Ingvar Kamprad, a prodigious entrepreneur from Småland in the south of Sweden who combined Åhrén's idealism with a ferocious business acumen, spending his schooldays reselling matches bought in bulk from Stockholm. As a high-school student in 1943, Kamprad started making replicas of his uncle's kitchen table under the brand name IKEA. The company that sprang from that enterprise would root its stern but malleable design principles on rural Scandinavian traditions and the demands of the simple peasant cottage, budget included. 'Beauty for All' was IKEA's first publicity slogan. The words might just as well have been carved into the marble façade of the Malmö Opera.

Functionalism has remained a steadfast component of Scandinavian and Finnish design from cutlery to airports – this in a region where an architect commissioned to design the latter won't think twice about taking charge of the former too. But functionalism is a big word with plenteous implications and inconsistencies. In a societal context, it suggests efficiency of organization: every aspect of a society serving an indispensible purpose. It speaks of stability, integration, effectiveness, of minimal waste and maximum harmony, of a deep satisfaction born of a lack of frivolous show – universally applicable values, maybe, but ones with which Brand Scandinavia seeks tirelessly to associate itself.

Much of this is messaging, but a lot of it is real. Public infrastructures in the Nordic region are built of undeniable clarity and efficiency. A simple example is the Danish social security or CPR number, a ten-digit code of which the first six digits are the resident's date of birth and the last denotes their gender (odd numbers for men, even for women). The code takes care of library loans, medical treatments and prescriptions, all fiscal exchanges including salaries and tax, indeed virtually every piece of interaction with the state, all of which is communicated via every citizen's individual, encrypted state email inbox. With a single codified input, a person can communicate a change of contact address or telephone number to almost every agency with which they interact, private and public.

If functionalism was a permeable enough theory to embrace both the workings of a society and the design of a coffee jug, it was also ripe for cooption by a new music scene facing its own aesthetic crises in the 1950s. With Nielsen no more and Sibelius silent, the Nordic region was once again forced to look south to mainland Europe and to musicians pursuing a radical modernist agenda. Denmark in particular was quick to show interest in the new modernism of the French composer Pierre Boulez, whose landmark piano work *Structures I* from 1951 was soon being played north of the Baltic.

Naturally, Scandinavian and Finnish composers took an interest in that music's central conceit – an advancing of Schoenberg's systematic techniques so that a formula or formulae now controlled every element of musical structure, not just pitch. Some Nordic composers visited the contemporary music mecca Darmstadt to study Boulez's methods; one or two continued on his path (perhaps most notably, the pioneer of electronic music in Denmark, Else Marie Pade). But the overwhelming majority felt uneasy with it, concluding relatively early on that it fell foul of the idea of music serving a useful societal purpose. A whole generation of Nordic composers admired the sturdy, systematic elements of Boulez's 'total serialism' and wanted to write progressive, uncompromising music. But they also wanted that music to chime with the times in which they lived and sit well with the social democratic promise that beauty was for all.

A pivotal movement born in Denmark suggested one way out of the impasse. The term 'New Simplicity' was first used in the country in 1966 to describe a stripped-down musical aesthetic with rigorously clear textures. This functionalist, objective music could easily show its workings because there weren't many of them to show. It used similar series and formulas to those deployed by Boulez, but here in the context of tonality – the major and minor scales embedded in our collective musical psyche. For the Danish writer and music historian Søren Schauser, it was a combination that 'according to Adorno could not exist: modern in structure but traditional in sound'. The reference is to the philosopher, sociologist and musicologist Theodor W. Adorno, who grew suspicious of the serialist techniques propagated by Boulez, predicting their path to fatal, self-defeating restrictions.

The genesis of New Simplicity can be traced back to 1964 and a largely forgotten piece titled *Perceptive Constructions* by a Danish composer named Henning Christiansen. The principles of functionalism and clarity that the movement would come to embrace soon delivered the formative experimental works of Hans Abrahamsen – and, before those, the bold, colourful early creations of Pelle Gudmundsen-Holmgreen that subjected the same stringent guidelines to the workings of a ferocious imagination. New Simplicity's founding fathers proved what a broad church it could be, not just for composers but for audiences. That may be one reason it's enjoying a comeback. Perhaps it never really went away.

Accordingly, New Simplicity's levelling tendencies didn't have to lead to short, austere and direct pieces of music – just as Sibelius had suggested, with *Tapiola*, that the functional didn't have to equate to the simple. The challenge Sibelius had laid down, in the mind of at least one Nordic composer, was that of creating beautiful, integral and progressive music that was wholly tangible but intensely modern; that was structurally impressive but emotionally bracing. After all, many of the great functionalist buildings springing up in Copenhagen, Gothenburg, Oslo and Helsinki weren't exactly 'simple', however orderly they looked.

◢

Per Nørgård was born in Gentofte, a well-heeled suburb of Copenhagen, in 1932. As a young man he became obsessed with *Tapiola* and Sibelius's symphonies, hearing something particularly Nordic in the Finnish composer's ability to subject small musical fragments to a steady process of metamorphosis. But Nørgård wasn't only interested in the way music was built from bar to bar. He also set significant store by the universal, embracing relevance it took on as a result of its broader solidity and consistency of form – the impression a piece of music could make as an 'object'.

In 1954, the 22-year-old Nørgård wrote to Sibelius at Ainola, outlining his theory that the Finn's music was 'in touch with the elementary, innermost and quite timeless forces of existence, with nature in the broadest sense'. Sibelius wrote back: 'Only rarely have I received letters that show such an understanding.' The challenge for Nørgård was that of taking Sibelius's ideas forward in the 1960s, when harmonic music was seen as old hat, and the European avant-garde was clearly approaching an endgame. In a Scandinavia expressing itself through design, Nørgård would develop a form of musical functionalism that breathed new and distinctly Nordic life into music's most structurally integral form: the symphony. In much of the rest of Europe, the symphony was already seen as dead in the water.

It was and remains Nørgård's belief that a symphony exists on two levels: a long and perhaps grand process of transformation that will make the room an audience is sitting in feel somehow different when the music has come to an end; and a tapestry of momentary activity that should readily engage that audience's minds so that they hardly notice such a transformation taking place. The task of writing a symphony, Nørgård understands, is that of coherently uniting the two.

As he grappled with that challenge, Nørgård had a breakthrough. He developed an architectural formula he refers to as the 'Infinity Series' – a potentially infinite constellation of predetermined notes mapped according to a mathematical pattern. This schematic grid subjects music to stringent restrictions but, given its infinite reach and its potential for fractal expansion or inversion, sets that music free at the same time. The Infinity Series can generate its own polyphony – the braiding of independent but complementary musical lines – by being superimposed on top of itself at different speeds. Nørgård had discovered an entirely new way of drawing his chosen musical motifs into a continuous process of metamorphosis. In a difficult climate for long-form notated music, most of Nørgård's peers were looking to innovate within the isolated domains of key, form, rhythm and harmony. Nørgård had stumbled upon a more fundamental structural solution.

Nørgård's Symphony No. 1, finished in 1955, shows him working towards that solution. The piece opens with a timpani roll and a woodwind solo and proceeds to include a quote from *Tapiola* – three obvious references to Sibelius that show the extent to which Nørgård considered the composer's works a touchstone. Within the austere, Nordic noir domain of the music that follows, you detect the faintest suggestions of a new technique – an almost frustrated desire to form connections through patterning and cross-fertilized layers of rhythms.

Four years later, Nørgård was sure of his Infinity Series. After more than a decade experimenting and preparing, the ground zero in Nørgård's search for structural coherence came in 1970 with his Symphony No. 2.[1] Here, the composer lays out the full symphonic potential of the Infinity Series for the first time, demonstrating in the purest terms how its structural rigour can induce the clearest, most organic process of metamorphosis imaginable – the consummate modernist answer to the natural unfolding heard in Sibelius's late works. Nørgård's Symphony No. 2 unfurls over the course of around twenty-two minutes in one movement, all according to a version of the Infinity Series mined from the simplest musical gesture there is: the leap from one note to its immediate neighbour.

At the start of the symphony, pitchless wind sounds on a flute slowly settle onto the note G, which strains pregnantly before hatching an A flat, one integer higher. That gesture is then inverted from the original pitch – stepping the opposite way, downwards – and multiplied to form an algorithmic pattern. A steady rhythmic pulse allows the music to spool out of itself as if induced by gravity. By adding extra layers to his self-perpetuating constellation of notes, Nørgård generates surrogate melodies and climaxes that are subtle enough not to distort what he calls the 'timeless objectivity' of the basic process. The symphony progresses through four sets of stacked musical rounds, separated for the listener's benefit by strips of repeated notes on brass instruments. These alert listeners to the shift, like the steel studs that tell drivers they are crossing lanes on a road.

Different sections of Nørgård's orchestra proceed at their own speeds – sub-divided strands of the symphony's steady 48-beats-per-minute. The composer has likened the effect to that of ships moving across a fjord in the same direction but at different rates of knots. 'It becomes the listener's own concern whether he will mainly follow one, the other or a pair of ships – or conceive the whole picture as a wave interference pattern,' Nørgård has written. A thundering climax comes when one last brass fanfare sounds, its bass anchor tumbling downwards through one of the very seams of pitches that stitch the whole canvas together. The symphony contracts back into its original G, and is soon just wind again.

You don't need to know any of that to be beguiled by the music, just as you don't need to be au fait with the structural engineering behind the Malmö Opera's amphitheatre to appreciate its form and benefit from its clear sightlines. As it happens, Nørgård's fractal symphony does indeed look fascinating in print, its pages filled with recurring V-shaped patterns like flocks of geese. But it was written to be played and to be heard. When you do hear it, you're less aware of the progress of the algorithm than you are of individual patterns bound by a larger scheme.

The effect is radiant, beguiling, coolly ecstatic. The music glistens, its textures shifting and shimmering like Debussy's, details emerging and disappearing again like foam on the surface of an undulating sea. It is the epitome of concord despite each instrument in the orchestra resolutely doing its own thing. In focusing in, the music actually opens up – a unification of Mahler's idea that a symphony must 'embrace everything' with Sibelius's insistence that it must enshrine a 'profound logic and inner connection'.[2] It's not difficult to hear this piece, and others like it, as a clear antecedent to the throbbing tapestries of Anna Thorvaldsdottir and others.

Blissed-out as Nørgård's Symphony No. 2 might sound, it rests entirely on the structural integrity of the composer's breakthrough method. 'Since my earliest youth I had cherished a dream of a new kind of music where everything was interconnected in a kind of delicate latticework that radiated out in all sorts of wave forms, yet which still formed one melody,' the composer said in 2003, in an interview concerning the prototype for the Symphony No. 2, a piece from 1968 titled *Voyage Into the Golden Screen*. The ideal, Nørgård continued, was 'a clear conception of the qualities music needs to emancipate itself from rigidity and still retain its links with the past'. Adorno would have approved.

Since then, the Infinity Series has continued to guide the composer through all manner of works including six more symphonies. These days it's less the be-all-and-end-all it was in 1970, more a chassis upon which further experiments have been laid, from which more truths have been gently gleaned. It has undeniably lent Nørgård's music a selfless, universal quality. It has also proved extraordinarily influential. The idea of a tightknit pattern setting its own boundaries, however explicit or concealed, has self-evidently seeped into the wider consciousness of Danish music. As Nørgård consolidated his teaching presence at the Royal Academy of Music in Aarhus from the 1980s, he garnered a cult-like status that saw the influence of the Infinity Series baked into the structural thinking of many who passed through the Academy's composition faculty. And plenty who didn't.

Some composers of the so-called 'Aarhus School' developed their own variants on the series. Karsten Fundal hit upon what he called the 'Feedback System', a dynamic layering of several seams of music in which lower, slower layers of predetermined notes influence the contours of the faster layers above – an algorithm that could determine even the duration of a piece (best heard in *The Wings of a Butterfly*, a 1997 score for clarinet, violin, viola and accordion). Poul Ruders developed a technique shaped by the 'change ringing' tables used by English bell ringers in which small motifs are linked together to induce slow, incremental variations.

The change ringing system, which Ruders no longer uses, was a means of erecting large musical structures according to a lucid, predetermined formula. It reached a high point in Ruders's own Symphony No. 2 of 1989, titled *Symphony and Transformation*. 'You get rid of all the notes you don't need and if every note is needed, every note will be right,' the composer told me at his old farmhouse in the Danish countryside in November 2018, discussing his general approach to composition while outing himself as a card-carrying functionalist. His most famous work, *Concerto in Pieces* from 1995, demonstrates that with relish. It has a symphony orchestra perform a living autopsy on itself using a well-known fragment of Henry Purcell's *Dido and Aeneas*.

▲

On a grey Helsinki day in November 2018, I ran into the conductor John Storgårds. We were both in town for the Nordic Music Days, a festival of contemporary music held in one of the Nordic nations each autumn. In 2015, Storgårds made his own invigorating recording of Per Nørgård's Symphony No. 2 with the Oslo Philharmonic. On this occasion, he was fresh from Pittsburgh where, with the city's symphony orchestra, he had just conducted *Kuutamo Jupiterissa* ('Moonlight on Jupiter') by the Finnish composer Väinö Raitio.

Persuading an American symphony orchestra to play a work by a composer unknown even to many Nordic music enthusiasts struck me as some achievement. By way of explanation, Storgårds described a burgeoning interest in Nordic music among the many American orchestras he conducts. Sometimes, the impetus to schedule what he described as 'obscure' Nordic works (not Grieg, not Sibelius) came from the orchestras themselves, he suggested. Usually, orchestras in the United States exercise extreme caution when programming music by unknown or living composers. Likewise the ultra-conservative Vienna Philharmonic. But even that orchestra has taken a liking to the music of Per Nørgård recently. In 2014, it recorded two of his symphonies.

That afternoon, Storgårds took part in a panel discussion during which a respected Danish music publisher discussed her 'frequent use of the Nordic brand' when promoting new music from the region, even recounting how a composer had jokingly offered to wear a Viking helmet in his publicity photographs. Apparently, the Anglophone world's fetishizing of Nordic lifestyle and design extends even to the niche that is contemporary classical music. A cursory glance through the last decade of concert listings from big British and American symphony orchestras suggests that contemporary works from Scandinavia, Finland and Iceland are far more prevalent than their equivalents from classical music's 'legacy' (and far more populous) nations of Germany, Austria, Italy and France. Anyone who has marketed orchestral concerts to American and British concert audiences knows that a piece of contemporary classical music on a concert listing can easily dissuade audiences even from coming to hear some popular Rachmaninoff billed alongside it. Either Nordic contemporary music is somehow less off-putting, or the soft-power work done by Brand Scandinavia has made audiences feel at home with the idea of that music, irrespective of how it actually sounds.

The panel discussion opened with an acknowledgement of Nordic classical music's global success, couched in the sort of self-congratulatory tones that Finns and Scandinavians are normally psychologically programmed to avoid. The panellists agreed that the Nordic countries have become a powerhouse in the dissemination of high quality classical music and its contemporary sub-genre, though admittedly the most glowing words of all came from the one speaker who was visiting from the outside – a journalist from Scotland.

Back home, the Nordic funding model allows orchestras to play what they like and trains audiences to accept contemporary music, claimed one panellist, the manager of a Finnish orchestra who was fresh from four years working in the heart of Europe. He went on to describe Finland's extensive network of professional orchestras as 'part of the social welfare system'. Next, the Danish music publisher came straight out with it: 'We have the best education system in the world and we have the best funding for arts in the world, so of course we are punching above our weight. If we were not, we would be a sorry lot.'

Soon the panellists were again trying to get to the bottom of contemporary Nordic music's success abroad – the wealth of festivals and one-off seasons that feature it, the orchestras from Seattle to Seoul who play it. They tied themselves in knots attempting either to define a common sound or deny that one existed, drawing inadvertent parallels in the process. Various themes emerged including some well-worn classics: Nordic music's strong voices formed with patience over time; Nordic music's air of self-confidence resulting from empowerment through stable funding; Nordic music's willingness to explore dark, depressive thoughts.

There was much talk of how difficult it is to identify a piece of music as Nordic from listening alone (except in the case of music from Iceland, naturally). But there was insufficient time to discuss whether less immediately audible design features might reveal that music's provenance. 'Per Nørgård's sound is not a Nordic sound, it never was,' said one panellist. But the 'Nordic sound' may be difficult to define precisely because it constitutes a broad spectrum of approaches to a narrower spectrum of values. Even the very different-sounding symphonies written by exact contemporaries Jean Sibelius and Carl Nielsen would suggest that. Those composers apparently understood each other's desire, to some degree, to harness different forms of musical energy in highly distinctive ways.

The 'Nordic sound' comment reminded me of an article published in Oslo in 1992 by the British musicologist Richard Steinitz. In the essay, itself titled 'The Nordic Sound' and printed in the programme book for that year's Ultima Festival of Contemporary Music, Steinitz attempts to pin down what he describes as the 'vigour and purpose' of new Scandinavian music and how it stands in such marked contrast to the 'long, lanky, moth-eaten and mildewy' new music coming out of central Europe. Shy of naming names, Steinitz writes instead of the general attention paid by Nordic composers to timbre and harmony.

Two references ping out of his article, even three decades after it first appeared. One is to 'serious engineering', to 'shapes ... created out of an ingenious variety of components'. The other is to 'the physicality with which [Nordic] composers engage with their sonic material'. Functionalism may not have a unifying sound, but it can certainly have an effect on the clarity of impression made by a piece of music. Is good old-fashioned Scandinavian design helping to render contemporary classical music from the region less disorientating, less self-obsessed, less burdensomely literary, less gauche? And all that, irrespective of the actual noise it makes?

No institution can decide what guiding principles should lie behind a particular country's musical creativity, inadvertently or otherwise. Then again, no institution can decide how a populace should decorate its homes, but that doesn't stop Danes from across the social spectrum painting theirs a uniform chalk white and filling them with objects from the same list of approved design classics. The homogeneity of Nordic societies is the lubricant to their functionalism and is inevitably experienced by artists, however much they attempt to disrupt it. Whether or not Nørgård's sound is distinctly Nordic, elements of his music's design and conceptual basis have arguably been echoed by enough of his Nordic counterparts to make them so. The principle of imposing delimiting boundaries or technical restrictions on the creative process, in order to induce greater creativity and focus, is seen not just throughout Danish music of the last century but also in the country's design, literature and cinema. Likewise, Denmark's unofficially prescribed colour palette of blacks, greys, browns and whites extends from fashion and interiors even to children's toys.

Ideas are spread quickly and easily through the Nordic countries, a restless exchange fuelled by an aspirational press and a relatively small number of higher education institutions. This is also the only geopolitical union of countries on earth that gathers its composers together once a year for an exploratory concert series. The Nordic Music Days has been happening since 1888, its 1919 edition in Copenhagen providing one of the rare occasions on which Sibelius and Nielsen met. Just to ensure Nordic composers are familiar with one another from an impressionable age, there's now a youth edition too.

Creative freedom reigns within these festivals, and within the various composers' societies, ensembles and conservatories that are their main stakeholders. Even if the underlying purpose is the raising of standards and the cross-fertilization of ideas, an inevitable side effect is the engendering of trends, however individual and radical their seeds. As one Helsinki panellist observed: 'The greater interaction we have had has, in my experience, contributed to ... limited aesthetics.' Music export agencies in Iceland, Finland, Sweden and Norway competitively market their composers' wares to the world, involving some degree of exoticizing. International audiences are primed to receive it, aided by the same list of intriguing and resonant adjectives. If the tail isn't wagging the dog, the collective idea of what constitutes Nordic music, domestically and internationally, inevitably bears down on the music actually being written here.

Whatever *is* being written here, it wouldn't be heard without events like the Nordic Music Days, the region's unparalleled network of orchestras and its remarkable appetite for contemporary music festivals (four annually in Copenhagen alone). Perhaps the 'physicality' of engagement with material described by Steinitz, and the 'confidence' of the Nordic music described by the panel, both stem from the practical experience the region offers its composers early on. Britta Byström from Sweden and Outi Tarkiainen from Finland have both spoken of learning their trade by having local ensembles on hand to play what they write, drawing a telling geographical contrast. 'Anywhere else in the world, it seems to be much harder to even get your music performed,' Tarkiainen told *Finnish Music Quarterly* in 2020. A year later, in his final season as director of Helsinki's Musica Nova Festival, the German conductor André de Ridder told the music journalist Yulia Savikovskaya of the local orchestras' tendency to 'pick up young composers very early and give them commissions', citing their propensity to 'programme contemporary music all the time, for almost every concert. This is something you don't get in Berlin.' Audiences, apparently, respond to it. When we discussed the phenomenon in 2021, the Finnish Radio Symphony Orchestra's former chief conductor Hannu Lintu told me of more tickets sold the more experimental his programming.

◢

As with alcohol consumption and social customs, subtle regional variations colour what each Nordic nation expects of its contemporary art music – generally speaking. For years, Finland retained its wildness while Sweden clung to dogmatic levelling ideals that in the 1970s silenced some composers entirely – a sort of New Simplicity in overdrive. In the 1980s just as in the 2020s, Norway was exploring ways of integrating national folk music into formal concert works, often with a radical political agenda.

Denmark, Europe's most physically manicured nation, has proved just as true to type. Historians like to trace the country's distinctive cultural psyche back to 1864, when it lost the last remnants of its global power and a third of its own landmass in the catastrophic final days of the Second Schleswig War. By that time, the once powerful Danish empire had been reduced in size to the point of unrecognizability. The country reconciled itself to the idea that it would never be the major player it once was and resolved to make the best of what remained. It would lead, over a number of decades, to a focus on small domestic comforts and a determination to better understand everyday life through art.

Both are evident in Denmark's national obsession with interior design. The sleek, elegant and pale interior of longstanding Danish archetype is but one contemporary manifestation of this humble but inspired, self-serving but rigorous aesthetic, itself rooted in tradition yet fiercely progressive. Beauty didn't have to be chiselled out of huge blocks of marble, Denmark decided; it could be found in the dust particles floating through the domestic hallways painted by Wilhelm Hammershøi, or in the designer Finn Juhl's elevation of household objects to the status of sculpture.

Hardwired into that idea was the notion that inspiring things could be built from modest and easily graspable ingredients – a new idea of simplicity long before New Simplicity. In 1913, the architect Peter Jensen-Klint dreamed up Denmark's most spectacular basilica, Grundtvig's Church on the edge of Copenhagen, using nothing more than the humble rectangular brick – 6 million of them, very nearly one for every Dane by 2021's statistics. In the decade the church was finished, Denmark's most celebrated export, Lego, was born of the same principle.

The idea of building big from small ingredients – of a sense of delight wrought from understated beauty – is surely what led Per

Nørgård and Karsten Fundal to their respective algorithmic systems just as it had led Edvard Grieg to open windows onto the soul with extraordinary thrift. It lurks behind Hans Abrahamsen's whirring canons, Poul Ruders's deconstructed musical Meccano sets and Pelle Gudmundsen-Holmgreen's modular approach to composition that is happy to create a new score by simply stacking two existing ones on top of one another.

All three exerted a strong influence on their countryman Svend Hvidtfelt Nielsen, a Danish composer interested in the weaving of lucid polyphonic structures from which musical ideas might be thrown up and transformed. In 2010, that process delivered its first outright masterpiece, Hvidtfelt Nielsen's delectably simple Symphony No. 3, a symphonic Tower of Babel that journeys from low registers to high ones over a twenty-five-minute span, enacting a grand process of coalescence and dissolution in the process. A core of weaving orchestral activity lifts the music upwards while pockets of the orchestra throb and glisten with micro-machinations in support. The feeling is of Sibelius's symphonic river flowing in an anti-gravitational, upstream direction.

The composer subtitled his symphony *Watching Life*, and describes the 'many different persons set in motion ... connected only by their appearance in the same period of time' that inspired it, a starting point that echoes the openness and universality of Nørgård's own creative aims. When the music reaches pitches too high to sustain, or even sound, it evaporates. The symphony's final bars bring to mind another ecclesiastical structure on the edge of Copenhagen, Bagsværd Church. On the inside, the building's 'horizontal' tower, designed by Jørn Utzon, recreates the theological notion of ascending into the blazing whiteness of clouds with astonishing but unassuming power. From the outside, the structure resembles a power station – a blunt, suburban answer to the billowing white sails of the building Utzon designed immediately before it, the Sydney Opera House.

Some years before the panel discussion in Helsinki, I made my first visit to the building that hosted it – the concert hall complex known as the Musiikkitalo. The occasion was the building's inauguration on 31 August 2011. At a concert that evening, John Storgårds conducted the Helsinki Philharmonic Orchestra in a brooding performance of *Tapiola* at the bottom of the building's bowl-like main auditorium. A few hours later, almost alone in one of the smaller auditoria, I watched as the building's lead architect Marko Kivistö entered, sat down, crossed his arms and closed his eyes while the party buzzed on outside. He remained in still contemplation for some time, listening to a student organist playing Bach.

Kivistö, of Finnish firm LPR Architects, labelled his design concept for the Musiikkitalo 'mezza voce': a building that would hunker down by Helsinki's main traffic artery, Mannerheimintie, as if cowering in the face of the Finnish parliament that eyeballs it in severe granite from the other side of the road. The steel exterior of the low-lying Musiikkitalo gives it the appearance of an electricity sub-station. As in Utzøn's church at Bagsværd, the interest is on the inside. The auditorium in dark woods and metals toys with the twentieth-century 'vineyard' concert hall format, ruffling it with asymmetry. Banks of seat rows are arranged at obtuse angles like logs floating in a river basin – a conscious reference to Finnish industrial traditions. Like the new opera house in Oslo inaugurated a few years earlier, this angular, sleek urban building references the untidiness of the natural world. Inside the main auditorium there is hardly a right angle to be seen.

The morning after the inaugural concert, a minibus was hired to ferry a group of journalists from the Musiikkitalo to the Finnish Ministry of Foreign Affairs in Katajanokka. The fifteen-minute trundle through downtown Helsinki started more-or-less opposite Storyville, the legendary jazz club on Aurorankatu. As we crawled down Mannerheimintie towards the art-deco cinema and restaurant complex at Lasipalatsi, the conductor Sakari Oramo took hold of the bus's microphone and started to point out landmarks. Oramo had also appeared at the opening concert the night before, leading the Finnish Radio Symphony Orchestra in a performance of Stravinsky's *The Rite of Spring*.

'On the right is the Forum shopping centre, built in the 1980s, with its lovely brown glass windows,' said Oramo, his tongue lodged firmly in his cheek. He gestured towards Stockmann on the opposite side of the street, adopting a mock-advertising tone as he described 'the oldest and finest department store in Helsinki' (it had recently sold its renowned academic bookshop to an American capital fund). At the elegant white Swedish Theatre, Oramo joked about Swedish-speaking Finns still holding the reigns of cultural power in the city; 'Isn't that right, Sebastian?' he directed in jest at the Swedish-speaking Finnish composer Sebastian Fagerlund, also along for the ride.

Oramo saved his most freighted comments for the moment we turned off Esplanadi, crossing the short bridge onto Katajanokanlaituri to be momentarily confronted by the stark white façade of the Enso-Gutzeit Building. This monolithic white box is Helsinki's mezza voce answer to the Doge's Palace, sitting between the flat water (or ice) of the city's harbour and the onion domes of its Orthodox Cathedral. 'It was designed by Alvar Aalto,' explained Oramo, 'a man who all orchestral musicians in Helsinki love.'

Finns do deadpan irony well. There is little love lost between Helsinki musicians and the celebrated Finnish architect, who was responsible for the country's most beautiful yet dysfunctional concert venue, Finlandia Hall. The hall's acoustic shortcomings, which meant orchestral musicians could barely hear what they were playing on stage, necessitated the construction of the Musiikkitalo in the first place. Aalto was born in Ostrobothnia in 1898, arriving in a booming Helsinki for the first time eighteen years later. What he failed to grasp about acoustics, Aalto made up for in aesthetics. Even without a Sydney Opera House to his name, his legacy is far more globally significant than Utzon's.

Like Sibelius, Aalto progressed from a traumatic, affection-deficient childhood to become a spendthrift more attached to alcohol than to his long-suffering wife. Like Sibelius, he was an individual who seemed perpetually confused about his own place in the world, slipping into an oscillating self-aggrandizement and self-hatred in response. Like Sibelius, he was a needy egomaniac unsettled by the coolness of his native country's emotional temperament, interpreting celebration abroad as a sign of neglect at home.

Also like Sibelius, Aalto would bestow on his discipline a whole new grammar, one that replaced weight and mass with lightness and delicacy. Both men were artists sceptical about wholesale breaks from the past, the extent of whose genius would only be realized some way into the future. Both sought refuge from the torment of life in the forest as well as the bottle, allowing it to shape their works. Both became convinced that nature's growth processes were the purest form of functionalism there is. Aalto's manipulation of forest wood into the modernist material par excellence echoed Sibelius's transformation of rune-song repetition into an advanced form of musical metamorphosis.

Aalto's breakthrough came in 1939, when he was asked to design the Finnish Pavilion for the New York World Fair. He delivered a shockingly atmospheric solution in which a wave-form wall cuts through the space while leaning into it, like a frozen image of the Northern Lights. Sibelius's *Andante Festivo* was performed inside the pavilion at its inauguration that year. As the academic and architect Sarah Menin has written, the orchestra should really have played *Tapiola*.

The New York Pavilion had its prototypes. In 1927, for the meeting room of his library in Viipuri – an eastern outpost of Finland later ceded to Russia after the Winter War – Aalto had designed a wooden roof that undulated in one giant rippling wave from back to front (in Finnish, 'aalto' literally means 'wave'). It was, writes Aalto's biographer John Stewart, 'the first original motif in Finnish architecture since the heyday of national romanticism: the counterpoint between a free, undulating line and a firm melodic base'. Gestures like this would become Aalto's architectural hallmark. Its musical equivalent – a held pedal note in the bass with an oscillating melody waving away above it – was already Sibelius's.

Parallels with Sibelius persist. For Aalto, the combination of a firm bass line with undulating waves would be developed in the auditoria of Finlandia Hall and, most dramatically of all, at the opera house in Essen, Germany. The Essen theatre, with its leaning balconies echoing the timber waves of the New York Pavilion, conjures up the foreboding atmosphere of a forest clearing. What had started out as a source of raw materials for Aalto soon came to shape his very idea of architectural space, no more obviously than in his various asymmetrical auditoria where, for Stewart, 'the sinuous contrasts with the orthogonal'. A lot of architecture prompts admiration or wonder, but Aalto's is intensely dramatic. 'Frozen music' indeed – Sibelius's specifically.

Aalto moved architectural functionalism to a new place and did so with vitality and subtlety, much as Sibelius had done with traditional harmonic thinking as it stood at the turn of the twentieth century. Finland found it a little easier to get to grips with Aalto's manifestations of that process than Sibelius's – only to be expected, given the architect was producing tangible objects and the composer abstract symphonies. Those who were prepared to look and listen deeper were intrigued as much by the strange counterpoint of levels and angles in Aalto's buildings as they were by Sibelius's apparent ability to write music occupying major and minor keys – and fast and slow speeds – at the same time.

Britain and the United States found both craftsmen fascinating from the get-go. While the Americans offered Aalto a visiting professorship at MIT and commissioned Sibelius's last great tone poems, the London journal *Building Design* hailed Aalto as 'the last great form-giver of our era' just as British conductors, including Thomas Beecham, were performing *Tapiola* when their German counterparts wouldn't go near it. The Royal Institution of British Architects bestowed its gold medal on Aalto, citing his creation of 'simple, good, undecorated things ... which are in harmony with the human being and organically suited to the little man'.

Certainly, much of Aalto's work was underpinned by the idea of social obligation. His famous chair for the Paimio Sanatorium, still in production for domestic use and found in homes rural and metropolitan across the world, was consciously designed to improve the breathing of whoever found themselves seated in it. At the same time, Aalto saw no conflict in combining functionalism with a sense of free-form fantasy. In much the same way, Sibelius would extend the imaginative remit of the symphony – often, ironically, by radically reducing its dimensions and streamlining its form.

Both pursued a tougher, more conscious control of their materials. Aalto's buildings appear to float free, even when cut sternly into sloping rocks or hillsides. Many are infused with the spirit of the forest whether or not, like the Essen opera house and the New York Pavilion, they consciously evoke forest or tree forms. When the architect designed his pavilion for the 1937 Paris World Fair, he placed a series of timber-clad structures among the trees that already populated the allocated site, saluting their formation. The organizers had presumed the trees would simply be uprooted and discarded. Soon enough, the patterns of the forest would come to infiltrate the most fundamental aspects of Aalto's thinking. Buildings, he concluded, must grow from their smallest idea. Much like the music of *Tapiola* does.

I wasn't lucky enough to hear *Tapiola* played at Finlandia Hall – nor at Aalto's other Helsinki concert hall, the House of Culture – before the Musiikkitalo's opening effectively put an end to orchestral performances at both venues. But I have often dreamed of hearing the score recounted live inside the Essen opera house, where orchestral music is still played, and have long had a sense of what synergies and parallels such a performance might throw up. The score's waving gestures, the fragments of melody that turn back on themselves, would reflect the snaking form of the theatre's balconies. The music's vertigo-like swaying and awesome disposition would provide a soundtrack to those balconies' teetering, angular lean. The undulating form of the auditorium's roof would adumbrate the coming waves of meteorological turbulence from the orchestra's strings, while its slatted patterning might echo Sibelius's screens of instrumental arabesque – the soil in which he grows his themes. The music's pedal notes would seem to control space and time just as the false perspective of the auditorium manipulates focus onto its proscenium – momentum given physical form.

Aalto and Sibelius may have taken the hint from nature's repeating patterns, but the works they produced as a result didn't always wear those biophilic tendencies on their sleeves. They often sought to evoke something else entirely. The significance was technical: natural forms used not for Romantic inspiration but for methodological advice. This guidance from the natural world lay behind the fashionable metropolitan creations that made Aalto a household name – the plywood chairs and benches that remain a firm fixture in so many Finnish and Scandinavian homes. To the Nordic functionalists, imitating natural forms was a technical solution first and foremost; far more rational to learn from nature than to bask in its beauty.

◢

In 2013, Finland experienced its own miniature crisis of identity with what looked, to all intents and purposes, like the gobbling up of its most beloved home-grown business, Nokia, by Microsoft. Brand Finland has been steadily ramping up its projection of a distinctive national aesthetic ever since, though the process probably got going far earlier.

Before making its name as a manufacturer of mobile phones and rubber boots, Finland's most historically successful brand started out as a pulpwood plant on the banks of the River Nokia near the Tammerkoski waterfalls – as Finnish an operation as any, and one absolutely of the forest. Even after that period straddling the turn of the millennium when every other adult in the developed world possessed a Nokia mobile phone, the company's spiritual significance to Finns far outweighed its economic value (plenty of Finns remained loyal to Nokia boots long after switching to the iPhone). When Nokia as a technology firm seemed gone forever after the buy-out by Microsoft, Finland wasted no time looking to other creative success-stories for internal sustenance and external messaging.[3] Tourism emerged as a lucrative growth area. Visit Finland duly rebranded, adopting a new logo clearly inspired by the Savoy Vase designed by Aalto for a fashionable Helsinki restaurant – itself based on the form of a typical Finnish lake.

The best crash course in contemporary Finnish aesthetics you could get post-2013 was to hop aboard a plane operated by the country's flag-carrier, Finnair. Organic brown gauze separated the business and economy cabins. Blankets and napkins carried the repeating floral patterns developed by Maija Isola for the Finnish textile company Marimekko. Drinks glasses were from Tapio Wirkkala's Ultima range, designed for the airline in 1968 and now manufactured for general sale, each resembling an intricate hanging ice formation. If you were lucky, one of your crew might have formed part of the only touring vocal ensemble operated by an airline, the Finnair Singers – a sure sign of the country's fondness for ensemble performance. All of this was wrapped in a fuselage of stark ice-white, the tonal baseline of Finnish modernism as established by Aalto, born of his penchant for semi-translucent Italian marble. On the plane's belly, the giant letters spelling out the name FINNAIR were formed in a bespoke typeface by the Helsinki branding agency Sek & Grey that seemed to evoke a half-familiar alphabet from far, far away.

In fact, that typeface strategically referenced the linguistics and aesthetics of the airline's fastest growing market, Asia. Many hundreds of years before Finnair got in on the action, merchants noticed that the quickest route to the Far East from Europe was via the chunk of rock now known as Finland, giving the two landmasses a link since ancient times. It was long believed the peoples of Asia and Mongolia shared genetic origins with the Sámi and, by the association of their common genetic mutation, with the Finns. But the assumptions were made on the basis of two telling misunderstandings: that the Finnish language contained elements of Asian dialects, and that obvious phenotypic distinctions such as high cheekbones revealed a genetic connection. Those distinctive cheekbones came, in fact, from chewing: both cultures erred towards tougher food, which resulted in a change in the development of masseter muscles, pushing cheekbones up.[4]

That hasn't stopped telling bonds emerging, particularly between Finland and Japan, two of the most distinctive homogenous cultures in the world. Numerous tendencies unite the two island-strewn nations including a penchant for wood, fish, the outdoors, solitude, minimalism, classical music, hard liquor, high-quality design and architecture, social order and the notion that tradition and modernity can fruitfully coexist. Finland has an unusually high population of expatriate Japanese. Meanwhile in Tokyo, two Moomin Cafés cater to Japanese citizens obsessed with the mythical characters invented by the Finn Tove Jansson. Marimekko textiles are sold all over the country, viewed as the pinnacle of good taste. A wider interest in all things Nordic has seen household brands including Kraft foods commission Nordic designers to create bespoke packaging for the Japanese market. One of them is Lotta Kühlhorn, who also designs for the confectionary manufacturer Fika – an imitation Nordic brand that exists solely in Japan.

More striking still is the musical synergy that exists between the two countries' languages, one that lay behind those incorrect assumptions of a genetic connection. Japanese citizens may not understand a word of spoken Finnish, but they reportedly find the language phonetically and syllabically sympathetic to their own, especially Finnish names. I can't have been the only European to have read Sakari Oramo's name on a concert listing in the 1990s and presumed he was Japanese.

In 2012, Finnair wrapped one of the aircraft serving its Helsinki–Tokyo route in Maija Isola's most famous floral pattern, Unikko. Isola's subtler, more abstracted designs, like those of her compatriot Ritva Puotila, play with the sort of organic arabesque that helped Sibelius establish a schematic order in his music that could be worked or repeated until its meaning transformed. The designer Johanna Gullichsen's creations extend the concept, compressing and expanding the rate of rhythmic activity as if visualizing the undulating density of a Sibelius score. Fragmentary, linear patterns like those found in Gullichsen's designs are found all over the straight surfaces of Aalto's buildings and have re-emerged with striking prominence in contemporary Nordic architecture. They are etched into the flat surfaces of almost every one of the concert halls opened in the region since the turn of the century – unobtrusive patterns in relief that conjure up the vitality of repetition and reproduction.

◢

True to form, the biggest collective development in Finnish art music after Sibelius was ignited not by a noisy protest but by a promise to listen harder. Korvat Auki ('Ears Open') was a movement spearheaded in the late 1970s by the composers Esa-Pekka Salonen, Magnus Lindberg and Kaija Saariaho. Among other objectives, it sought to steer contemporary Finnish music away from its anomalous obsession with operas on heroic, historical and mythological themes.

Salonen sealed his status outside the Nordic region after a stint as chief conductor of the Los Angeles Philharmonic that spanned the two decades either side of the turn of the millennium. In that time he introduced a strong diet of contemporary music to the ensemble, including plenty of his own. Much of it inherited the lyrical and luminous sheen characteristic of his teacher Einojuhani Rautavaara, himself a protégé of Sibelius. Otherwise, Salonen moves into the foreground the sort of filigree musical patterning that Sibelius so often placed in a hinterland. Salonen's is nature music by design as much as by inspiration.

The composer's Violin Concerto, finished in 2009, feeds off a perpetual weave that tricks the listener into thinking the music was active even before it became audible. The soloist hops on, exploring the whole range of the instrument with continuous patterns of arpeggios (chords broken into their constituent notes). In the third movement, the most discernible patterns are rhythmic, the solo violin chasing its own tail with inward-twisting figurations conjuring up images of Isola's design known as Joonas. The concerto's entire solo part is really just elaborated figuration, patterns pulled or pinned into shapes. The threads gradually unwind in the last movement, described by the composer as 'the very basic process of nature, something coming to an end'.

Organic, scientific life cycles like this direct much of Salonen's music. His orchestral showpiece *Helix* is a nine-minute fuse-out based on its own anti-Infinity Series, in which the speed of the music increases as its note and phrase lengths are correspondingly stretched. The faster the music gets, the more the instruments try to hide the fact. Two tunes, forced into ever decreasing concentric circles, grow more and more frantic as the music runs out of space and time. It is a thrilling piece of display-functionalism that almost always quickens the breath of the audience listening to it.

Salonen's Korvat Auki co-conspirator Magnus Lindberg would become the most high-profile Finnish composer of orchestral music in the new millennium and one of the most commissioned in the world. On the surface, his monumental orchestral works seem to spring from the virtuoso orchestral tradition of the late-Romantic

German Richard Strauss. But key elements of their design are rooted in the more ascetic Aalto/Sibelius principle of letting a steady foundation or pedal note fling open large expanses of musical space and time above them. Like his great inspiration, Sibelius, Lindberg looked for a way to write original music based on the principle of the primitive made structurally useful.

In 1985, Lindberg's work *Kraft* was first performed at the Helsinki Festival. It immediately raised eyebrows and pierced eardrums, introducing a symphony orchestra to the sonic apparatus of Lindberg's favourite German heavy metal band, Einstürzende Neubauten. Some of *Kraft*'s breeze-block chords contain no less than 72 notes, mapped by a computer program that could imitate and expand the composer's own harmonic tendencies. Most listeners come away from *Kraft* with the impression of music powered by primitive, earthbound rhythms machined-out by a colossal battery of junkyard percussion. Finland hadn't heard anything quite like it. Nor had the world. Lordi's Eurovision moment had been pre-empted in a classical concert hall, helping to fix a wider idea of the sound of a wild, far-flung country in impressionable minds.

As compelling as *Kraft* sounded in 1985, over time it started to feel a little hollow – over-reliant on the big gesture. Lindberg noticed that before most. In the 1990s, his music became freer and more expressive, even if it still traded in the aggressive rhythms the composer so relished. *Kraft* had proved to Lindberg that computers could be useful in the spelling-out of complex chords. And if computers could do that, they could surely help him do something more sophisticated: mimic the complex patterns of the 'overtone' series, the mostly inaudible notes that certain frequencies naturally radiate. Much like Aalto imitating the floor plan of the forest, Lindberg wanted to map the natural acoustic properties of a musical note to create more resonant harmonies.

That suited Lindberg's fascination with large ensembles. With an extended symphony orchestra as his primary instrument, Lindberg's music became richer and more radiant. It also became more climactic. His pieces started to move with apparently thrilling inevitability towards huge ruptures, building and releasing tension as they went. His orchestra would momentarily split open to reveal gaping chasms or colossal vistas. Much of his music would use that trusty device, the sustained bass pedal note. For Lindberg, held pedal notes are the 'primitive' (the drones of folk music, the hum of the earth) that facilitate the 'complex'. The music billows and blossoms out above them like forests teeming with life and complexity.

Interest in all things Finnish surged after Lordi's 2006 Eurovision victory. But it was less the Finland of Aalto and Sibelius that caught the wider international imagination, more that of hard metal and the cool, plastic modernity of the Nokia phone. Still, that same decade, Lindberg's residencies at the philharmonic orchestras of London and New York were helping to create a parallel vision of Finland in sound that chimed with the mythology of a wild, expansive and foreboding land either completely dark or bathed in strange, magical light. For British, American and Asian concert audiences with a deep-rooted regard for Sibelius and even Strauss, Lindberg offered audible and biographical links to the music they already knew and loved. His music became easy to programme.

Japan wanted a slice of the action. In 1994, the Suntory Foundation presented the first performance of *Aura*, its own Lindberg commission, at its concert hall in Tokyo. *Aura* is blessed with design features that would satisfy both schematic modernists and misty-eyed Romantics. Like *Tapiola*, it is a symphony in all but name that finds release courtesy of a final, hymn-like theme despatched by luminous strings. But it also draws its audience in with cold mathematics: the music appears to contract from its first two, twelve-minute movements into its last two, six-minute ones. Like the velocity games of Sibelius's Symphony No. 7, the music appears to get slower while actually getting faster.

A decade later, Lindberg wrote a new work for his friend Salonen, inspired by the architecture of the Los Angeles Philharmonic's new home. The most distinctive feature of Frank Gehry's Walt Disney Concert Hall is a roof that billows outwards in convergent aluminium sails. In Lindberg's *Sculpture*, the orchestra throws down a series of pedal notes like plinths. Unlike Gehry's roof, Lindberg's sound sculptures initially remain squat and dark, his orchestra devoid of violins and stuffed instead with low woodwind instruments. Its driving force comes from an energy field created by combining the first pedal note, D flat, with higher material in the key of C – just a semitone away on the scale, but pitched octaves higher to trick the ear. The tension is sustained until an exhaling organ hauls the music magnificently up into the key of C once and for all, finally acknowledging the aerated lightness of the building that inspired the music. In the meantime, the space in between the C/D flat clash is filled with the writhing instrumental abundance that puts concert audiences on the edges of their seats.

◢

The bass pedal note has proved persistent in Nordic orchestral music from Grieg onwards. It is easily associated with landscape: with clear views through long, wide vistas; with the stillness and stasis that spilled over into Nordic music from equivalent oil painting well over a century ago. We can cite the pedal note as a central ingredient of musical functionalism that seeks, first and foremost, to establish clarity and foundation. Unsurprisingly, the bass pedal note has also come to signify some degree of general security – level horizons, steady waters, the assurance of gravity. The old rules sticking fast. Nature holding out.

The dubious privilege of existing at the sharp end of the climate crisis has forced Nordic composers to confront scientific realities more immediately than most. Nature, in fact, is not holding out. And nor is the once-trusty bass pedal note. The Swedish composers Jan Sandström and Allan Pettersson were among the first to place long, fixed notes in their musical scores that would subsequently drift alarmingly off-pitch, as if the stage of our consciousness were listing dangerously to one side or entire landscapes were curling upwards or falling away before our ears. The gesture can be heard in swathes of contemporary Icelandic music.

The pitch-bending pedal note, along with entire chords that slip and slide out of position, has become a favourite device in a certain strand of music for film and television, adept at suggesting disorientation, distortion, horror and psychosis. Finland has long harboured a faction of composers who feel twelve notes are insufficient for capturing the distinctive colours they see all around them, and have therefore slipped free from the chromatic scale's temperate moorings altogether. Some Finnish musicians have even pioneered new instruments that can readily access these 'notes between the notes', the ultimate response from a posse of wild-hearted composers to the music theory taught so rigorously inside their country. There's not much that sounds so provocatively yet beautifully disorientating as Sampo Haapamäki's Quarter Tone Piano Concerto from 2019, a work that listens more to the earth than to the tempered scale.

The composer from Finland most obviously following in Magnus Lindberg's footsteps is Sebastian Fagerlund, one of the passengers on Sakari Oramo's architectural minibus tour of downtown Helsinki. As composer in residence at the Royal Concertgebouw Orchestra in Amsterdam in 2015, Fagerlund wrote an orchestral piece titled *Stonework* built of firm bass pedal foundations and fixed horizons. Two years later, his orchestral work *Drifts*, written for the same orchestra, subjected those same structural devices to exertions that prove too great to bear. In *Drifts*, pedal notes no longer step clearly up or down as they do in *Stonework* – as they do, indeed, in Sibelius, in Lindberg and in Aalto's architectural bass lines. In *Drifts*, bass pedals bend, twist, creak and falter into positions of increasing precariousness. A horrifying, teetering danger courses through the music.

'Perhaps the idea of large fields of music or large arc forms, of something emerging from underneath, can be traced back to the influence of Sibelius,' Fagerlund told me in 2015 as we discussed his own work in the context of his forbear's 150th birthday year. In the same conversation, Fagerlund distanced himself from the composer. He even pointed to Einar Englund and the Finnish composers of the generation immediately after Sibelius who tried to resist that composer's influence by consciously doing something different.

In truth, Finland's most exported contemporary classical music has long embraced the scale, topography and techniques pioneered by the country's most celebrated creative figure. Recent outings for new Finnish music at the BBC Proms have profiled a new generation of composers, personified by Lotta Wennäkoski and Outi Tarkiainen, who still cleave to the sound of a large orchestra and appear intensely engaged in the ideas of silence and instrumental colour. One takes her lead principally from textiles, the other from the extremities of her country's northernmost reaches.

Tarkiainen's *Midnight Sun Variations*, premiered at the BBC Proms in 2019, is a response to the forest light explored in *Tapiola* but in this case experienced in Ivalo, a village nearly 300 kilometres north of Rovaniemi on which the midnight sun shines 70 nights a year. At one point in the score the composer inscribes a quote from Robert Crottet's book *Fôrets de la lune*, in which the Swiss adventurer addresses Finns directly: 'In your country, dream and reality are so closely bound together that one cannot well distinguish one from the other.' Long have we been drawn to Finnish music that appears to look down on the earth from as near as possible to its point of rotation – opening up vistas we have never seen, facing down phenomena that would freeze us in fright. What the rest of us consider dreams, many Finns experience as very real indeed.

◢

A vast amount of Finnish art and creativity has little to do with the sort of marketable aesthetic outlined above, even if an uncanny proportion of it bears an umbilical connection to animals, light and weather. Plenty of Finnish artists and composers take their inspiration from elsewhere in the world and indeed elsewhere in the world of music. Nor is there anything so imposing as those huge, variegated orchestral canvases in Maija Isola's textiles, which these days constitute more of a cultural touchstone to the Finn on the street than anything from the pen of Fagerlund or Lindberg.

And yet, a great deal of Isola's deep-rooted work echoes the base forms Sibelius and others employed to tease-out melodic material or alter states of mind through circular repetition. Isola's recurring shapes and patterns are intensely rhythmic, malleable and musical – desk-designed metropolitan entities that, like those of Aalto and Sibelius, borrow from the natural world. Many of Isola's textiles were given exposure at world fairs and exhibitions, much like Aalto's had been decades earlier. Her silk-screened works for Marimekko and its sister company Printex were influenced by patterns she saw in African, Slovakian and Karelian folk art.

Some of them, like the patterns known as Unikko and Kaivo, feature bold and obvious organic shapes. Silkkikuikka and Lokki evoke the sort of wave forms harboured in countless works of Finnish music from the early 1900s. Albatrossi suggests a florid little melodic cell stepping through adjacent notes, the basis of the linguistically distinctive motifs that course through pages of Sibelius and are all over Björk's *Homogenic* and *Vulnicura*. The more elegant Putkinotko evokes the screens of string figuration that take root in Sibelius's orchestra. The pattern known as Muija, a precise grid using two similar forms altering minutely in specification, speaks of the micromechanisms that power forward Symphony No. 3 by the Finnish composer Seppo Pohjola – a symphonic argument built entirely of canons, whereby a motif is overlapped with an imitation of itself at staggered chronological intervals.

Plenty of musicians only recognised the long-term significance of Sibelius's unorthodox structures long after the composer had proved himself unable to conjure up any more of them. In the decades since his demise, conductors have become steadily more intrigued by the composer's apparently idiosyncratic ability to establish and control musical momentum, a conjuring trick with the manipulation of repeating patterns at its heart. Constantly working and turning his motifs in the manner of a rune singer, Sibelius was able to establish a sense of circular metamorphosis in his music, which in turn facilitated that music's apparent ability to dredge up melodies and emotions from deep within itself.

The composer's distinctive manipulating musical momentum is best heard in his odd-numbered symphonies but is explored in earlier works including *The Wood Nymph* and *Lemminkäinen and the Maidens of the Island*. These pieces can appear to flow like rivers. For Sibelius, ragging the orchestra's rhythmic synchronicity, or letting the bottom of the orchestra pursue a marginally separate rhythmic agenda to the rest of it, was equivalent to changing the shape of the symphonic riverbed – thereby subtly altering the music's rate and density of flow. Often, the most significant structural pivots in Sibelius's symphonies are buried deep in metre and figuration, allowing the music to shift course almost imperceptibly. Sibelius's sleight of hand means our perception of the shift is often delayed, delivering a wondrous sense of sudden enlightenment when it arrives later on.

We are conditioned by popular music to presume rhythmic complexity means overt syncopation – music in which a strong, foregrounded rhythm is temporarily and obviously displaced. Much of the structural strain and cumulative power built up in Sibelius's orchestral music comes from a gentler combination of rhythmic displacement and reunification. In the Symphony No. 5, different cohorts of the orchestra are made to pursue slightly divergent rhythmic agendas at the same time with a purposeful ambiguity of dominance, which invests their eventual, cumulative 'coming together' with colossal power. It can be heard throughout the first movement of the symphony, by concentrating your ears on the lowest sounding notes.

These idiosyncrasies explain why some musicians find the music difficult to play and understand – at first, at least. They are also reasons, surely, why Sibelius's scores have struggled to gain a foothold in whole swathes of Europe used to a different form of musical architecture. 'Strings are playing completely new textures, especially from the Symphony No. 5,' the Finnish chief conductor of the Orchestre de Paris and Oslo Philharmonic, Klaus Mäkelä, told me in 2021. 'The notation hardly makes any sense when you first look at it. Any orchestra has to learn how to approach this distinctive sound and make everything coherent.'

Watching an orchestra attempt to do so is an education in itself. 'The feeling in much of the Symphony No. 5 is of activity that's entirely inhuman,' the American conductor Michael Stern told me in 2019, as I witnessed him drill an orchestra of capable student instrumentalists in Guangzhou, China, preparing for a performance of the symphony a few days later. Very few of them had ever played Sibelius before. 'This is music unbounded by time,' Stern continued. 'Sibelius uses deep syncopation to consciously displace our feeling of earthbound stability, which means you're always reaching for something that is, in the end, unknowable. You'd think those chords at the end of the Fifth Symphony would be definitive. But they don't sound definitive to me. Right up to that point, there's no strong beat.'

That's tricky enough. But orchestral musicians are also programmed to hear structural hierarchies in the music they play; to know which parts of the orchestra are supposed to be in charge at any particular moment. This presents another challenge in Sibelius's scores, where musical patterning is often neither exclusively material (tune) nor accompaniment (background). Sibelius said of all that patterning that its notated form was less a forensic communication of what should be played, more the clearest possible way of writing something intangible down – not so much strict rhythm as much as general pulsation. He wanted listeners to be left with the impression of a musical 'soup', a broad sense of sound rather than a musical kit of parts.

Sibelius's ubiquitous instrumental patterning forms a sort of musical subconscious as much as it steers the discourse of a piece. This, like the composer's circular working of his themes as a potter at a wheel, is connected to the often cited 'internalized' emotions in Sibelius's music. Stern, who has made some illuminating recordings of Sibelius's orchestral works with his Kansas City Symphony, returned consistently to rhythm – to those moments when different parts of the orchestra appear to be veering away from each other, momentarily on different tracks. 'It comes back to something essential: the disquiet that comes from the rhythmic displacement against the clarity of the actual line.' It's these unsettling devices, Stern insisted, that feed the music's monumental tectonic shifts.

If it's tricky to play, it was fiendishly difficult to write. Even by the time of *The Wood Nymph*, Sibelius had come a long way from the bluntly mechanistic, episodic music of his narrative choral symphony *Kullervo* of two years earlier, though his more radical techniques can be traced directly to some of the base repetitions and static melodies presented naked in that piece. Getting something to sound organic and inevitable took not only a shift in concept – and probably some whisky – but hours of deskbound distilling, cutting and stitching. Not to mention an ability to hear the results amid the silence of Ainola.

That much is evident from the now-published original version of Sibelius's Symphony No. 5. The notes are more or less the same, just not necessarily in the best order – thus obscuring the essence of a self-perpetuating journey. The leap Sibelius made from this decent first draft to the symphony's inspired final version was that of streamlining momentum by mimicking the impulses of improvisation, the essence of all folk music. It was the first step towards the sort of distilled natural clarity in the composer's music that would reach its apex in *Tapiola*. In the process, the 'self' disappeared from the picture altogether – the composer's technique suddenly illusory, the architect's hand invisible. A sort of vaporous, apparently formless, impressionistic yet entirely coherent music emerged. The impression, more and more, was of music unbound by time, musical and historical.

▲

Genuinely reactive improvisation, from an ensemble of musicians, is one of the purest forms of musical functionalism there is. One Finnish composer has convinced himself that Sibelius's Symphony No. 7 was an invitation to future generations: a challenge to extend the concept of musical fluidity and 'designed improvisation' in a symphonic context. It is a challenge, Leif Segerstam claims, that Finns are better placed to meet than most.

'The flow must always go on in our own lifescore,' writes Segerstam in a typically eccentric introduction to his own Symphony No. 288 (subtitle: 'Letting the flow go on . . .'). The symphony was probably composed some time in 2016, but keeping track of Segerstam's oeuvre is as tricky as following him in conversation. He is one of the Nordic music world's great characters, a lauded conductor of the old school who looks just as likely to have stepped out of the pages of the *Kalevala* as from a scene from *The Muppets*. Despite both, he has conducted Sibelius's orchestral works with a level of emotional intelligence few have matched.

Segerstam's circa 400 symphonies (and counting) tend to last, like Sibelius's Seventh, a little under twenty minutes. They are performed without a conductor or even a conventional score, challenging orchestral musicians to enter a new level of conscious listening that Sibelius surely prepared the ground for.[5] Contrasting energy fields course through Segerstam's music, compressing and expanding its rate of flow from all angles – Sibelius's structural riverbed turned upside down and inside out. The result is a sort of controlled polyphonic chaos that could never be forced into the rhythmic straightjacket of standard musical notation. Besides, according to Segerstam, 'Time doesn't exist, it's just a way of comparing continuities.' So he told me when we met in Aarhus in 2019.

True enough, time shape-shifts wildly in Segerstam's symphonies. On the page, musical time doesn't exist at all. Players are allocated stretches of non-rhythmic time by the clock, within which they work through or repeat prescribed cells of musical material on their instrument. Often that material is strictly organized despite its relative freedom – instruments as chess pieces, permitted to move only in set directions or through certain integers. The orchestra musters at predetermined points of coalescence. Silences hang in the air, but not even these are officially counted out. 'Nothing is,' Segerstam insists. Even so, his sketched-out plans result in symphonies with discernable forms that plot tangible journeys.

Sibelius would spend years perfecting twenty minutes-worth of organic symphonic logic. Segerstam dashes his symphonies off in a matter of hours. Some are more successful than others. No. 295 is particularly beautiful, written in memory of his colleague, the conductor Ulf Söderblom, but to some degree broadly representative. The elegiac message of the music helps, but in its density of emotional content, the symphony approaches the residual power of Sibelius's Seventh. It packs a lot in before a broad, luminous farewell that appears to float unconstrained – music of centrifugal inevitability, time as distant as hope. Halfway through the score, the entire orchestra deflates, instruments sliding uniformly down off their individual pitches.

A heightened sense of listening is demanded of everyone involved in Segerstam's music, whether on the stage or in the audience. You can't read the score in your head and you certainly can't consult any rational programme notes. Segerstam's are symphonies 'in the moment', never structurally the same twice. Aalto claimed, tongue in cheek, to have represented the shape of the archetype Finnish lake in the form of his Savoy Vase. Segerstam enjoys the fact that in the real world, the Savoy Vase's lake never existed and never will.

Interviewing Segerstam in 2019 was like attempting to keep a severely damaged aircraft in the air. He repeated well-worn ideas about his music's goal in tethering the essence of human existence to quantum mechanics, on which he can be judged a partial success solely on the evidence of his symphony for Söderblom. But his generally grumpy demeanour saw him spout sexist comments and react badly to my questioning about the parallels between his own music and that of Per Nørgård, which he once championed. 'He doesn't give a fuck if the notes are good or bad, they go according to his scheme,' huffed Segerstam dismissively of his Danish colleague. 'I don't go according to a scheme; I listen for everything. Which is the next note? Downwards or upwards? One step or two steps? The situation gives the answer. I am not a composer, I am a tone chooser. It is not building, it is surfing.'

According to Segerstam, Finns are uniquely gifted in that regard, a privilege of their country's coordinates. He outlined his theory: 'In our music, we are deciding to go this way or that way, up or down, or are waiting until we are ready to make a decision. This is natural for a Finn, because we are between Orient and Occident and we take inspiration from both. This is *life* for a Finn. But it means something for a Finnish musician following the instinct of how he expresses himself rhetorically.' He proceeded to explain the Finnish privilege of being born with a 'ternary shape mechanism between the ears.' At least that could explain Sibelius's obsession with melodies based on three notes.

I have long suspected there is an element of genius concealed somewhere within Segerstam's eccentric and frequently incoherent ramblings. He is preoccupied with the idea that Sibelius's opus number for *Tapiola* would become Finland's emergency telephone number, 112. One pertinent theme he returned to time and again during our conversation in Aarhus was that of freedom through restriction. It felt like an appropriate topic to be discussing in the town from which Per Nørgård exerted such a strong influence. As Segerstam posited in a moment of lucidity: 'What is music? Music is not that which sounds. Music is why that which sounds sounds like it sounds when it sounds.'

The Sámi divide the year into eight seasons. Scandinavians tend to warn foreigners that there are really only two: dark and light. The schemes aren't mutually exclusive. Even at the comparably low latitude of Copenhagen, November gloom at 3 p.m. is entirely different to February gloom at the same time. Summer sunlight in Gothenburg has a piercing whiteness around midday that gradually assumes a more fulsome glow as the day lingers on, drawing colour from everything it meets. A sunset in Spain may last twenty minutes, but it can stretch to two hours in Trondheim while embodying a totally different palette of colours in June to those offered up in September. The periodic non-existence of daytime light higher up is as significant as that light's varying qualities from April to October, even further south. Often it's not the absence of light that affects the mind so much as the absence of the sun – a teasing blue glow suggesting there is a light source present, you're just not authorized to see it. In November, you'd happily trade the semblance of light on one day for the simple luxury of a blue sky on another.

Indeed, it is hard to capture the Nordic light's kaleidoscope of colours and moods in words, which is why so many composers have attempted to do so in sounds. 'The changes in sunlight throughout the year [in Finland] are so drastic they affect everyone,' the Finnish composer Kaija Saariaho said in 2014, 'you can't escape its influence.'[6] Saariaho has built her career reflecting on the sanctity and variability of Nordic light, on what gradually seeps out from beneath the 100-plus days of murk referred to in Finland as 'kaamos'. While classical composers generally look out from the darkness, their counterparts in metal music have tended to look the other way (one Finnish metal band has even taken Kaamos as its name).

The higher a country's latitude, the sharper the angle of its sunlight and the wider the distribution of the sun's beams when they meet a horizontal surface. On the night I moved to Scandinavia, I was transfixed by the late-April light as I was driven up the slender curve of Amager Beach in a taxi from Copenhagen Airport. It had a piercing, all-seeing quality, the very antithesis to Los Angeles haze. A century and a half earlier, painters had gathered at Skagen, Denmark's northernmost tip, where they formed an outpost of French Impressionism prompted by an extreme version of this limpid light combined with open skies and long beaches facing north. Led by the Norwegian-born P. S. Krøyer, the Skagen painters got wise to the particular moment on summer evenings when the water and the sky appeared to merge into a single shade, the so-called 'blue hour'. If you sense the difference in the angle of the sunlight in northern Denmark, you feel it strongly in Oslo and fiercely in Stockholm. In Helsinki it is all embracing. In Rovaniemi, it's as though the whole world is being projected cinematically from behind your shoulder.

Aalto sought to replicate the feeling of sunlight filtered sideways through forest trees – architecture as the management of natural light in a defined space. As the tentacles of Nordic architecture have reached out into the world in parallel with the region's music and musicians, cities from Riyadh to Shanghai have seen quintessentially Nordic structures rise from sand and soil. Angular rock, wood and glass have been put to work in the manipulation of sunlight, finely calibrated according to latitude. Standing amid the slatted wood, obtuse pillars and honeycomb pods that form the foyer of Snøhetta's Oslo Opera House, you learn a little about the sanctity of the sunlight that pours through the building's colossal wall-windows (if you're lucky). In the same firm's library for the Egyptian city of Alexandria, light is filtered through soft wooden surfaces and acid-stained bronze paneling – light not so much indulged as tamed.

Composers were playing with equivalent luminous techniques in music long before Sibelius, Saariaho and others got in on the act in the far north. In his oratorio *The Creation*, Joseph Haydn managed to conjure up the transformative magnificence of a sunrise within the aesthetic limitations of Viennese classicism. In the nineteenth century,

Richard Wagner perfected the idea of light graduating from the faint to the glowing to the saturating. Claude Debussy had his light shift in colour and intensity momentarily, as if reflecting on the undulating surface of an orchestral ocean. Anders Hillborg, a Swede, has written plenty of semi-narrative orchestral works in which massive consonant chords invade more opaque, elusive textures – harmony and tonality as an image of sudden, overwhelming white light.

As Hillborg's musical language has developed, so the various luminous techniques in his writing have increased in eloquence and nuance. He is now Sweden's most performed living composer, a craftsman with a rare ability to perceive how the listener will hear his music while never compromising its integrity. He manages to sound like himself even in works that bear little comparison to their predecessors. Hillborg composes with the clarity of the pop music he initially wrote, with the cool objectivity of a classic Scandinavian functionalist and with more than a hint of the narrative Nordic noir.

His orchestral work *Beast Sampler*, finished in 2014, is a thrillingly manipulative piece for orchestra that tints its own surface textures by degrees, layering planes of brass, woodwind and strings on top of one another. Marginal shifts in the music's bass foundations gently rotate the music that towers vertically above, altering the light that appears to glint off it. Musicians are instructed to play and sing without vibrato – the wobbling of the note for expression – resulting in a crystalline sound quality. Notes bend, slide and sweep through the orchestra like shafts of light thrown onto a landscape by shifting clouds. *Beast Sampler* is all texture, all sound. But it can't resist culminating in a stirring hymn for strings, according to Nordic custom.

At around the same time he was writing that piece, Hillborg was also completing a new work to order for the flagship orchestras of Berlin, Los Angeles and Chicago. In *Sirens*, Hillborg sharpened his idea of instrumental and vocal light still further. The piece plants distinctly Nordic fingerprints on the sort of pained mysticism associated with music from Estonia, across the Baltic Sea from Hillborg's

Stockholm. To the clear white light of its already clean orchestral and vocal textures, Hillborg adds the sound of human whistling. His 2002 piece for the Swedish mezzo-soprano Anne Sofie von Otter, '... *lontana in sonno* ...', combines a shimmering glass harmonica with vibrato-light strings that curl themselves stealthily around the female voice. Each instrumental or vocal component, including sculpted, marbled brass, is asked to imitate its companions. As the aperture gradually widens, the music's surface serenity takes on a gripping unease. The mood, like many a Scandinavian sky, threatens to turn at any moment.

Hillborg knows his Lindberg, and has evidently reacted to techniques used by his colleague in neighbouring Finland. In 2010 he wrote *Cold Heat*, an orchestral ice mountain with a warm glow. Some way into the piece, blocks of brass begin to move through a particular constellation of notes. The constellation is derived from the overtone series – the same set of mostly inaudible frequencies mapped and reproduced by Lindberg after *Kraft*. For both composers, the patterns of the overtone series provided the obvious tools with which they could aerate textures and tint timbres. They sensed how this most natural series of notes might do for our perception of sound what light does for our perception of image.

Harbouring the natural properties of the overtones series is a technique often said to have originated in France, the land that gave us impressionistic painting. In 1970s Paris, the composer Gérard Grisey pioneered so-called 'spectralism': using the timbral, acoustic or overtone properties of notes, often mapped by a computer, as a means of structuring a work or establishing its fundamental sound. As the British composer Julian Anderson has suggested, the technique can be traced back further, to the 1960s Denmark of Per Nørgard. In the first movement of his *Voyage Into the Golden Screen* written in 1968, Nørgård develops a particular constellation of pitches by superimposing one overtone series over an identical one tuned a quarter of a note higher. As its title suggests, the result is a searching work that hunts for something formally perfect, all the while foregrounding listener perception over any hint of a composer's message.

Can the basic idea of spectralism be traced back further still? It is surely adumbrated in Sibelius's taxonomical arrangement of instruments and instrumental groups according to timbre in *Tapiola*. It could even lie behind the idea of inaudible metamorphosis in a work like Sibelius's *The Wood Nymph*, and the heightened listener perception demanded by the plain repetitions and blunt narratives of his *Kullervo* – a work in which our minds do much of the conceptual legwork. If spectralism's central conceit is the sound of music as a state of mind, Sibelius got there first.

The twenty-something Kaija Saariaho heard Grisey's music at the summer school in Darmstadt in 1980, which led her almost immediately to Paris. She, too, analysed the acoustic overtones produced from a single frequency – in this case, the note produced by the bow of a cello pressed hard onto one of the instrument's strings. Again, Saariaho made a computer analysis of the inaudible frequencies produced by that sound and scored the results into her 1986 work for large ensemble, *Lichtbogen*. As she started work on the piece during a trip back to Finland, Saariaho saw the Northern Lights in the Arctic sky. 'When looking at the movements of these immense, silent lights which run over the black sky, first ideas concerning the form and language of the piece started to move in my mind,' wrote the composer in her own analysis of the piece.

The best translation of *Lichtbogen* is something approximating 'light arc', though in Scandinavian languages the word looks tantalizingly close to 'the book of light'. Whether or not its music conjures up a mental picture of the shimmering curtain of the Northern Lights – a long shot – it does home in on the idea of one colour or light source imperceptibly shifting onto another, and so on. Already, in works like *Laconisme de l'aile* from 1982, Saariaho had started to explore the idea of structuring a piece on an axis of transforming textures and timbres, rather than seeing texture and timbre as the final layer of icing on the cake.

From the late 1980s, Saariaho's music became more overtly beautiful, as if adapting to its creator's life in Paris. Colour and translucency were now its overriding concern, the transfiguration of one shade into another a rapidly developing technique. Textures became more active and vivid, the notes tending to pass by at a faster rate even if base speeds felt unerringly slow. The colour spectrum of the cello, a touchstone theme for Saariaho since *Lichtbogen*, found new expression in the cello concerto *Notes on Light*, written for Anssi Karttunen and the Boston Symphony Orchestra in 2007. Across five movements, the piece gradually casts away the shadows of darkness only to discover a light no less uneasy.

Critics didn't fail to notice the tough, rigorous, 'Nordic' outer layers falling away from Saariaho's music, to be replaced, apparently, with something softer but no less geographically specific – an obsession with light and its absence. What they might have dismissed as frivolous or decorative from a French composer was accepted, in Saariaho's music, as a reaction to the geographical extremes to which Finns are inevitably subjected. But Saariaho's deep sensitivity to light has as much to do with form as feeling – a delimiting structural boundary in the manner of Nørgård's Infinity Series. France may not have softened the composer's Finnish tendency towards self-discipline or even self-flagellation. But it's often when leaving your homeland that you get a sharper eye on it.

◢

In 1995, Berlin hosted an architectural competition with a difference. The five autonomous Nordic nations were to erect new embassy buildings on a single site in the German capital. Each country would get to design its own, but within strict parameters laid down by the winner of the competition, who would draw the footprint and establish the wider unifying plan.

Appropriately enough, that winner was an Austro-Finnish firm run by Alfred Berger and Tiina Parkkinen, who proposed a 226-metre louvred copper wall, snaked into an organic shape resembling a squat keyhole. It would allow for the maximum permeation of natural light and views of the Tiergarten trees that surrounded the site. Inside it, the hamlet of five embassies would be arranged according to geography. From Denmark in the south-west corner, the complex moves clockwise through Iceland, Norway, Sweden and Finland, arriving at a communal reception and conference hall positioned roughly where Estonia and Latvia would be on the map. There's even a central water feature symbolizing the Baltic Sea in miniature.

According to the parameters laid down by Berger and Parkkinen, each of the embassy buildings would be 15 metres tall with a flat roof. Otherwise, each is locally designed and conforms to type – from chosen materials to stylistic subtleties. Iceland's is the only structure whose façade is hewn from stone, though Norway's does include a single 120-ton piece of raw-cut granite behind which the interiors aim to evoke the 'coolness of glaciers'. Denmark's embassy, lined with metropolitan steel, is that bit more European – the only building of the five to boast a physical link to German territory in the form of a glass façade that lines the Rauchstrasse. Ever musical, Finland's embassy has an exterior of rhythmically slatted larch inspired by the physique of the country's national musical instrument, the kantele. Sweden's was designed by personality-architect Gert Wingårdh. Like much Swedish design, it's a touch more blingy and transatlantic than that of its neighbours, with a façade of gloss black and a showpiece spiral staircase that offsets glass-walled conference rooms shrieking Swedish democracy.

A sixth building, the communal house or 'Fellehuset', presents a more universal view of the Nordic region and mindset. It is open to the public yet intriguingly closed to the world, its narrow strips of glazing punctuated by far wider strips of impermeable timber. Once inside, the building shows its workings with visible joints, sharp contours and frosted glass partitions bolted to suspended floors. Sunlight fills its central atrium discretionally, where the fundamental structure semaphores a pan-Nordic combination of progress and tradition in concrete and wood.

The broader complex appears to acknowledge the international community's perennial mental merging of the five biggest Nordic nations while concurrently indulging the deep separations, rivalries and cultural peculiarities that permeate an old union of autonomous lands. Only when viewed from above does the fundamental schematic structure thought up by Berger and Parkkinen reveal itself in full: an Aalto-like radiating grid of two sets of non-parallel lines, largely invisible from the six isolated structures that follow them but picked out in the communal space in between. These non-parallel lines originate from two points beyond the exterior walls, dictated by the suggested flow of light through two open points within them. The grid, more than the copper wall, is the unifying feature despite it remaining largely hidden. It's a subliminal scheme rather like Nørgård's Infinity Series. But when you know about it, it's a beautifully simple one that anchors and rationalizes all. If anything suggests the Nordic nations are keen to look formally disciplined in the eyes of their great cultural and intellectual surrogate Germany, this complex does.

What is it about the buildings themselves that we take to be so distinctly Nordic? Their materials project shiny metropolitan progress while also referencing natural truths and rural hard work. Their cladding speaks the language of calming, motivic patterning in pallid colours that filter the light inside. Various sharp contours and non-right angles outline their stark shapes. As for the austere geometric structures themselves, each knows its place and height and yet each feels somehow monolithic, as if it had always been – sturdiness and severity in proud prows formed of hard rock and steel.

In the Tiergarten, the buildings appear as distant from the prevailing design tradition as Aalto's Essen opera house must have half a century earlier. Entirely contemporary, they give the impression of having existed for centuries. Meticulously designed, they seem untouched by human hands. They play on our collective idea of what makes the Nordic region mythical yet real, strange yet rational, individual yet inseparable – European but so inherently separate from Europe. The geographical scheme helps us ascertain which of these interchangeable countries are which; the design tells us just a little of their individual cultural histories, if we're willing to look hard enough.

The embassies also echo much of the deliberately constrained Nordic music discussed – works that set delimiting parameters only to explore fully what might be achieved within them. They do so across six linked but independent movements, not striving for triumph as much as for order, clarity and union. They are a mezza voce reminder, just a stone's throw from the ostentatious home of the Berlin Philharmonic, that in the twenty-first century, large-scale symphonic music hasn't, in fact, fallen out of fashion. It has just migrated north.

Postlude. Silence

Kierkegaard's best-known aphorism is that life must be lived forwards but can only be understood backwards. Anyone too young or too naïve to grasp his meaning was given a helping hand in 2020.

For a few hundred Copenhageners, a warning shot was fired on 19 February that year. We made our way to an awkwardly positioned suburb and up one of the region's only hills, to the brick basilica that is Grundtvig's Church. Inside, a new piece by the Icelandic composer Bára Gísladóttir was to be performed. It had attracted an audience far bigger than anyone expected. Inside the church, new sections of seating were hastily being uncordoned to accommodate the hoards.

I had come across a few of Gísladóttir's works before. In one of them, a piece from 2015 titled *Jódynur*, a solo flute accompanies video footage of twelve dead horses being craned out of an Icelandic lake. All twelve animals had trotted onto the frozen water in 2014, but temperatures were unusually high for the time of year. The ice was too thin to support their weight and the horses drowned.

This time, we were assembling for the first performance of Gísladóttir's new work *Víddir* – its title another of those Icelandic words that stretches far beyond the confines of an already broad definition, 'dimensions'. What we heard was a monolithic sound landscape lasting an hour and scored for nine flutes, electronics, percussion, organ, bass guitar and Gísladóttir's own double bass. The one instrument the piece sought to play above all others was the one we were all huddled inside: the immense reverberating acoustic of Denmark's most spectacular church.

First the herd of flutes puffed, whistled and sang into the ether, as if invoking the work itself with their ominous breeze. When the same instruments returned later it wasn't to sing like avian creatures but to bray and caterwaul like four-legged ones, marking *Víddir*'s most obvious point of existential crisis. At its most overwhelming, the piece resembled a treeless *Tapiola*, roaring through the church's tall nave like a gale. Its primeval rumbles and judders appeared as snapshots of a bigger process, one whose naturally recurring cycles don't begin or end. Or didn't, until humankind got involved.

Eventually *Víddir* did end. It came to rest, like *Tapiola*, on a tranche of distinctive light – not so much the warm glow of forest safety as the white light of general annihilation. I wasn't the only audience member to cycle back to Copenhagen spooked. The performance had felt less a warning than a prophecy – rationally Scandinavian in its assertion that the demise of humanity was a done deal; darkly Icelandic in its willingness to examine, in sound, precisely what that might entail.

Once upon a time, nature was the bosom to which composers hurried for comfort – the portal through which a symphony could transcend into bliss, the restful idyll in which it might seek momentary repose. Nordic 'nature music' has long been more complicated than that – a reminder that, in the north, the natural world was always the great enemy as much as the great inspiration. *Tapiola* is freighted with nature's awesome power. After the freewheeling energy of his *Sinfonia Espansiva*, Nielsen's later symphonies sound sick and overwhelmed. The rumblings of a pandemic are never quite silenced in No. 5. One viable interpretation of No. 6 is that only the spirited will survive.

POSTLUDE

Whether or not Sibelius and Nielsen consciously anticipated it, the tables have now turned almost fully. We are fast coming to terms with a world in which nature as the comfort blanket of romantic pastoral or Mahlerian transcendence no longer exists. Nature is a cornered, injured animal prone to lashing out. We are both assailant and lifeline, guilty party and only hope.

Plenty of Nordic music has taken up the mantle of concern. Bent Sørensen's works suggest the purest forms of beauty are already lost to the world. Hans Abrahamsen's retreat into the domain of all our childhoods – where it still snows, where the story turns out good but the good people don't always survive. Others, like Gísladóttir, are looking forwards. Maja Ratkje's 2010 sound installation *Desibel* positioned the world's loudest speaker system on the side of a Norwegian mountain overlooking a salmon fjord earmarked for mining, raising the alarm courtesy of a wall of amplified trombones. Helge Iberg's *Songs from the Planet of Life* (2018) presents a delicate landscape of melancholy and vitality in which we sense a creeping discomfort, the rug pulled from under nature-nostalgia by science and reason. Niels Rønsholdt's *Archive of Emotions and Experiences* (2019) takes a circuitous view of mass extinction, imagining a time when the world has been purged of life as we know it – when an oracle-pianist must imagine what the previous ecosystem's creatures known as 'birds' might have sounded like.

As birds and beasts check out of that ecosystem with ever more regularity, an early manifestation of potentially irreversible climate change looks set to be Planet Earth's steady decrescendo. Nordic music apparently saw that coming too – from *Tapiola*'s structural dissolution, its muting of its own composer, to the slow but steady quieting-down of new music from the last two decades or more. Never has the silence of annihilation felt closer, scientifically or creatively. Music by Christian Winther Christensen and Johan Svensson urges us to set an ear to the ground and listen to the soil, where there might just be some last scratches, snuffles and scurries left to hear.

THE NORTHERN SILENCE

▲

The global classical music community has long proved adept at speculating if and when, in a world moving culturally and economically further and further from the historical traditions in which it is rooted, its own music will stop. Nobody predicted that the bandwagon would judder to an abrupt halt in mid-March 2020. Whether or not the experience of the following year will prove a useful drill for climate change's coming havoc, it did provide the world with a resonant general pause – a 'fermata', to use the musical term. The silence was crushing, until we got used to it. As the months dragged on, it forced the classical music community to ask the sorts of questions it had been avoiding for decades.

Exactly half a year after the first Covid-19 lockdowns halted performances in Copenhagen, I caught a train across the Øresund Bridge to hear the Malmö Symphony Orchestra play Sibelius's Symphony No. 5. There were only five spectators in the orchestra's oak-lined concert hall: four administrative staff and me. Its American chief conductor Robert Trevino looked directly into a camera as he addressed everyone else, watching the live broadcast from home. Sibelius's symphony, he said, is a work in which overbearing trauma and overwhelming hope appear to co-exist. Asking his musicians to play a tiny snippet of the first movement, he demonstrated the harmonically elusive music's ability to teeter between major and minor keys – walking the tightrope of fear and confidence, anxiety and freedom.

The Nordic model served the region's culture sector relatively well during the pandemic's shutdowns. With ticket income always secondary, established orchestras were able to adapt. The Aalborg Symphony Orchestra quit its concert hall Musikkens Hus ('The House of Music') and climbed aboard a bus painted to resemble the building's distinctive architecture, 'Musikkens Bus'. For weeks, its members trundled around north Jutland playing in care homes and nursing homes.

Other Nordic orchestras were shaken from their complacency – but far from all. One that remained on stage was Trevino's Malmö

Symphony Orchestra. At the end of April, it was the last orchestra in Europe left playing at full strength, live streaming its weekly Thursday concerts from an empty hall. Trevino's agency in Vienna started to refer to their client as 'the last man standing'. When concert life in Denmark and Finland got going again in the autumn, those conductors who normally ply their trade in Seattle, San Francisco, London, Paris and Glasgow suddenly found themselves working at home, leading Danish and Finnish orchestras in front of Danish and Finnish audiences. The Russian music director of the Royal Danish Opera, Alexander Vedernikov, became one of many thousands of musicians for whom the actual disease proved tragically more significant than its societal repercussions. He died of Covid-19 in Moscow at the end of October 2020, aged 56, seven weeks after conducting the season opening at the Copenhagen Opera House.

Meanwhile Sweden's governmental approach to the pandemic, unique in Europe, provided the Nordic region with its biggest rumbling of geopolitical disquiet for decades. It was felt acutely along the Øresund Bridge. Sweden imposed no formal lockdowns, closing neither schools nor businesses but eventually restricting attendance at large sports and cultural events. The country's death rates soared far beyond those of its neighbours. For the first time in modern history, Denmark and Sweden closed ranks on one another, even imposing reciprocal travel bans. Denmark labelled Sweden irresponsible. Sweden castigated Denmark as protectionist. The usual good humour that buffers tensions between the two nations very nearly evaporated.

As 2020 groaned into 2021, it became clear that Sweden was set on playing a long game with Covid-19, however reluctant the country's officials were to admit it. In a society prizing stability, order and the bigger picture of social welfare above all else, excess deaths from the disease among the elderly were evidently seen as a fair price to pay for protecting wider mental health and societal stability – for keeping business going, keeping education going, keeping some form of social and cultural life going. Most Swedes trusted their government to have made the right judgement, with the implication that the lockdowns enforced everywhere else in Europe would wreak economic, social and mental health havoc in the long term. It will take years to say with any certainty whether Sweden called it right.

Music, meanwhile, proved its agency. Sweden's orchestras and opera companies gathered and played, streaming their performances online. From the first days of the first lockdown in Denmark, the conductor Phillip Faber, seated at a grand piano, led the nation in daily, televised communal singalongs. Each episode of Fællesang ('communal song') would begin with breathing exercises before Danes were taken through a litany of well-known numbers, the line-up underpinned by the dual icons of the country's song tradition, the composer Carl Nielsen and the rocker Kim Larsen. Teitur Lassen made an unforgettable appearance on the show, playing live on the side of a Faroese mountain as the low sun illuminated a tranche of the glistening North Atlantic behind him.

Migrating to Friday nights, Fællesang proved immensely popular and became a permanent fixture on the schedules. DR television executives touted the show as the very definition of public service broadcasting – pandemic or no pandemic – in an age when hostile politicians were increasingly demanding that definition be clarified. In February 2021, the show's TV trailer included appearances from politicians straddling the ideological divide, all endorsing the value of communal singing.

As Fællesang effectively took the place of *X Factor*, plenty of Danes were reminded that music can exist without the trappings of the music industry – music not as the narcissistic pursuit of individual success, but as a communal activity, a cross-generational bonding agent, a non-financial commodity that might be appreciated for its own empowering strength and beauty no matter who is delivering it. For a time, it felt as though the pandemic had done the very opposite of silencing Denmark. Once a society lets go of songs that can be sung together by every generation alive, suggested Fællesang, there isn't much left to bind it together – an echo of the 'original' Fællesang meetings: expressions of democratic resistance in Nazi-occupied Denmark. Nobody was talking about genre, but the constant presence of Faber and DR's various in-house choirs set the tone. By Christmas 2020, the Danish Government had passed a budget increasing culture funding across the board – beyond the rescue packages already agreed – and halting planned cuts to DR. Both had long since been promised, but now even the detractors seemed to get the point. Parliament waved the relevant bills through.

◢

Stability underpins the Nordic region's cultural life, from inbuilt complacence to infrastructural brilliance. It is as much the stability of political consensus as that of cultural idealism. Anticipating the biggest political upheavals in several generations after the disruption of the pandemic, Robert Trevino bent my ear about the 'disproportionate sense of stability' felt across the Nordic countries and the complacency it engenders. 'We have seen how easily priorities can change,' he said on the phone from Malmö in April 2020, as he continued to conduct his orchestra there and lobby local politicians to allow it to keep playing. The reference was to the constant threat hanging over the Copenhagen Philharmonic, the one orchestra in Denmark for which politicians have consistently passed the buck of financial responsibility. 'The presumed social contract is only that: presumed,' warned Trevino. As Fredrik Österling had argued up the coast in Helsingborg, local government spending on opera companies and orchestras is not insignificant. Officials are increasingly likely to ask for tangible returns on their investment.

In a Denmark where the political climate has grown more suspicious of such ensembles, audiences for classical music and opera increased significantly in the decade to March 2020. The growth was fuelled, in part, by an awareness of that suspicion among the institutions themselves and their determination to future-proof. In a Sweden far less prone to questioning culture funding – where the arts remain an undisputed element of the social democratic project – audience figures have been heading in the opposite direction. As with Covid-19, it's difficult to say whether Sweden's blind idealism or Denmark's cautious hesitance will prove more enlightened in the long term.

Trevino had some ideas. It wouldn't be long, he assured me, before Denmark's increasing political cynicism surrounding culture funding found its way into Sweden and even Finland, 'though Finland will be the last to get it', said the conductor, who once served as an assistant to Leif Segerstam in Helsinki. He spoke of the need for orchestras like his to reinforce their place at the heart of the societies that fund them, justifying their existence and ensuring they are well positioned to lead local people, at short notice, in times of societal need and distress. 'The world is going to divide into orchestras that start to recognize that reality and get on board with it, and those who don't,' Trevino said. 'And we're not going to hear about the ones who don't, because they won't exist.'

Even from within sometimes-cynical Denmark, the Nordic region can feel like a societal utopia – a collection of progressive, wealthy countries in which 'the market' and 'profit' remain elements of life rather than reasons for it. Despite their frequent intolerance, these nations have managed to resist the pervasive rush in the other direction even as they have climbed from the bottom of Europe's economic ladder to the top of it (or perhaps because of the fact). And apparently, they are clinging on. Facing a perfect storm of labour segmentation, globalization, privatization and profiteering – irrepressible flies in the ointment of social democracy for a decade or more – Denmark, Norway, Sweden and Finland had all returned Social Democrat-led governments by the end of 2021.

If electoral habits haven't changed all that much, the parties themselves have. It was a coalition government led by the Social Democrats that imposed the first of successive cuts to Denmark's culture budget from 2011; that privatized the country's national energy firm and sold off its postal service. Forced to pander to various forms of populism, individual Social Democrat politicians in Denmark have shifted as much to the right on culture policy as the wider party has on immigration, citing an 'elitist' focus on opera and classical music and even criticizing high spending on public libraries. Neither Finland nor Denmark have proved themselves immune from the elitism flag of convenience, a cross-party position which derides expertise and seeks to cordon cultural life off into identity-oriented, commercially viable silos – the beginning of the end for probing and unifying creativity.

It has been left to morally objectionable, nativist parties in Denmark to fight against the closure of orchestras (unsuccessfully, in the case of the 2014 disbanding of the DR Chamber Orchestra) while advocating high tax and high spending, just as long as the welfare money makes its way to white, Danish-speaking Europeans. Across the Nordic countries, these parties are scared for the future of their homogenous, functional societies and perhaps with good reason. But their proposed solutions tend to look backwards not forwards, culture policy included. The far-right Danish People's Party's bookish culture spokespeople enjoy holding forth on the repertoire of the nation's opera companies and symphony orchestras, with a disdain for the avant-garde and a nostalgic fondness for works from the Golden Age. But at least their blind idealism allows them to talk about culture on its own terms, with real belief in its non-economic value. In 2020, the party's rising star in the Danish parliament, Morten Messerschmidt, proposed the development of a new classical music TV platform offering the best of the Nordic region's state-sponsored concerts and operas, modelled on the French-German arts channel Arte. Now there's an idea.[1]

At the opposite end of the political spectrum to the new far right – enacting a pincer movement on social democracy – is a resurgent Nordic libertarianism, keen on deregulation and insistent that the rich should be allowed to keep far more of their money, thus inspiring greater ambition among the rest of us. It is this movement, arguably, that has proved most hostile to the traditional place of culture within the public sector.

And yet, like the venture capitalism of early 1990s Sweden under Prime Minister Carl Bildt, Nordic libertarianism has never quite maintained traction. North of the Baltic Sea, something about it just doesn't seem a good fit. For three years until 2019, the movement's main exponent in Denmark, a party currently labelled Liberal Alliance, had control of the country's Culture Ministry as part of a coalition government. With the support of the Danish People's Party, its minister dreamed up all sorts of plans for the nation's artistic life, advocating the merging of choirs and orchestras and even voicing a free-market argument against symphony orchestras performing Handel's *Messiah* at Christmas. Even as Danish society has become ostensibly more narcissistic, the Liberal Alliance's message that 'nobody fights harder for lower tax' evidently felt alien. The party was annihilated at the ballot box in 2019 and now barely exists. Its former Culture Minister quit politics to join the priesthood.

▲

The River Harrestrup skirts the western edge of Copenhagen, flowing through nondescript suburbs down to the city's newly fashionable South Harbour. In the Middle Ages, the river was dammed at what is now the district of Rødovre, creating a large pond known as Damhus Lake. King Frederick II handed ownership of the lake over to the University of Copenhagen in 1561 and for the intervening five hundred years it has proved a favourite walking and twitching spot. At its south-westerly tip sits a proud stone building that once served as the tollhouse for traffic heading into the capital from Roskilde, the town whose cathedral entombs seven centuries of Danish monarchs.

Since the 1800s, the tollhouse has gone by the name of Damhuskroen ('The Damhus Inn'), the name spelled out proud in broad black lettering between two regimented ranks of windows. For years it was a much-loved and much-mocked venue for unaffected celebration, conducted in that uniquely Danish style that sees inhibition and prejudice left at the door. In 2020, it was sold to an investor. These days, it goes by the name of The Old Irish Pub – indistinguishable from thirty-five other such hostelries across Denmark, Norway and Finland (and counting) and an establishment neither old, Irish nor even strictly definable as a pub – to an Englishman, at least. Its interior is filled with uniform green-gold paraphernalia aping the imagined traditions of a country far, far away. In place of the gingham tablecloths and brass candlesticks is a fixed interior of booths and dance-floors that, if you've been in any other branch of The Old Irish Pub, you'll have seen before.

Despite its homogenous population, even in the 2020s Denmark was largely holding out against the homogenization of its high street and its retail sector. Central Copenhagen had just three non-concession branches of McDonalds in 2021 and the nation's only other prominent hospitality giants were homegrown ones. Chain bars were a new phenomenon, lending enterprises like The Old Irish Pub the feel of a charming novelty – a place where, for once, you knew what you were getting and could get it relatively cheap. Still, the selling of The Damhus Inn to investors looked to many like proof that anonymous venture capitalism had more than a foot in the door; that this small country's wholesale surrender to the global corporate conveyer belt was all but inevitable.

This corner of the Damhus Lake seemed like a good spot to meet with local resident Maria Frej, whose unique view of Scandinavia's cultural life straddles the political, the musical and the geographical. A straight-talking south Jutlander, Frej was elected as a Copenhagen councillor in 2014 and spent seven years fighting incessantly for culture at the town hall. I first encountered her in 2015 when, as Head of Music at Tivoli Gardens, she was responsible for programming the biggest classical music festival north of the BBC Proms. In

February 2020, she began commuting across the Øresund Bridge to Sweden as Chief Executive of the Malmö Symphony Orchestra and its concert hall, Malmö Live.

On the March morning in 2021 when we circumnavigated the lake, anemones were blossoming. Copenhagen appeared to be returning to something resembling normality, the second of its national lockdowns about to be eased and the faint warmth of the sun finally allowing friends, families and colleagues to meet outdoors. 'Hopefully in May or June I will be able to invite you to Malmö to see the orchestra again. But that's just a hope,' Frej proposed, indulging the spirit of optimism generated by the weather. After that, we talked about the bigger political picture, where things weren't so sunny.

Politics, Frej lamented, had become a short-term game – the promising of quick fixes in return for votes. Long-term vision was in short supply, even in Denmark. She compared campaigning to 'offering people sugar and white bread; you are not motivating them to look any deeper'. She pointed to one of the original tenets of social democracy: that citizens engage themselves in the serious consideration of society's challenges throughout the year, whether an election was looming or not. 'When social democracy started, people bought a ticket to a whole package of meaningful values,' she said. 'They don't do that today. Nobody feels a responsibility to ask themselves whether something is good for society. And if you are not encouraged to see the bigger picture, then we all have a problem.'

What of the old idea of culture as lifelong irrigation for the mind – the foremost stoker of democratic thinking? Echoing Trond Aarre's words in Nordfjord, Frej suggested not so much a dissolution as a splintering. 'The Social Democrats have left that position, even though they were the ones to introduce it. Now you find people who believe in culture in all parties – people who believe in culture as a way of forming people, uniting them and allowing them to make wise decisions. But it's a minority of people in all parties, to the extent that you could even make a separate Culture Party out of them.'

Political stability and consensus, said Frej, lay behind the preservation of Denmark's cultural infrastructure and particularly its network of orchestras. 'The orchestras are maintained, not because there's a great cultural vision anymore, but because of the fear of tampering with a legacy. It's such trouble to take them away, so why not keep them?'

Others disagree, predicting Denmark's network of regional symphony orchestras will be wound down as the century rolls on, with Sweden's not far behind and potentially Finland's too. Only in Norway does that seem somehow unthinkable, probably as it's the one Nordic nation establishing and expanding orchestras rather than simply preserving them.

It is easy to confuse pragmatism with pessimism when talking to a Dane, even more so one as wearied by the attrition of politics as Frej. Her sense of dissatisfaction with the workings of democracy is typical in Denmark, and probably the very thing that keeps that democracy so virile. Besides, her own political legacy would indicate not the imminent dismantling of cultural infrastructure, but rather the opposite. As a councillor, she oversaw a general uplift in culture and music education funding for Copenhagen and its districts. Just a few months after our walk at the lake, she secured the first tranche of cash for a new, dedicated centre for chamber music in the city.

Elsewhere in Europe, a fundamental shift in philosophy has affected not so much the allocation of money for culture as the reasoning behind it. In the United Kingdom, spending on culture is increasingly justified not on creative, civic or humanitarian terms but on economic ones – on the baseline notion of a return on an investment. A whiff of this has come to the Nordic countries too; a crack down the façade of the principle that culture be paid for by the public for the sake of its sustenance, its educational and democratic nourishment and its own creative inspiration. 'It feels like we are constantly trying to make the case for why the arts matter in a language that is made for businessmen,' the Finnish violinist Pekka Kuusisto told me in 2017, 'that the conversation about art in society has been sidetracked by people who are just so desperate to make it sound like a good investment. Which I suppose it is, but that's not what it's about.'

Kuusisto was talking to me as his brother, the violinist Jaakko, participated in the political redrawing of Finland's cultural map – a process aimed at securing the financial future of the country's unparalleled network of orchestras while increasing support for free-form genres including poetry, dance, circus arts and so on. That agenda alone appears to return the horse to its rightful position before the cart: to considerer the creative value of the actual art before auditing its economic dividend.

And yes, culture does appear to have retained its almost sacred place in Finnish society, as in Swedish, and despite eyebrow-raising cuts to the nation's culture spending in the autumn of 2021. Even the difference in language is striking. 'I'm probably one of the worst Culture Ministers ever,' the Finnish incumbent Paavo Arhinmäki told me on the record in 2013, lamenting his own inability to increase his ministry's budget in line with a decade-long trend rather than pandering to the popular notion, prevalent elsewhere, that any money it spent was an indulgence. Frej talked of 'a whole different tone of voice' to the culture conversation in Sweden, where she felt able to discuss the central, soulful significance of the arts to the wider populace 'without being laughed at'.

And in Denmark? 'They find it more difficult to value those long perspectives than in Sweden,' Frej observed. 'But I'm positive about it coming back on track. The whole culture debate has become far more prominent in the last ten years in Denmark, especially in newspapers and on the radio. It's more common, and more politically interesting, to talk about culture and to demand answers on it from politicians.' The discussion may well have been stoked by a decade of cuts to the country's culture budget, only halted or in some cases reversed in 2020. As we spoke, even long-term security for the Copenhagen Philharmonic seemed to Frej within touching distance.

'I could have landed a real deal there, but then Covid-19 happened and the orchestra changed leadership, so I kind of had to let it go.'

As we arrived back at The Old Irish Pub from the opposite direction, we addressed the elephant in the room – whether the Nordic region's orchestras were not themselves part of the problem: uniform, inflexible, expensive, impersonal – offering largely workaday performances of the same narrow spectrum of easily-quaffed music with the same peripatetic cohort of soloists and conductors; as indistinct and anodyne as anything on offer inside the pub. We talked of Frej's erstwhile colleague Fredrik Österling in Helsingborg. We talked about the hunger, innovation and restlessness that enlivens the classical music scene in London, where relatively low funding levels mean almost every ensemble has to fight for its audience and its existence.

Frej insisted it was her mission to make the Malmö Symphony Orchestra distinctive and indispensable – to turn its interaction with citizens from passive to active. 'No orchestra has a licence to survive,' she said. 'Why should it? Surviving in itself is not a purpose. The purpose of an orchestra is to make an impact on the society it is in.' In Malmö, reckoned to be the most diverse city in Scandinavia and home to 187 different nationalities in 2020, that seemed both a huge opportunity and a colossal challenge.

As we unlocked our bikes outside the pub, Frej outlined her plans to quit politics, frustrated by the fragility of its victories and the painstakingly slow speeds with which they materialize. 'Working in culture, I can develop strategies to move entire institutions forwards. In politics, I am constantly disappointed,' she said with a resigned smile and a pragmatic shrug. But she shifted tack by way of a farewell: 'I still believe in the bigger project, that people want more from life, even if you find many politicians who are afraid to put that into words. I entered politics because I believe in equality, because you don't get to choose where you are born. Culture evens out the chances people have to lead a quality life, and that leads to a better world.'

In the Nordic region's far north, where the indigenous Sámi herd reindeer in sync with the shifting rhythms of nature, there was no need of Covid-19 to provide an hors d'oeuvres to the havoc of climate change. Curious, unseasonal weather, much of it significantly warmer than usual, has been steadily syncopating and deregulating those rhythms for years. In 2020, a fourth of the reindeer population in the districts of Troms and Finnmark died as unusual weather patterns trapped their food under layers of ice and snow. At the same time, warming temperatures significantly disrupted the Sámi's ability to herd reindeer over frozen rivers, marooning the animals out of the reach of food.

As if none of this were happening, Finland and Scandinavia's growing obsession with tourism was trouncing habitats and communities. In the decade since my first visit in 2010, the Arctic town of Tromsø sprouted handfuls of chain hotels while souvenir shops effectively commandeered its high street. Cruise ships would release their payloads into the town for a matter of hours, prompting a rush to consume as much as possible in the shortest space of time without investing in an overnight stay – the very antithesis to the way of life that once held sway here.

For many in Tromsø, 2020 provided the deceleration they thought would only come when it was too late. Before the pandemic, the tiny city had set its sights on welcoming a whopping 2 million visitors annually by 2030, while its development plan sought to green-light more hotel builds and a new shopping mall on the harbour side. The people of Tromsø appear to be divided on whether this is much-needed modernization or greedy corporate whitewashing. Either way, the Sámi didn't stand to benefit all that much, even if the newly formed Arctic Philharmonic, on balance, probably did.

One composer could see the environmental catastrophe in the Arctic unfolding with her own eyes. I first met Outi Tarkiainen in

Helsinki in the summer of 2015, while making a documentary film for the Society of Finnish Composers. The encounter lingered in my mind long after the event. She had described the piece in-progress on her desk at the time: a song-cycle for voice and orchestra titled *Eanan, giđa nieida* ('The Earth, Spring's Daughter') setting words by Sámi poets – the first notated song cycle to use the language. Since recorded by John Storgårds's Lapland Chamber Orchestra and mezzo-soprano Virpi Räisänen, it is a monodrama that rails with varying degrees of politeness against the oppression of the Sámi and the plundering of the earth. The piece takes the form of a symmetrical cycle reflecting the Sámi's traditional belief in continuous renewal – a belief that finds itself under increasing strain.

During that interview in 2015, Tarkiainen had spoken slowly and determinedly in English, narrowing her eyes as her voice took on a sort of stoic fervour. She described wandering the streets of London long into the night some years previously, having seen a performance of Alban Berg's opera *Lulu* at the Royal Opera House. 'I was thinking: can a person, at such an old age of 25, change her life's direction, and start to do something really different?' As a female composer in a man's world, she began to interpret her own struggle as an echo of that of the Sámi in and around her hometown of Rovaniemi, their traditional ways largely ignored by governments in Helsinki, Oslo and Stockholm set on a standardized view of modern life. From its basis in the world of the jazz orchestra, Tarkiainen's music veered into a lyrical, pained, Alban Berg-influenced aesthetic lined with a distinctive sense of longing that the composer rationalizes as 'for the north'. Just being in conversation with her was a moving experience. 'I see the best music almost as a force of nature, which can flood over a person and change entire destinies,' she told me.

The following summer I made good on my promise to visit Tarkiainen's Silence Festival in Kaukonen, and in the intervening years we have stayed in touch. In one email in 2019, she told me she had moved with her husband to Ivalo, a village in the Inari district of

Lapland, around 300 kilometres north of Rovaniemi. 'Somehow it had been our dream for many years and now we're here, looking at the clear sky filled with so many stars and the Northern Lights,' she wrote. I found it intriguing that a person would move to such a place for almost exclusively creative, intangible purposes.

Over the course of 2019, from her composing desk in Ivalo, Tarkiainen fulfilled the terms of a commission from BBC Radio 3 and the National Arts Centre Orchestra in Ottawa for a new orchestral work. The resulting piece, *Midnight Sun Variations*, is described by the composer as 'a set of variations on the light when the sun never sets in the arctic summer night ... the infinitely nuanced colours that, as the summer draws near, become veiled in shadow until darkness descends and the sun ceases to rise above the horizon.'

In Ivalo, Tarkiainen experienced a flush of creativity. 'We were going into nature every day. It was purifying as an artist – I could listen to my inner voices and be very honest with myself – but also as a human being,' she told me in the spring of 2021, having moved south to Kuhmo. From near the top of the planet, Tarkiainen could easily see the cycles and habits of nature she had known from childhood changing. 'The Arctic has already warmed much faster than southern and central Europe, with average winter temperatures rising two or three degrees,' she explained. 'The weeks of minus 30 and minus 40 have almost gone. Now there are just a few days of that here and there. The snow comes about a month later than I am used to and you get heatwaves in May. You notice a great deal just from the feel of the ground.'

The Sámi have felt it most. 'They are out there in nature for weeks and weeks, all year round. The herding culture gives them a far deeper connection to the earth,' Tarkiainen said. 'The Sámi talk now about the "new weather", something I have also been thinking about, though probably not as much as the rabbits and reindeer have been. The difference with humans is that we know it's happening because of us.' One message of *Midnight Sun Variations*, Tarkiainen explained, was that we consider what nature would tell us if we could listen to it. 'Finns and the Sámi are related from thousands of years back. So what exactly is it that we Finns have forgotten over the centuries that the Sámi still remember?'

Tarkiainen, her husband and their first son arrived in Ivalo on 22 December 2018, in the depths of the arctic winter. It was one day after the solstice and one month into a two-month stretch in which there would be no natural light at all. The first phase of their existence there equated to a journey from darkness to light – a two-month sunrise. 'I struggled with the lack of light, for weeks and even months,' the composer recalled. Then came incessant light. 'In the summer I remember thinking what a waste of light it was. The nights were really, really bright; the sun was more in the centre of the sky than it had been, even in Rovaniemi.' When the darkness came again, she barely noticed it encroaching.

Tarkiainen finished the score for *Midnight Sun Variations* in May 2019, 'when the light starts to really open up in Ivalo'. The word 'variations' in the title refers not to the musical form but to the varied range of colours revealed by Ivalo's lucid summer light, 'infinitely-nuanced hues that become veiled in shadow until darkness descends,' according to the composer's own programme note. As she wrote the piece, Tarkiainen became aware of the growth of her second child in her womb.

Ivalo in June is an extraordinary place to be. The evening light, in particular, has a bleaching purity to it on clear nights, though not yet the piercing quality that comes later in the summer and in early autumn, when the sun has started to lower in the sky once more. At its highest, the sun glistens and dazzles like the woodwinds, harp, celeste and tectonic percussion that tangle in the opening pages of *Midnight Sun Variations*. The work had its premiere at the BBC Proms in London on 19 August 2019, its score dispatched from Ivalo to Manchester earlier that summer for the BBC Philharmonic and conductor John Storgårds to start rehearsing it.

At first, the piece appears to hold up a hand, shielding eyes and ears from the light's unfiltered strength. After some minutes, block harmonies appear, rooting the music's otherwise vaporous textures; woodwind chords moan as if blown through their instruments by the wind. A kettledrum rumble curls upwards, and the chords transfer from cool winds to warming strings. The whole orchestra steels itself during the keening ascent that follows, using those chords for traction, urged on by bending trombones slicing upwards through the ensemble's midriff. After a moment of rupture that speaks of nature's awesome and indiscriminate power, a chorale-like gesture emerges on strings. It turns through a series of chords before, slowly but surely, taking the form of the unifying motto from *Tapiola* – 'the dense coniferous forests mystified by Jean Sibelius, bathed in countless shades of light', according to Tarkiainen.

Midnight Sun Variations revels in the intense beauty of Tarkiainen's Ivalo, but not without a feeling of terrible underlying concern. The impression is of a beauty that cannot last – fading with the slow, seasonal onset of winter but also in the face of something altogether more seismic. 'We can't know what is ahead of us,' Tarkiainen told me, reflecting on the state of the wilderness all around her after decades witnessing its abuse at human hands. 'I feel artists have been saying this for quite a few years now.'

The composer has also spoken of her work's connection to giving birth, its capturing of 'the moment the woman and the child part'. There's a sense of separation in the score's final sixty seconds, as a lonely trumpet, on a now-familiar tune, is sent out into the unknown to make its way. Woodwinds and a solo violin flutter at the edges of the orchestra, and a held string chord eventually disappears into a sonic whiteout – the silence of Europe's biggest wilderness brought to four thousand people inside a London concert hall.

Notes

Prelude. *Tapiola*

1. *Tapiola* refers to the realm of Tapio - in Finnish mythology, the god or 'spirit' of the Forest.
2. Goss, Glenda Dawn (2009). *Sibelius: A Composer's Life and the Awakening of Finland*. Chicago: University of Chicago Press.
3. Walter Damrosch, director of the New York Philharmonic Society, commissioned *Tapiola* for his society's orchestra; it was first performed in New York on 26 December 1926.
4. Hans Abrahamsen and Bent Sørensen (see Chapter 4).

Chapter 1: Landfall

Epigraph: Gill, A. A. 'Nordic Exposure', *Vanity Fair*, August 2012 (Condé Nast Publications).

1. Known as the Norske Nationaldragter.
2. Original title: *Ældre og nyere norske Fjeldmelodier: samlede og bearbeidede for pianoforte*.
3. In 'Hvad est du dog skjøn' ('How Fair is Thy Face') the soloist sings in the minor to major key backing; in 'Guds søn har gjort mig fri' ('God's Son Has Set Me Free') the soloist sings in the major to minor key backing.
4. Most notably in No. 5 of *Six Impromptus for Piano* and in the opening pages of the *Kullervo* Symphony.
5. 'Hvad udad tabes, skal indad vindes'.
6. Rowell, Lewis (1995). *The Nielsen Companion*, ed. Mina F. Miller, Portland: Amadeus Press.
7. This theory is proposed by Petra Garberding in '"We Take Care of the Artist": The German Composers' Meeting in Berlin, 1934', *Music and Politics,* Vol III No 2.

Chapter 2: Performance

Epigraph: Pekka Kuusisto in conversation with the author, 12 August 2017.
1. 'Hvordan styrker vi landskabet for professionelle klassiske ensembler og orkestre i Danmark?' ('How can we strengthen the landscape for professional classical ensembles and orchestras in Denmark?'), *Artana, Kultur & Strategi*, 2017.
2. The Royal Danish Playhouse was eventually built in 2008 and won that year's RIBA European Award.
3. A selection of composers from the orchestra's 2019/20 season.
4. Max Granström: 'Vi ska förvalta det [modernisering] och se till att det fortsätter'. Helsingborgs Dagblad, 11 February 2021. https://www.hd.se/2021-02-11/fredrik-sterling-slutar-som-konserthuschef-gar-till-sametinget
5. Andrew Manze, chief conductor 2006–2014.
6. May 2018, rehearsing Berlioz's *Grande Messe des Morts* at the Grieg Hall, Bergen.
7. Osmo Vänskä, Thomas Dausgaard and Stefan Solyom have held titles at the BBC Scottish Symphony Orchestra; Jukka-Pekka Saraste was chief conductor of the Scottish Chamber Orchestra and John Storgårds regularly conducts there.
8. 'Zoo official on Marius the giraffe: Conservation isn't always clean', CNN, 11 February 2014. https://edition.cnn.com/2014/02/10/world/europe/denmark-zoo-giraffe/
9. Statoil has since rebranded as 'Equinor'.
10. BBC Radio 3, *Building a Library*, 11 February 2017.
11. Previously the DR Chamber Orchestra, the ensemble was closed by the broadcaster DR in 2014 but re-established as an independent entity later the same year.
12. The term 'bygdedyret' was coined by the Norwegian writer and journalist Tor Jonsson (1916–1951).
13. In 2021, British-born Nicholas Collon became only the second non-Finn to lead a Helsinki orchestra when he took over the chief conductorship of the Finnish Radio Symphony Orchestra.
14. *The Tempest* was written for the Royal Danish Theatre in 1926, Sibelius's last orchestral score before *Tapiola*.

Chapter 3: Off Piste

Epigraph: Jakob Möller, interview with Jón Leifs. First published in *Vikan*; translated into English in *Jón Leifs and the Musical Invention of Iceland*, by Árni Heimir Ingolfsson.
1. The Eurovision Song Contest is known throughout Scandinavia as the 'Melodi Grand Prix' (with spelling variations).
2. Johnson, Julian (1999). *Webern and the Transformation of Nature,* Cambridge: Cambridge University Press.
3. The shape of the building was inspired by the images of elves' palaces from Icelandic folklore.
4. In Iceland's morning newspaper, *Morgunblaðið*, 4 June 1926.
5. Ingólfsson, Árni Heimir (2019). *Jón Leifs and the Musical Invention of Iceland*, Bloomington: Indiana University Press.
6. An ambiguous, unsettling interval consisting of a note and the note three whole tones above it, traditionally used by composers to signal unease.
7. The last remained unfinished at the composer's death in 1968.
8. A structural reference also used by the architect Samúelsson and seen in Olafur Eliasson's exterior shell to the Harpa in Reykjavík.
9. *Vestsvenska Dagbladet*, 29 January 1931 (as cited by Ingólfsson in *Jón Leifs and the Musical Invention of Iceland*).
10. Áksell Snorrason, *Dagur*, 9 June 1932 (as cited by Ingólfsson in *Jón Leifs and the Musical Invention of Iceland*).

11. Icelandic surnames follow a distinct formula: girls add the suffix 'dottir' or 'dóttir' to their father's first name, while boys add the suffix 'sson'.
12. Rasmussen is a Faroese DJ, living and working in Iceland.
13. The existence of a single radio or television channel, which persisted late into the twentieth century across the Nordic region, has fed into the region's cultural homogeneity but also the breadth of its artistic experience across genre boundaries.
14. 'With this song, I really had a sort of National Anthem in mind. Not the National Anthem but certain classic Icelandic songs – very romantic, very proud.' Björk interviewed by *Record Collector* no. 276, 1 August 2002.
15. Björk interviewed Karlheinz Stockhausen in 1996. https://www.sonoloco.com/rev/stockhausen/Bjork/bjorkfr.html
16. The gesture resembles the opening sequence of 'Jóga' flipped upside down, or 'in retrograde'.
17. Adriane Pontecorvo, 'Nico Muhly and Teitur: *Confessions*' in Pop Matters. https://popmatters.com/nico-muhly-and-teitur-confessions-2495404722.html
18. The score was written for the South Jutland Symphony Orchestra as part of Rasmussen's residency marking the orchestra's first season at the Alsion concert hall (see Chapter 2).
19. The band's most famous song, 'Regin Smiður', is a straight rendition of the ballad of the same name.
20. Wagner borrowed the idea of a 'world tree' for his cycle *Der Ring des Nibelungen*; the idea of an 'all-encompassing tree ... constantly threatened and devoured as it grows and flourishes' is cited in the ensemble's biography. https://www.kristianblak.com/yggdrasil

Chapter 4: Nordic Noir and Snow White

Epigraph: Kierkegaard, Søren: *Begrebet Angest* ('The Concept of Anxiety'), 1844.
1. The dramaturge and theatre researcher Nila Parly has written in detail about the concept behind Von Trier's *Ring* and how the production plans derailed: see 'Lars von Trier's Lost *Ring*', *Cambridge Opera Journal*, Vol 30 Issue 1, March 2018.
2. Strindberg's 'Intima Teater' was both a physical theatre on Stockholm's Barnhusgatan and also a theatrical presentation style, in which audience and actors would be confined to the same, unadorned space making use of innovative lighting techniques.
3. The work's given name is in Italian: *L'isola della Città*.
4. The words are by Nikolaj Grundtvig: 'My Jesus, let my heart receive thee'.
5. The song tells of a road-mender who worked his whole life at chipping and shaping stones, but for whose own grave no stone could be found.
6. February 2014, the *Guardian*: 'Pelle Gudmundsen-Holmgreen, the composer who finds beauty in absurdity'. https://www.theguardian.com/music/musicblog/2014/feb/26/pelle-gudmundsen-holmgreen-composer-interview
7. Grimley, Daniel (2011). *Carl Nielsen and the Idea of Modernism*, Woodbridge: Boydell & Brewer.
8. As cited in Booth, Michael (2014). *The Almost Nearly Perfect People: Behind the Myth of the Scandinavian Utopia*, London: Jonathan Cape.
9. Winstock, A.R. et al. (2021). 'Global Drugs Survey 2020: Psychedelics Key Findings Report'. https://www.globaldrugsurvey.com/wp-content/uploads/2021/03/GDS2020-Psychedelics-report.pdf
10. Koski-Jaunnes, Anna. 'Alcohol and Literary Creativity: The Finnish Experience', *Journal of Creative Behavior*, June 1985, Vol 19 Issue 2.
11. Saarikallio, Suvi. 'Music: A Meaningful Resource at Turning Points and in Times of Crisis', *Finnish Music Quarterly*, 18 June 2020. https://fmq.fi/articles/music-meaningful-resource

Chapter 5: Scandinavian by Design

Epigraph: Stewart, John (2017). *Alvar Aalto: Architect*, London and New York: Merrell.
1. The symphony was revised the following year, 1971.
2. Jean Sibelius and Gustav Mahler met in 1907, on which occasion they discussed the concept and construction of their respective symphonies. Mahler reportedly argued that 'A symphony must be like the world... it must embrace everything!' while Sibelius suggested that a symphony should be born of 'profound logic and inner connection'.
3. The deal's small print ensured that Nokia as a small Finnish entity focused on design would survive; it has since retaken its place in the mobile phone market.
4. Melissa Stroud's research on the subject has been published by the University of Texas. 'The Origin and Genetic Background of the Sámi'. https://www.laits.utexas.edu/sami/dieda/hist/genetic.htm
5. Segerstam's unconducted symphonies extend a certain feeling in Sibelius's late works that the conductor's art must remain as hidden as possible: 'If the music sounds like it's not being conducted, then the conductor has done a good job,' the leading Sibelius interpreter Osmo Vänskä told me in 2016.
6. Clément Mao-Takacs 'A Conversation with Kaija Saariaho', *Music & Literature*, No. 5, 25 September 2014. https://www.musicandliterature.org/features/2014/9/22/a-conversation-with-kaija-saariaho

Postlude. Silence

1. Messerschmidt was elected Leader of the Danish People's Party in January 2022.

Acknowledgements

One or two of the journeys included in this text took place when colleagues at orchestras were encouraging me to write, even though they had employed me to do more useful things. I am grateful to Sue Colvin, Timothy Walker, Emily Smith, William Norris and Frances Cook at Manchester Camerata and the London Philharmonic Orchestra for doing so, thus nudging me onto another career path for all our benefits.

I owe a debt of gratitude to John Evans for bringing me into full-time journalism and for the three years of thorough training and good times that followed on *Classic FM* magazine. James Inverne and Martin Cullingford, my successive editors at *Gramophone*, picked up where John left off, nurturing my interest in Nordic music and allowing me to accept invitations to cover events in the region, often meaning time away from my desk. I am particularly grateful to Martin for tenaciously extolling the virtues of the Nordic embassies in Berlin and remain indebted to his entire staff at *Gramophone* for their continuing friendship, expertise and superior attention to detail – thank you James Jolly, Sarah Kirkup, James McCarthy, David Threasher, Tim Parry, Esther Zuke and Marija Duric Speare.

Most of the interviews referenced and quoted in the text originally took place at the behest of *Classic FM* magazine and *Gramophone*, or that of the *Guardian, Financial Times, The Strad, International Piano, Opera Now, Opera, Classical Music, Choir & Organ, Songlines, Limelight, Klassisk, Seismograf, Finnish Music Quarterly,* Glyndebourne Festival Opera and Decca. I am grateful for permission to reproduce parts of them here or use previously unpublished material gathered on those assignments. Specific thanks to Imogen Tilden, Jan Dalley, Richard Fairman, Charlotte Smith, Jo Litson, Jo Frost, John Allison, Ashutosh Khandekar, Maggie Hamilton, Owen Mortimer and Kimon Daltas.

Lucy Breaks and Joanna Wyld at the Philharmonia Orchestra, Rachel Williams at the London Philharmonic Orchestra and Didier Martin and Amélie Boccon-Gibod at Alpha Classics have conveniently commissioned plenteous programme book essays at the heart of my area of interest. Marina Vidor, also at the Philharmonia, has been a generous collaborator and was kind enough to put questions to Esa-Pekka Salonen on my behalf while making a series of beautiful films on Finnish music. Hugo Shirley at Idagio in Berlin allowed me to delve deep into dark corners of Nordic music by commissioning playlists and articles on imaginative themes.

Certain Finns and Scandinavians generously encouraged my interest in Nordic music even before I lived in the region. They include Kristian Lønsted, Henrik Rørdam, Denise Burt, Esben Tange, Christina Åstrand, Per Salo, Bent Viinholt Nielsen, Jens Rossel, Birgitte Ebert, Bo Gunge, Sten Cranner, Sofie Ringstad, Einar Indsøe Eidsvåg, Steinar Larsen, Åse Våg Aaknes, Ingrid Røynesdal, Alex Taylor, Liv Beate Skavdahl, Heli Lampi, Reijo Kiilunen, the late Hjarne Fessel and the incomparably knowledgeable and kind Jens Cornelius. The Trondheim Soloists and Oslo Philharmonic have been charitable with invitations and ideas, facilitating numerous encoun-

ACKNOWLEDGEMENTS

ters. I am grateful to Matt Groom and Paul Thomas at Presto Music for allowing me to extoll the virtues and vices of the Nordic countries on their wide-ranging podcast series.

Cecilie Rosenmeier, Annina Kivikari and Kathryn Naish Hjesvold have been as indispensible for their friendship as for their advice and help. I am sincerely grateful to my friend and colleague Philippa Chamberlayne, who fixed my first trip to Iceland and later organized visits to Stockholm, Örebro and the Carl Nielsen Project in New York, all with her inimitable sense of fun. Nicky Thomas has facilitated my interactions with The Gothenburg Opera while Lucy Maxwell-Stewart has been a constant source of ideas and contacts and a consistently friendly British presence on western Scandinavian soil. Patricia Price, always full of warm and helpful words, organized my visit to Guangzhou, China, where I encountered the orchestra of Youth Music Culture Guangdong playing Sibelius.

It is humbling to be asked to comment on a foreign country's creativity by a professional native to that country. I am thankful for the trust placed in me by Merja Hottinen and Anu Ahola at *Finnish Music Quarterly*, Annu Mikkonen and Olli Virtaperko at the Society of Finnish Composers, Nikolaj Skinhøj and the late Per Rask Madsen at *Klassisk* magazine, Jens Povlsen and Mie Petri Lind at Dacapo Records, Leif Hasselgren and Robert von Bahr at BIS Records, Hege Wolleng and Vegard Landaas at LAWO Records, Per Sjösten at Footprint Records, Erik Gard Amundsen at Grappa, Christian House at the Royal Norwegian Embassy in London, Henning Målsnes and Oddmund Økland at the Bergen Philharmonic Orchestra, Sune Anderberg and Sanne Krogh Goth at Seismograf, Trine Boje Mortensen and Elvira Mormino at Edition Wilhelm Hansen and Solveig Lindeskov Andersen and Eva Havshøj Ohrt at Edition-S. In some cases, this book uses interview or research material originally gathered at their behest. Some ideas in the final chapter were originally sketched out as reviews and essays for Seismograf, all of them scrupulously commissioned, guided and edited by Sune Anderberg.

ACKNOWLEDGEMENTS

Sam Wigglesworth at Faber Music and Sam Wilcock at Wise Music Group were kind enough to help with scores and pictures. Torgny Nilsson at Malmö Opera has been helpful and patient with my pleas for help with architectural images, while his company's artistic director Michael Bojesen was kind enough to fill me in on its history. My Copenhagen colleagues Thomas Michelsen, Jakob Wivel, Michael Bo, Celine Haastrup, Tatjana Kandel, Kim Bohr, Nikolaj Fine de Fine Licht, Lars Hannibal, Marie Rørbech, Ane Skak, Peter Lodahl, Katrine Nyland Sørensen, Jacob Soelberg, Rie Koch, Michael Emery and John Fulljames have been generous with encouragement and insights.

The foreign ministries of Finland and Denmark, Music Finland and Music Norway funded some of my early visits to those countries. The Augustinus Foundation in Copenhagen generously supported two final research trips, to Iceland and Finland, in the late stages of writing. I am grateful to the staff of Silence Festival in Kaukonen for allowing me to volunteer in the summer of 2016 and covering my travel costs.

This book wouldn't exist without those musicians and other professionals directly quoted in the text. I am indebted to each of them. Everyone mentioned by name took time to share their thoughts and many did rather more.

Christopher Tarrant of the University of Newcastle's International Centre for Music Studies, himself a fount of knowledge in the field of Nordic music, was kind enough to read excerpts of the manuscript and offer helpful advice. Søren Schauser at the Royal Danish Academy of Music took extensive time out from his own teaching and writing schedule to read the entire text and suggest improvements. Tryggvi M. Baldvinsson of the Icelandic University of the Arts was kind enough to respond thoroughly to my queries. Outi Jokiharju helped prevent misunderstandings of Finnish language and popular culture while Aksel Tollåli gave me access to his engrossing thesis on Nielsen's *Maskarade*. Vanessa Blander Hedegaard has been an invaluable contact inside the Royal Danish Orchestra. My colleague Philip Clark took time to offer advice just as he was fighting to finish his own monumental biography of Dave Brubeck.

I am indebted to Daniel Grimley of the University of Oxford for past encouragement, advice and expertise. His own unparalleled understanding of Nordic music has opened many doors and facilitated my own; his books on Edvard Grieg and Carl Nielsen are essential reading. Sarah Menin's writing on Alvar Aalto and Jean Sibelius made an indelible impression and is remarkable in its connective thinking. Glenda Dawn Goss's beautifully written, nation-themed biography of Sibelius has proved pivotal to my understanding of the composer, while Andrew Barnett's is justifiably known as the 'Sibelius Bible' (its author was kind enough to respond to my queries surrounding Sibelius's various travel itineraries). Robert Ferguson's engrossing book *Scandinavians* suggested to me, in its unusual form, that a similar narrative approach might be viable in a musical context. Michael Booth's *The Almost Nearly Perfect People* – irreverent, funny and uncannily accurate – is just about the best Nordic sociocultural primer in existence. I am grateful for fertile conversations with Paul Binding as well as his illuminating writings and translations. Andrew Brown's *Fishing in Utopia* is surely the most beautifully written, keenly observed English-language book on the Nordic mindset ever committed to paper.

I am immensely grateful to Marta Tonegutti at the University of Chicago Press for her significant time, advice and advocacy in the project's early stages, before it moved east. It has been a joy to work with such an encouraging editor as Julian Loose at Yale University Press and I am thankful for the work done by his team, in particular to Frazer Martin, Felicity Maunder, Eve Leckey and the book's cover designer, Luke Bird, who has succeeded in achieving with his imagery what I have tried to with my words. Sincere thanks are due to the two anonymous reviewers who provided vital criticism, corrections, direction and encouragement.

ACKNOWLEDGEMENTS

I owe a final debt of gratitude to my family. To my parents, sister and brother-in-law in England for their tireless logistical and conversational support, but most of all to my partner Sarah, for her constant words of encouragement and cultural enlightenment, all offered while negotiating the significant stresses and strains of a proper career.

Copenhagen, January 2022

Index

12 Tónar (shop) 129
200 (band) 155

Aalborg 68, 69
Aalborg Symphony Orchestra 69, 264
Aalto, Alvar 2, 3, 165, 212, 231–6, 238, 240, 243, 250, 253
    Savoy Vase 236, 250
Aarhus 42, 43, 44, 64, 249–51
Aarhus School 222
Aarhus Symphony Orchestra 42
Aarre, Trond 79, 272
Abba 18, 55, 78, 180
    'Lay All Your Love On Me' 180
Abrahamsen, Hans 110, 185–7, 189, 190, 217, 229, 263
    Double Concerto for Piano and Violin 110
    Let Me Tell You 186–7
    Schnee 185–8
    The Snow Queen 187
    Walden 189
Academy for Culture and Business (Nordfjord) 77
Acerbi, Giuseppe 121
Adorno, Theodor 217, 221
Aftenposten (newspaper) 34
Åhrén, Uno 50, 214

Ainola 202–3, 218, 248
Alaska 22
alcohol 23, 129, 171, 173, 201–6, 209, 227
Aldará, Jón 154
Aldubáran (ensemble) 157
Alenius, Louise 210
    Silent Zone 210
Alexandria 253
Alfvén, Hugo 49, 51
Alsion Concert Hall, Sønderborg 62, 65, 68, 101, 283
Alssund Straight 62
Alta (river) 121, 122
Althing (Icelandic parliament) 130, 136
Amager Beach, Copenhagen 253
Amalienborg Palace, Copenhagen 72
Amati (luthier) 111
Amper, Emilia 27
Amsterdam 243
Anda peninsula 74
Andersen, Hans Christian 41, 107, 169, 187, 194–6
    The Snow Queen 187
Anderson, Julian 180, 255
Andsnes, Leif Ove 59, 93, 94, 101, 102–4, 177
Another Round (film) 204
AP Møller Foundation 72

INDEX

Arctic Philharmonic Orchestra 80, 276
Ärhinmäki, Paavo 274
Arockalypse (album) 124
Arte (television channel) 269
Ásgeirsson, Ásgeir 136
Ashkenazy, Vladimir 128
Athens 124
Atterberg, Kurt 51, 52, 53, 54, 55, 57, 132
   Symphony No. 1 53
   Symphony No. 6, *Dollar Symphony* 52–3, 57
Augestad, Tora 91, 100
aurora borealis (Northern Lights) 21, 22, 232, 256, 278
Aurorankatu, Helsinki 230

Bach, Johann Sebastian 16, 31, 82, 103, 129, 143, 176, 179, 185, 230
   Goldberg Variations 185
   Mass in B minor 104
Bachke, Christian 24
Baez, Joan 34
Bagsværd Church, Copenhagen 229, 230
Baltic Sea 39, 45, 58, 210, 254, 258, 270
Barbican Centre, London 150
Barenboim, Daniel 112
Bartók, Béla 152
Bauhaus 50
Bayreuth 158
Bayreuth Festival 169, 184
BBC 9, 63, 92, 93, 143, 170, 181, 244
BBC National Orchestra of Wales 95
BBC New Generation Artists Scheme 93, 102
BBC Philharmonic 80, 188, 279
BBC Proms 180, 244, 271, 279
BBC Radio 3 93, 278, 282
BBC Scottish Symphony Orchestra 92, 282
BBC Symphony Orchestra 95, 150
Beck, Martin 168
Beckett, Samuel 192, 198
Beecham, Thomas 51, 234
Beethoven, Ludwig van 6, 43, 81, 85, 130, 132, 157, 166, 172, 176, 177
   Symphony No. 3, *Eroica* 43, 44
   Symphony No. 9 157
Berg, Alban 91, 277
   Lulu 277
Bergen 13, 15, 16, 17, 23, 26, 58, 59, 62, 74, 91, 102, 109, 171
Bergen Cathedral Choir 17

Bergen Philharmonic Orchestra 58, 59, 60, 62, 66, 87, 109
Berger, Alfred 258, 259
Bergh, Richard 172
Bergman, Ingmar 168, 209, 210
Berlin 51, 53, 55, 89, 106, 129, 227, 257
Berlin Philharmonic Orchestra 52, 112, 161, 254, 260
Berlioz, Hector 84, 282
Bernstein, Leonard 112
Biafra 34
Bier, Susanne 210
Bildt, Carl 270
Bjarnason, Daníel 139–40, 180, 210
   Brødre 210
   From Space I Saw Earth 180
Bjerre, Sys 125
Björk 5, 129, 142–5, 148, 160, 245, 283
   Björk (album) 142
   Homogenic 143–5, 245, 283
   Vulnicura 145, 245
Black Water 124
Blågårds Plads, Copenhagen 192, 198
Blak, Kristian 155–6, 158
Blixen, Karen 106
Blüthner 103, 104
Bobrikov, Nikolay 34, 35
Bodø 79, 80
Bolshevik Revolution 33
Bombin, Jaana 31
Boogie (television programme) 125
Booth, Michael 49, 283
Boston Symphony Orchestra 257
Boulez, Pierre 216–17
   Structures I 216
Bournonville, August 39
Bowie, David 118
Brahms, Johannes 43, 50, 85, 198
Branagh, Kenneth 46
Brantelid, Andreas 93
Breivik, Anders 79, 108, 184
Breivik, Anita 162
Brennevín 204
Bridge, The (television programme) 167
Brinkmann, Svend 99
Britten, Benjamin
   Peter Grimes 106
Brorson, Hans Adolf 17
Brown, Andrew 27, 174
Bruch, Max 89
Bryars, Gavin 148
Buene, Eivind 183
Building Design (journal) 234

INDEX

Bull, Ole 14, 15
Bush, Kate 147
Buxtehude, Dietrich 18, 82, 179
Bygdedyret 106, 282
Byström, Britta 227

Cage, John 81, 84
Cambridge University 157
Campus Allegro, Pietarsaari 4, 6
Capri 209
Carlsberg 42, 44
Catalonia 22
chain dancing 146–7, 149, 154
Chang, Han-na 86
Chernobyl (television programme) 140
Chicago Symphony Orchestra 254
Christensen, Christian Winther 180, 263
Christian Democrat party (Norway) 79
Christian I, King of Denmark 39
Christian X, King of Denmark 132
Christiansen, Henning 217
    Perceptive Constructions 217
cimbalom 28
citizenship test (Denmark) 211
Clausen, Marianne 159–60
Cohen, Leonard 147
Collon, Nicholas 282
Columbia Phonograph Company 52, 53
commedia dell'arte 199
Concerto Copenhagen 104
Conservative party (Norway) 79
Copenhagen 15, 39–41, 43–5, 56–61, 70, 101, 103, 109, 110–13, 138, 157, 159, 167, 174, 176, 177, 184, 187, 192, 204, 206, 211, 217, 227, 228, 229, 252, 253, 262, 270–3
Copenhagen Central Station 43
Copenhagen Council 71
Copenhagen Old Opera House (Gamle Scene) 105
Copenhagen Opera House (Operaen) 39, 71, 127, 211, 265
Copenhagen Philharmonic 70, 86–7, 267, 274
Copenhagen University 100, 270
Copenhagen Zoo 99
Covid-19 pandemic 68, 70, 104, 264–8, 275, 276
CPR number (Denmark) 215
Crottet, Robert 244
Croydon 48
Cullingford, Martin 127
Culture Bank (Stavanger) 88

Dadaism 91
Damhus Lake 270–1
Damhuskroen 270–1
Damrosch, Walter 188, 281
Danish Chamber Orchestra 105, 282
Danish People's Party 269, 284
Danish String Quartet 93
Dannelse 67
Danny and the Veetos 153
    'Alright' 153
Dark Music Days 140
Darmstadt 216, 256
Dausgaard, Thomas 147, 282
Davey, Alan 93, 96, 97, 98
Davidsen, Lise 93, 100, 101, 184
Dazed & Confused 143
De Beer, Lotte 106
De Ridder, André 227
Deadache (album) 124
Deadwind (television programme) 167
death penalty 197
Debussy, Claude 185, 221, 254
Delay Trees 126
    Doze 126
Den Klassiske Musikquiz (television programme) 67
Desert Island Discs (radio programme) 181
Deutsche Grammophon 137
Die Hard (film) 34
Dodge, Daniel Kilham 178
Dogma 95, 169
Dowland, John 39, 167, 193–4
    'Flow My Tears' 193–4
DR (Danish Broadcasting Corporation) 67, 70, 125, 266–7
DR Chamber Orchestra 269, 282
DR Concert Hall (Copenhagen) 70, 176
DR Girls' Choir 150
DR Symphony Orchestra (Danish National Symphony Orchestra) 67, 70, 150
Dreisig, Elsa 93
Dudamel, Gustavo 61

Edda (award) 130
Edda (poem) 134
Eid 75
Einstürzende Neubauten 240
Eisenhower, Dwight 178, 209
Ejersbo, Jakob 210
    Nordkraft 210
Elgar, Edward 98

INDEX

Eliasson, Olafur 101, 127, 211, 282
Emergence (album) 139
English National Opera 60
Englund, Einar 244
Enso-Gutzeit Building, Helsinki 231
Equinor 282
Eric Ericson Chamber Choir 31
Essen Opera House 233, 235, 259
European Broadcasting Union 67
Eurovision Song Contest 5, 23, 119–21, 124, 180, 240, 241, 282
Eysturoy 147

Faber, Phillip 266
Fællesang 266–7
Fagerlund, Sebastian 210, 243–5
  Autumn Sonata 210
  Drifts 243
  Stonework 243
Fálkinn (record label) 142
Faroese Music Awards 149, 152, 154, 158
Faroese Music School 156
Faroese Symphony Orchestra 157
FCK (FC Copenhagen) 9
Feedback System 222
Fellows, John 99
Ferguson, Robert 166–7
Fernström, John 213
Fika 237
Financial Times 101
Finlandia Hall, Helsinki 231, 233–4
Finnair 236–8
Finnair Singers (ensemble) 236
Finnbogadóttir, Vigdís 141
Finnish Civil War 33
Finnish Ministry of Foreign Affairs 230
Finnish Music Quarterly 227
Finnish National Opera 29, 197
Finnish Radio Symphony Orchestra 227, 231, 282
Finnmark 121, 122, 276
First World War 25, 45
Fischer, Ádám 105
Fjelstad, Lise 161
Fjelstad, Øivin 161
Flagstad, Kirsten 101
Fløyen, Bergen 16, 17
Flyum, Magni 77
Folk High School (Denmark) 78
Forum, Helsinki 231
Foss, Lukas 84
Frang, Vilde 93, 161

Fredericia 198
Frederick II, King of Denmark 270
Frederick IX, King of Denmark 112
Frej, Maria 271–5
Fröst, Martin 93
functionalism 49, 213–22, 225–6, 232, 233, 239, 242, 249
Fundal, Karsten 222, 229
  The Wings of a Butterfly 222
Funen 41, 62
Furtwängler, Wilhelm 51

Gade, Niels 41, 108
  Elverskud 108
Gallen-Kallela, Akseli 206
Garbarek, Jan 171
Garberding, Petra 281
Gardner, Edward 60, 61, 87, 106
Garvey, Michael 95
Gehry, Frank 242
Gentofte 218
German Composers' Meeting, Berlin 1934 54
Gillett, Meherban 111–13
Gimse, Øyvind 163
Giske, Trond 80
Gísladóttir, Bára 261–3
  Jódynur 261
  Víddir 261–2
Gislinge, Katrine 177
Glasgow 157
Global Drug Survey (2020) 203
Gloppefjord 74
Gloucester 141
Goodman, Irwin 206
Gorrlaus 23
Goss, Glenda Dawn 281
Göta (river) 51
Gothenburg 50–1, 56, 61, 134, 140, 217, 252
Gothenburg Opera 50
Gothenburg Symphony Orchestra 86, 87, 201
Gould, Glenn 90
Gragnani (luthier) 111
Gramophone (magazine) 42, 61, 80, 127, 152
Grand Hotel, Stockholm 47
Grawemeyer Award 9, 175, 177, 186
Greenland 148
Grieg, Edvard 14–21, 23, 26, 29, 37, 39–41, 44, 45, 49, 59, 101, 103, 129, 151, 157, 182, 223, 229, 242

INDEX

Four Psalms 17–21, 31, 163, 183
Haugtussa 37
'Lyric Pieces' 182
Piano Concerto 15, 59, 103, 104, 157
Violin Sonata No. 2 23–4
Griffiths, Paul 186, 193
Grimley, Daniel 199, 200, 283
Grisey, Gérard 255–6
Gröndal, Ragnheiður 129
Grundtvig, Nikolaj 283
Grundtvig's Church, Copenhagen 228, 261–2
Guadagnini (luthier) 111
Guangzhou 247
Guardian (newspaper) 187, 191
Gudmundsen-Holmgreen, Pelle 191–9, 217, 229
   Company 193
   Moving Still 194, 197
   Plateaux pour Deux 191, 193
   Run 193
   Triptykon 192
Guðnadóttir, Hildur 140
Gullichsen, Johanna 238
Gustav III, King of Sweden 48

Haapamäki, Sampo 243
   Quarter Tone Piano Concerto 243
Hætta, Mattis 121
Hagen, Lars Petter 182–4
   concerto for Hardanger fiddle 183
   Lament 183
   'Norwegian Archives' 182
   The Artist's Despair Before the Grandeur of Ancient Ruins 184
Hagerup, Nina 59, 101
Hako, Pekka 1, 2, 4, 6
Hallgrímskirkja, Reykjavík 127
Hallgrímsson, Jónas 133
Hamar 159
Hamburg Philharmonic Orchestra 130, 145
Hämeenlinna 125–6, 165
Hamferð 154, 283
Hammershøi, Wilhelm 228
Hamrahlid Choir 142
Handel, George Frideric 103, 172, 270
   Messiah 270
Hanseatic League 39, 58
Hansegård, Hallgrim 23, 24
Hansen, Per Boye 78
Hardanger fiddle 14, 23–4, 26, 27, 160, 183

Harding, Daniel 61, 86
Harley-Davidson 72
Harpa, Reykjavík 101, 127–9, 282
Harrestrup (river) 270
Haugesund 12–13, 16, 17, 74, 88, 90, 102
Haydn, Joseph 253
   The Creation 253
Heinesen, William 146, 154, 156, 158
   The Lost Musicians 146, 158
Helgefylla 204
Helldén, David 212
Helseth, Tine Thing 93
Helsingborg 82–4, 275
Helsingborg Concert House 82–3
Helsingborg Symphony Orchestra 82, 84–5
Helsingør 82
Helsinki 1, 4, 29–30, 45, 64, 68, 81, 94, 118, 125–6, 135, 170, 173, 203, 207–8, 217, 222, 226, 230–1, 243, 253, 268, 270, 277
Helsinki Baroque Orchestra 104
Helsinki Cathedral 34
Helsinki Philharmonic Orchestra 94, 230
Helsinki University 203
Hemsing, Eldbjørg 97
Hemsing, Ragnhild 23, 26
Hendin, Herbert 209
Herheim, Stefan 106
Hermann, Bernard 84
Hettarher 155
Hiisi 28
Hillborg, Anders 254–5
   '. . . lontana in sonno . . .' 255
   Beast Sampler 254
   Cold Heat 255
   Sirens 254
Hille, Sid 171
Hillier, Paul 195–6
Historically Informed Performance (HIP) 103
Hitler, Adolf 25, 51, 132
HJK (Helsingin Jalkapalloklubi) 9
'Højt på en gren en krage' (song) 100
Holland Baroque Ensemble 150
Holst, Bengt 99
Holst, Hans Peter 40
Holten, Kasper 107
House of Culture, Helsinki 234
House of Music (Aalborg) 68, 69, 264
Houston 88
hurdy-gurdy 27

INDEX

Hvidtfelt Nielsen, Svend 229
   Symphony No. 3 (*Watching Life*) 229
hygge 197, 205

Iberg, Helge 263
   Songs from the Planet of Life 263
Ibsen, Henrik 106, 169, 172
Iceland Symphony Orchestra 127, 128, 136, 139–40, 156
Icelandic Opera 127
Icelandic University of the Arts 142, 148
Ich ruf' zu dir, Herr Jesu Christ (chorale) 176
Idenstam, Gunnar 120–1
Ihle Hadland, Christian 102,109
IKEA 49, 215
Inari 171, 277
Infinity Series 218–21, 257, 258
Ingólfsdóttir, Þorgerður 142
Ingólfsson, Árni Heimir 132, 143, 282
Intersport 75
Intima Teater 169, 283
Isola, Maija 236, 238, 245
   Albatrossi 245
   Joonas 239
   Kaivo 245
   Lokki 245
   Muija 245
   Putkinotka 245
   Silkkikuikka 245
   Unikko 238, 245
Ivalo 244, 277–9

Jacobsen, Arne 8, 190, 214
Jakobsson, Thorbjörn 120
Jansons, Mariss 112
Jansson, Tove 237
Jantelov 71, 73, 86, 105, 107, 108, 197, 198
Japan 237–8
Jårgalæddji (record label) 121
Järnefelt, Eero 35, 172, 209
Järnefelt, Elli 209
Järvenpää Woods 202
Järvi, Neeme 61
Järvi, Paavo 93
Jastrau, Ole 206
Jensen-Klint, Peter 228
Jesu, meine Zuversicht (chorale) 90
Jóhannesson, Lárus 129
Jóhannsson, Magnús Blöndal 139
Johansen, Petter Udland 22
Johnson, Julian 126, 282
Jonsson, Tor 282

Jónsdóttir, Þuríður 139
Jotunheim Mountains 16, 19
Juhl, Finn 228
Jukkaslåtar (album) 120–3
Julebryg 204
Jutland 42, 61–2, 69, 130, 155, 198
Jutland Post 196

Kaamos 252
Kajaani 30
Kajanus, Robert 206
Kakooza, Melvin 198
Kalevala 28, 32, 36, 123, 125, 169, 249
Kallio 126
Kamppila, Sade 117
Kamprad, Ingvar 215
Kamu, Okko 170
Kansas City Symphony 248
Kantele 27–8, 35, 37, 258
Karelia 35, 36
Karmøy 13
Karsh, Yousuf 38
Karttunen, Anssi 257
Kass, Konni 153
Kaukonen 114–18, 277
Kaukonen Village Band 118
Kaurismäki, Aki 117, 206
Keflavík 126
Kenyon, Nicholas 104
Kierkegaard, Søren 19, 106, 125, 145, 166, 168, 178–9, 261, 283
Killing, The (television programme) 167
King's Cross, London 191
Kingo, Thomas 159
Kingosálmar 159
Kiruna 120
Kittilä Airport 117
Kivistö, Marko 230
Kjelsberg, Sverre 121
Klami, Uuno 123
   Kalevala Suite 123
Klein, Yves 75
Klemperer, Otto 112
Knausgaard, Karl Ove 106
Kokkonen, Joonas 81
Koli 171–2
Kongens Nytorv, Copenhagen 176
Korundi House 80–1
Korvat Auki 238, 239
Koski-Jaunnes, Anja 206, 283
Kosonen, Sanja 115
Kraft foods 237
Kraggerud, Henning 93

INDEX

Kraus, Joseph Martin 48–9
Kringvarp Føroya (Faroese Broadcasting Corporation) 157
Kristensen, Tom 206
  Havoc 206
Kristiansand 74, 109
Kristiansand Symphony Orchestra 74, 109
Kristiansund 75
Kronos Quartet 195
Krøyer, P.S. 253
Krýsuvík, Iceland 138
Kühlhorn, Lotta 237
Kuhmo 30, 32, 34, 278
  Hotel Kalevala 32
  Kalevala World 32
  Kuhmo Arts Centre 31
  Kuhmo Chamber Music Festival 31, 32
Kulning 171
Kutajärvi (lake) 174
Kuula, Toivo 116
Kuusisto, Jaakko 274
Kuusisto, Pekka 9, 58, 93, 98, 102, 123, 273–4
Kvæði 146, 154

Labour party (Norway) 79
Lagerlöf, Selma 106
Lagom 205
Lahti 165–70, 173–4, 207
Lahti Symphony Orchestra 165, 173
Lahti Television and Radio Museum 166
Lakes, Copenhagen 44
Lallerstedt, Erik 212
Langridge, Stephen 61
Lapland (Finnish) 80, 171, 278
Lapland (Swedish) 120
Lapland Chamber Orchestra 80, 81, 277
Larsen, Gjermund 160
Larsen, Henning 72, 127, 211
Larsen, Kim 266
Lassen, Teitur 149–50, 154, 155, 266
  Confessions 150, 283
  Poetry and Aeroplanes 149
  Story Music 154
  The Singer 150
Laurinus, Laurentius Laurentii 17
Lauritzen, Vilhelm 70
Laxness, Halldór 142
Lego 228
Leifs, Jón 114, 131–6, 137–8, 141, 151, 282
  'Dettifoss' 133
  Edda oratorios 134, 151
  Elegy 134

'Geysir' 133
'Hafís' 133, 138
'Hekla' 133, 135
Iceland Overture 135
'Torrek' 134
Leipzig 15, 16, 41
Lenin, Vladimir 33
Lennon, John 84
Léonie Sonning Music Prize 110, 112
Leroy, Nolwenn 150
Lewerentz, Sigurd 212
Lewis, Michael 140
Liberal Alliance party (Denmark) 270
Liberal party (Norway) 79
Lillehammer 159
Limfjord 68
Lincoln Center, New York 42
Lindberg, Magnus 238, 239–43, 245, 255
  Aura 241
  Kraft 240, 255
  Sculpture 242
Lindeman, Ludvig Mathias 19, 20, 24
Lindström, Emmy 84
Linstrand, Vicke 213
Lintu, Hannu 61, 94, 95, 188, 227
'Little Frog, The' (song) 57
Løgting 155
London 17, 45, 64, 92, 102, 156, 191, 265, 275, 280
London Philharmonic Orchestra 241
London Sinfonietta 192
Lordi 124, 135, 240, 241
  Hard Rock Hallelujah 124
Los Angeles 4, 253
Los Angeles Philharmonic 180, 238, 241, 254
Lost Wallet Test 170
Løvlid, Unni 162
Low Roar 129
LPR Architects 230
Lübeck 58
Lundbyvassen 51
Luther, Martin 18, 161, 179
Lutheranism 18, 34, 35, 49, 63, 66, 73, 76, 90, 160, 179–80, 195
Lutosławski, Witold 52
Lykke, Signe 210

Madagascar 89
Maderna, Bruno 81
Madsen, Allan Gravgaard 189–90
  Nachtmusik 189–90
Mærsk 71, 73, 211

INDEX

Mahler, Gustav 43, 166, 221, 263, 284
Mäkelä, Klaus 97, 188, 247
Mälkki, Susanna 61
Malmö 46, 212, 267, 272, 275
Malmö Live 272
Malmö Opera 47, 106, 212–13, 215, 220
Malmö Symphony Orchestra 264–5, 271, 275
Manchester 157, 279
Mangersnes, Magnar 17
Mankell, Henning 46
Mann, Thomas 187
Mannerheimintie, Helsinki 230–1
Manze, Andrew 61, 282
Mao-Takacs, Clément 284
Marainen, Simon 120, 121
Marble Church, Copenhagen 72
Margrethe II, Queen of Denmark 42
Marimekko 236–7, 245
Massachusetts Institute of Technology 233
Match of the Day 68
Matre, Ørjan 162, 182–3
Mattila, Karita 93
Maunula, Miikka 68
McCartney, Paul 84
McDonalds 17, 271
Mendelssohn, Felix 15, 16, 59, 65, 213
  Elijah 59
Menin, Sarah 232
Merikanto, Oskar 206
Messerschmidt, Morten 269, 284
Michigan 75
Microsoft 235–6
Minnesota 208
Miskimmon, Annilese 74
Mjørkadalur (Faroe Islands) 153
Möller, Jakob 282
Møller, Mærsk Mc-Kinney 71, 72
Molleson, Kate 97
Monk, Thelonius 84
Monroe, Marilyn 148
Montesquieu 145
Monteverdi, Claudio 105
  L'Orfeo 105
Moomins 237
Morgensang 45
Mørk, Truls 93
Mortensen, Lars Ulrik 104, 105, 107, 108
Mortensen, Otto 181
Mortensen, Trine Boje 178
Moscow 23
Mount Esja 127
Mozart, Constanze 39

Mozart, Wolfgang Amadeus 31, 48, 157
  Symphony No. 35 157
MTV 125
Muhly, Nico 150
Múm 129
Munch, Edvard 106, 172, 209
Munich 187
Muppets 249
Musica Nova Festival 227
Musiikkitalo, Helsinki (Helsinki Music Centre) 68, 71, 230, 231, 234
Musikselskabet Harmonium 59

Nansensgade, Copenhagen 44
National Arts Centre Orchestra, Ottawa 278
National Core Curriculum for Basic Education in the Arts (Finland) 94
National Day (Norway) 66, 88
National Day (Sweden) 82
National Theatre of Iceland 127
Nationaltidende (newspaper) 198
New Simplicity 190, 216–17, 227–8
New York 51
New York Philharmonic 42, 136, 241
New York Philharmonic Society 281
New York World Fair, 1939 232
Newman, Ernest 37
Nickler, Reto 29
Niels Finsensgøta, Tórshavn 156
Nielsen, Carl 38, 40, 41–5, 49, 52, 99, 100, 107, 110, 125, 131, 132, 151, 180, 185, 198–201, 216, 225, 226, 262–3, 266
  'Jens Vejmand' 180, 283
  Maskarade 44, 200–1
  My Childhood 41
  Suite for Strings 41
  Symphony No. 3, *Sinfonia Espansiva* 43–5, 50, 180, 262
  Symphony No. 4, *The Inextinguishable* 110, 132–3
  Symphony No. 5 180, 262
  Symphony No. 6, *Sinfonia Semplice* 198–200, 262
  'Tit er jeg glad' 125
  'Min Jesus, lad mit hjerte få' 180
  Wind Quintet 180
Nielsen, Jens 67
Nielsen, Kai 192
Nielsen, Nielsen & Nielsen Architects 65
Nielsen, Thorvald 200
Nobel Prizes 48

INDEX

Nokia 2, 72, 235–6, 241, 284
Nordfjord 74–5, 79, 272
Nordic embassies, Berlin 257–60
Nordic Music Days 135, 190, 222, 226–7
Nordic noir 167–8, 210, 254
Nordlysfestivalen 22
Nørgård, Per 218–22, 223, 224, 226, 228–9, 251, 255, 257
   Symphony No. 1 219
   Symphony No. 2 219–21, 284
   Voyage Into the Golden Screen 221, 255
North Sea 73
Norwegian Soloists' Choir 100, 160–3
   White Night 160–3
Norwegian Opera 78
Nouvel, Jean 70, 176
Nyckelharpa 26–7, 48, 56
Nyhavn, Copenhagen 98
Nyman, Marzi 115, 118
Nyman, Michael 84

Occurrence (album) 139
Odin 134
Ólafsson, Víkingur 93, 97, 127–8, 129–30, 141, 157, 208
Old Irish Pub (company) 271
Old Irish Pub, Rødovre 271, 275
Olympic Games 70
Opera Nordfjord 75–9, 88
Oramo, Sakari 95, 98, 231, 238, 243
Orchestre de Paris 247
Øresund 56
Øresund Bridge 46, 56, 264, 265, 272
Orlow, Benjamin 6
Orrefors 213
Orthodox Cathedral, Helsinki 231
Oslo 25, 59, 73, 78, 79, 90, 100, 109, 122, 159, 182, 184, 217, 253, 277
Oslo Chamber Choir 162
   Veneliti 162
Oslo Opera House 73, 74, 230, 253
Oslo Philharmonic Orchestra 161, 182, 188, 222, 247
Oslofjord 73
Österling, Fredrik 82–6, 267, 275
Ostrobothnia 231
Ounasjoki (River) 114, 118

Paasikivi, Lilli 197
Paasilinna, Arto 174, 189, 206
   The Year of the Hare 174–5, 189
Pade, Else Marie 216
Paimio Sanatorium 234

Pajunen, Sara 208
Paleface (Karri Pekka Matias Miettinen) 38
Pálsdóttir, Eivør 147–9, 155, 158
   Lava 148
Pálsson, Páll Ragnar 139
Panula, Jorma 93–4, 102
Pappano, Antonio 73
Paraske, Larin 36
Paris 47, 141, 255–7, 265
Paris World Fair, 1937 234
Parkkinen, Tiina 258, 259
Parly, Nila 283
Pärt, Arvo 143
Pavelich, Michael 75, 76
Peder Hiort Mathus (Røros) 161
Pedersen, Grete 160–3
Peltonen, Matti 203
Pensola, Minna 116
Pettersson, Allan 242
Philharmonia Orchestra 86, 87
Piazzolla, Astor 84
Pietarsaari (Jakobstad) 1, 4, 6, 9
Pietarsaari Music Institute 6
Pietarsaari Sinfonietta 6
Pilen 98
Pittsburgh Symphony Orchestra 222–3
Pohjola (Kalevala) 32
Pohjola, Seppo 207, 245
   Symphony No. 3 245
Pontecorvo, Adriane 283
Porra, Lauri 125
Porvoo 36
Printex 245
Progress party (Norway) 79
Prokofiev, Sergei 128
Puccini, Giacomo 29
   La Bohème 29–30, 47
Puotila, Ritva 238
Purcell, Henry 144, 222
   Dido and Aeneas 144, 222
Putaansuu, Tomi Petteri 124

Queen Louise's Bridge, Copenhagen 44, 192

Rachmaninoff, Sergei 223
Rae, Corinne Bailey 150
Räisänen, Tomi 81
Räisänen, Virpi 277
Raitio, Väinö 223
   Kuutamo Jupiterissa 223
Rapallo 208

INDEX

Rasmussen, Janus 140, 174, 283
  Vín 175
Rasmussen, Sunleif 150–3, 157, 158, 283
  Prelude for Brass 150, 283
  Symphony No. 2, *The Earth Anew* 151–2
Ratkje, Maja 263
  Desibel 263
Rattle, Simon 110–13, 161
Rauchstrasse, Berlin 258
Rautavaara, Einojuhani 116, 123, 239
Realdania 69
Recurrence (album) 139
Red Army 33
refugee crisis, 2015 46
Reykjavík 126–9, 130, 140–3, 145, 146, 148
Rieu, André 14
Rigshospitalet, Copenhagen 200
Riisager, Knudåge 42
Ringve 25–7
Riyadh 253
Rødovre 270
Roiha, Viivi 117
Rome 6, 209
Rønsholdt, Niels 263
  Archive of Emotions and Experiences 263
Rorbua Pub, Tromsø 22
Røros 159–63
Roskilde 270
Roskilde Festival 123
Roskilde, Treaty of 46
Ross, Alex 188
Rostin, Valentina 25
Rostin, Victoria 24, 25
Roundhouse, Camden 129
Rouvali, Santtu-Matias 86–7, 97
Rovaniemi 80, 81, 114, 116, 123, 253, 277, 278, 279
Rowell, Lewis 281
Royal Academy of Music, Aarhus 189, 221
Royal Concertgebouw Orchestra 243
Royal Danish Academy of Music 189, 190
Royal Danish Opera 39, 40, 107, 211, 265
Royal Danish Orchestra 39, 110–13, 167
Royal Danish Playhouse 282
Royal Danish Theatre 71, 72, 187, 200
Royal Festival Hall, London 92
Royal Institute of British Architects 234, 282
Royal Northern College of Music, Manchester 156–7
Royal Opera, Covent Garden 107
Royal Scottish National Orchestra 97
Royal Swedish Opera 47
Ruders, Poul 222, 229
  Concerto in Pieces 222
  Symphony No. 2, *Symphony and Transformation* 222
rune singing 35, 120, 232, 246
Rusten, Johannes 27
Rutherford-Johnson, Tim 184
RÚV (Icelandic Broadcasting Corporation) 127, 129, 142
Rwandan genocide 33
Rybak, Alexander 23

Saariaho, Kaija 238, 252, 256–7, 284
  Laconisme de l'aile 256
  Lichtbogen 256, 257
  Notes on Light 257
Saarikallio, Suvi 207, 283
Saraste, Jukka-Pekka 282
Sætren, Kristian Myksvoll 76
Sallinen, Aulis 123
Salonen, Esa-Pekka 4, 174, 238–9, 241
  Helix 239
  Violin Concerto 239
Salzburg Festival 5, 143
Sámi 22, 80, 118–22, 148, 237, 252, 276–9
Sámi Grand Prix 120, 122
Samúelsson, Guðjón 127, 282
San Francisco 265
Sandane 74
Sandemose, Aksel 71
Sandoy 151
Sandström, Jan 242
Savall, Arianna 22
Savikovskaya, Yulia 227
Saxell, Michael 46
Scala, La 77
Scare Force One (album) 124
Schauser, Søren 190, 217
Schierbeck, Poul 195
Schleswig-Holstein 40
Schmelzer, Johann Heinrich 103
Schnittke, Alfred 81
Schoenberg, Arnold 5, 50, 89, 90, 91, 143, 216
  Pierrot lunaire 91, 92, 143
Schubert, Franz 52, 84, 130
  Symphony No. 8, unfinished 52
  'Winterreise' 130
Schumann, Robert 15, 185

INDEX

Schütz, Heinrich 39, 103
Scottish Chamber Orchestra 282
Scruton, Roger 129
Seal 150
Seattle 265
Second Schleswig War 228
Second World War 25, 34, 157
Segerstam, Leif 249–51, 268, 284
   Symphony No. 288 (Letting the flow go on . . .) 249
   Symphony No. 295 250
Sek & Grey 236
Shakespeare, William 82, 167, 186, 188, 213
   A Midsummer Night's Dream 213
   Hamlet 167, 186
   The Tempest 188
Shanghai 253
Shern, Chris 95
Shetland Islands 12
Shostakovich, Dmitri 52
Sibelius Academy 93
Sibelius, Aino 201–2, 209
Sibelius, Jean 2, 3, 4, 8–10, 28, 29, 34–6, 38, 53–4, 63, 92, 110, 112, 116, 123–6, 131, 147, 151, 164, 166, 168–73, 180, 186, 188–9, 201–3, 206, 208–10, 216–19, 221, 223, 225–6, 229, 232–5, 238–41, 243, 245–8, 249–50, 262–4, 280, 282, 284
   Andante Festivo 232
   En Saga 36, 37
   Finlandia 33, 34, 35
   Kullervo 248, 256, 281
   Lemminkäinen and the Maidens of the Island 246
   Six Impromptus for Piano 281
   String Quartet in E minor 126
   Swanwhite 203
   Symphony No. 1 37
   Symphony No. 2 124, 208–9
   Symphony No. 4 172, 186
   Symphony No. 5 151, 164–5, 171, 188, 246–8, 264
   Symphony No. 7 110–13, 170, 201–2, 206, 241, 249, 250
   Tapiola 2, 3, 8–10, 32, 36, 64, 110, 126, 138, 188, 209, 217, 218–19, 230, 232, 234, 241, 244, 248, 251, 256, 262–3, 280, 281, 282
   The Tempest 188, 282
   The Wood Nymph 246, 248, 256
Sibelius, Kirsti 209

Sigfúsdóttir, Mariá Huld Markan 139
Sigur Rós 129, 136, 140
Silence Festival 114–18, 174, 277
Sirkus, Tórshavn 155
Sjaggo, Brita-Stina 121
Sjöblom, Jonas 120
Sjöqvist, Hans-Åke 77
Sjöwall, Maj 168
Skagen 253
Skagerrak Strait 74
Skåne 46, 57
Skanör 56–7
Skjaldur 146, 152, 154
Skúvoy 151
Småland 215
Snøhetta 253
Snorrason, Áksell 282
Society of Finnish Composers 277
Söderblom, Ulf 250–1
Sokos 30
Sólheimajökull glacier 138
Solyom, Stefan 282
Somby, Ánde 122
Sonata form 130
Sønderborg 61, 62, 64, 65, 66, 69, 80
Søndergård, Thomas 95, 97
Sørensen, Bent 81, 175–7, 180, 185, 190, 263
   It Is Pain Flowing Down Slowly on a White Wall 175–6
   L'isola della città 175, 177
   La Mattina 176
   Sounds Like You 176
   Sterbende Gärten 176
   Trumpet Concerto 176
South Harbour, Copenhagen 270
South Jutland Symphony Orchestra 62, 64, 65, 283
Sovereign Wealth Fund, Norway 73
spectralism 255–6
St Olav 149
St Petersburg 34
Standal, Kari 75, 76
Statoil 102
Stavanger 74, 88–91
Stavanger Chamber Music Festival 88
Stavanger Concert Hall 74, 89, 91
Stavanger Symphony Orchestra 89
Steen-Andersen, Simon 189
Steinitz, Richard 225, 227
Stemme, Nina 93
Stenhammar, Wilhelm 49, 50, 51, 52
Stern, Michael 247–8

INDEX

Stewart, John 212, 233
Stockhausen, Karlheinz 143–4, 283
Stockholm 27, 47, 50, 56, 83, 253, 255, 277, 283
Stockmann, Helsinki 231
Støjberg, Inger 197
Stokke 100
Stoltenberg, Jens 79, 181
Stóra Dímun 151
Storgårds, John 61, 80, 81, 188, 222–3, 230, 277, 279, 282
Storioni (luthier) 111
Storm Solomon 115, 118
Storyville, Helsinki 230
Stradivarius (luthier) 111
Strandvägen, Stockholm 47
Stratovarius 35, 124–5, 135
Strauss II, Johann 75, 91
  Die Fledermaus 75, 76, 77, 78
Strauss, Richard 54, 67, 100, 101, 124, 125, 184, 240, 241
  Also Sprach Zarathustra 184
  'Four Last Songs' 101
Stravinsky, Igor 50, 116, 231
  A Soldier's Tale 116
  The Rite of Spring 231
Streymoy 152
Strindberg, August 46, 169, 210, 283
  The Ghost Sonata 169, 172
Stroud, Melissa 284
Stutzmann, Nathalie 61, 109
suicide 65, 179, 209
Suntory Foundation 241
Suosalo, Martti 206
Svensson, Johan 263
SVT (Swedish State Television) 67, 68
Swedish Radio Choir 78
Swedish Theatre, Helsinki 231
Sydhavn, Copenhagen 55
Sydney Opera House 229, 232
Symposium (painting) 206

Talent Norway 102, 103
Tammerkoski 236
Tampere 29, 125–6
Tampere Philharmonic Orchestra 87
tango 116
Tarkiainen, Outi 116, 118, 227, 244, 276–80
  Eanan, giđa nieida ('The Earth, Spring's Daughter') 277
  'Kunnes kivi halkeaa' 116
  Midnight Sun Variations 244, 278–80

Tchaikovsky, Pyotr Ilyich 65, 81, 85, 88, 157, 172
  Piano Concerto No. 1 157
  Symphony No. 4 88
Tesla 89
Thirty Years' War 39
Thomissøn, Hans 17
Thoreau, Henry David 189
Thoresen, Lasse 23
  Yr 23, 24
Thoroddsen, Jón 97
Thorsteinson, Árni 130
Thorvaldsdottir, Anna 136–40, 144, 175, 221
  Aeriality 137–9
  Dreaming 137
  Rhízōma 136
Ticciati, Robin 61
Tiergarten, Berlin 258, 259
'Til Ungdommen' (song) 181
Tivoli Gardens 40, 43, 104, 271
Tokyo 237, 241
Tom and Jerry 200
Tómasson, Haukur 129, 139
Tønsberg, Christian 14
Torne (river) 120
Tórshavn 145–6, 149, 152, 155, 157
Torsteinsson, Torgrummur 142
Trainspotting (novel) 210
Trevino, Robert 264–5, 267–8
Troms 276
Tromsø 21, 22, 23, 30, 80, 276
Tromsø Big Band 23
Tromsø Culture House 23
Tromsø Savings Bank 22
Trondheim 24–6, 59, 252
Trondheim Cathedral (Nidaros) 162
Trondheim Soloists 27, 109, 163
Trondheim Symphony Orchestra 86
Tsar Nicholas II 34
Tutl 155–6
Tuusula (lake) 164–5, 203
Tvísöngur 133, 145
Twisting Torso, Malmö 46
Týr 154

UEFA Euro 2016 96, 139
Ultima Festival 182, 225
Ulvaeus, Björn 55
UNESCO 161
University of Applied Sciences, Pietarsaari (Centria) 6
University of Tromsø 122

INDEX

Unnila, Raimo 208
Uppland 27
Urbański, Krzysztof 61, 86
Ustvolskaya, Galina 84
Utøya 79, 184
Útúrdúr (television programme) 129
Utzon, Jørn 229, 230, 232

Väinämöinen 28
Vaka, Veronique 138
   Lendh 138–9
   Vanescere 138
Valdres 19
Valen, Olav Fartein 89, 90, 91
   Piano Sonata No. 2 90
   Violin Concerto 90
Valtaoja, Esko 81
Vanity Fair 140
Vänskä, Osmo 92, 165, 173, 282, 284
Vásquez, Christian 61
Vedernikov, Alexander 265
Venice 48
Verdi, Giuseppe 162
Versto, Berit Opheim 160
Vestergård Hansen, Matias 190–1
Vick, Graham 60, 211
Vienna 158
Vienna Philharmonic Orchestra 223
Vierula, Rami 126
Vigdal, Ragnar 160, 162–3
Viipuri Library 232
Viking Thunder Clap 96, 139
Villa Magia, Kaukonen 118
Vilmarsson, Hlynur Aðils 139
Vinterberg, Thomas 168, 204
Visit Finland (agency) 236
Vök (band) 140
Volvo 167
Von Karajan, Herbert 112

Von Otter, Anne Sofie 93, 255
Von Trier, Lars 106, 168–9, 283

Wagner, Richard 39, 67, 100, 106, 134, 254, 283
   Der Ring des Nibelungen 39, 134, 151, 169, 283
   The Flying Dutchman 106
Wahlöö, Per 168
Walt Disney Concert Hall 68, 242
'We Are Musicians' (song) 57
Webern, Anton 91
Weilerstein, Alisa 109
Weill, Kurt 211
   Rise and Fall of the City of Mahagonny 211
Weisser, Johannes 19
Welser-Möst, Franz 61
Wenck, Heinrich 43
Wennäkoski, Lotta 244
Westminster Abbey 156
Who Wants to Be a Millionaire? 71
Widor, Charles-Marie 121
Wilkinson, Bernharður 156–8
Wingårdh, Gert 258
Winter War, Finland 33, 232
Wirkkala, Tapio 236

X Factor 125, 266

Yggdrasil (ensemble) 155
YLE (Finnish Broadcasting Corporation) 68
Yli-Salomäki, Aki 207
Yoiking 118–23
Young, Simone 61, 109
Ystad 46

Zealand 41, 62
Zebeljan, Isidora 81
Znaider, Nikolaj Szeps 93